Twayne's United States Authors Series

EDITOR OF THIS VOLUME

Kenneth Eble

University of Utah

DuBose Heyward

TUSAS 392

DuBose Heyward

DUBOSE HEYWARD

By WILLIAM H. SLAVICK

TWAYNE PUBLISHERS
A DIVISION OF G. K. HALL & CO., BOSTON

Copyright © 1981 by G. K. Hall & Co.

Published in 1981 by Twayne Publishers,
A Division of G. K. Hall & Co.
All Rights Reserved

Printed on permanent/durable acid-free paper and bound
in the United States of America

First Printing

Frontispiece credit: Vandamm Studios
courtesy South Carolina Historical Society

Library of Congress Cataloging in Publication Data

Slavick, William H
DuBose Heyward.

(Twayne's United States authors series : TUSAS 392)
Bibliography: p. 189–93
Includes index.
1. Heyward, DuBose, 1885–1940—Criticism and interpretation.
PS3515.E98Z87   811'.52   80-27633
ISBN 0-8057-7342-8

For my parents, and for
Ursula, Susanne, Lisa,
Sarah, Stephen, Madeleine,
Ellen, and in memory
of John Henry

Contents

About the Author

William Henry Slavick, a native of Shelby County, Tennessee, received the A.B. degree from the University of Notre Dame in 1949, the M.A. in 1951, and, after studies at St. Bernard Abbey, Louisiana State University, and the University of Munich, the Ph.D. from the University of Notre Dame in 1971. He has written about Elizabeth Madox Roberts, William Faulkner, and Ralph Ellison. A member of the University of Southern Maine faculty, in 1977 he was Senior Fulbright Lecturer at the University of Kassel in West Germany. In 1978 he directed the Downeast Southern Renascence Conference in Portland, Maine.

Preface

For a brief moment in American literary history, around 1923, DuBose Heyward was, in the eyes of some, those who had yet to appreciate John Crowe Ransom's early work, the most notable modern southern poet. Two years later, with the publication of *Porgy*, he became for some the South's great fiction hope as a successor to the aging Ellen Glasgow. This reputation, merited only until Elizabeth Madox Roberts published *The Time of Man* a year later, continued, despite the appearance of William Faulkner and Thomas Wolfe in the interim, into the 1930s: "There is no finer English style in the South than Heyward's; there is no keener eye, no more discerning mind than his; there is no more honest and truthful writer," Gerald Johnson wrote in 1935.[1] The success of *Porgy* on the stage in 1927 and of *Mamba's Daughters* a dozen years later made him the South's most notable playwright until Lillian Hellman's reputation was established in the late 1930s. Now it is hardly remembered that Heyward did the libretto for *Porgy and Bess* or even that the opera is based on his novella and play. His poetry, fiction, and plays are all but forgotten. Heyward's poems have not been anthologized in decades. His fiction and plays are out of print. Only *Porgy and Bess* lives on.

Heyward might safely be forgotten, some will surely say. Beside the luminous figures in the canon of the Southern Renascence, from John Crowe Ransom and William Faulkner to Walker Percy, Heyward's eclipse may appear deserved. And some of the minor writers who published during Heyward's brief hour of importance—Jean Toomer, Julia Peterkin, and T. S. Stribling—today appear more deserving of attention.

On several counts, this is an inadequate assessment. No history of the Southern Renascence can be complete without due notice of the Charleston writers, of whom Heyward was foremost, and the Poetry Society of South Carolina, which he was largely instrumental in founding. Heyward's distinctive achievement as a southern writer, particularly in fiction, merits regard. And within the framework of the Harlem Renaissance—black writers from Kansas to the Indies as well as Eugene O'Neill, Sherwood Anderson, Carl Van Vechten, and Waldo Frank—Heyward remains a significant, even major figure.

Heyward's place in the Southern Renascence is not easily defined. As an answer to H. L. Mencken's insulting but all too accurate essay, "The Sahara of the Bozarts," the Poetry Society was far less effective than the poetry published in the *Fugitive* and the first novels of Thomas Wolfe, Roberts, and Faulkner. But Heyward was probably the single most influential person in opening the way for new southern writers in New York publishing houses.[2]

If Hugh Holman is right in dividing modern southern fiction into the ironic Piedmont writers, the democratic mountaineers, and the mythic authors of the transmontane states, Heyward's fiction fits none of these modes.[3] He may be called a chronicler or memorialist as he feels his way gingerly out of a world of the past he largely accepts and toward a much different future he recognizes, if with anxiety. The present he abides stoically and faithfully records, aware of what is inhuman and doomed, yet respectful of the tradition that makes the inhuman possible and the doom inevitable.

Heyward is, then, more than a late local color figure. Sometimes his luxuriating in the physical scene and exploiting of the quaint or historical is disturbing. But he does not engage in the regionalism of pride. His sense of place is distinguished by a firsthand experience of waterfront Negroes, mountaineers, several types of Piedmont and Low Country whites, and an appreciation of their traditional ways of life, what Wendell Berry calls the "continuity of environment."[4] His work, particularly his fiction, recognizes the humanity of blacks, the barren quality of mountain life, and the cultural sterility of Charleston whites, as well as the economic and social forces that surround them. Heyward sees the Negro's pursuit of dignity and fulfillment and in the process finds him freer, better attuned to the earth, his own cultural roots, and the channels of joy than southern whites.

Heyward's characters are representatives of their class and time, engaged in largely representative efforts. But, invariably, they work out their fates in tension with some change in the traditional order of society; the real world is, for Heyward, a changing world.

Neither is Heyward a doctrinaire southerner about the traditional order in his treatment of the South. Donald Davidson said Heyward wrote like a "latter-day Abolitionist"; Ransom thought he did not write like a southerner.[5] In a sense they were right. Like his Nashville cousins, Heyward smarted from Mencken's ridicule of the cultural wasteland south of the Potomac, and, like them, he both accepted the criticism and found it necessary to defend the southern way of life against Mencken's too sweeping condemnations. Unlike them, he did not recognize Mencken's insensitivity to the value of tradition, especially to the role religion played in shaping the South's tragic view of life. And so, while he clung nostalgically to his heritage, Heyward sought to follow Mencken's lead: he tried to write as a regionalist and as a critic worthy of Mencken's iconoclasm. Heyward's powers of observation were good, but he did not have the developed critical mind of the Nashville writers and Faulkner. He could not, as they, identify with the modernist alienation of Yeats, Joyce, Eliot, and Mann or find religious values in memory and history. But in all of his work appears an implicit criticism of the southern tradition's lack of vitality and some awareness of its causes, intellectual and social. Given his uncertain health, his lack of formal education, and the frozen thinking of Charleston, it is no mean achievement that Heyward captured, substantially and honestly, the Charleston world.

So Heyward is something more than a southern memorialist, "writing," as Ellen Glasgow observed, "in beauty and truth of a vanishing South."[6] His novels and plays and a number of his better poems come to focus on the struggle of lonely characters to find life—in rhythm, love, integrity, creative expression, freedom, or community—in a changing traditional society. That society is almost invariably inimical to his characters' quests, and the weight of its tradition, racism, bourgeois materialism, or religious hypocrisy forces their compromise or defeats them, or they must flee it to live. The exceptions are few. The experience of life in Heyward's work is reserved for those in harmony with the rhythms of nature and is sustained only in Catfish Row and on St. Croix, where harmony with nature includes harmony with the community's past—its traditions—and its present.

Heyward's intention was, in the end, romantic, and his view of life is somewhat sentimental. But his pervasive social realism, which leads to his juxtaposition of the sterility of white Charleston aristocracy and the possibility of life in the black community, deserves recognition as one of the influences that freed Southern Renascence writers of earlier stereotypes and defensiveness about the South. And after two decades of renewed stereotyping of blacks, now as all-good or blameless, Heyward's appreciation of the humanity of his black and white characters takes on new importance.[7] Heyward's interest in the personal struggle for life against the realistically apprised background of Charleston and the changing South, if somewhat attenuated in his work, an interest carried forward by the younger generation of writers but unique with Heyward in his, alone justifies a study of his achievement.

The significance of Heyward's work in the Harlem Renaissance is much more readily identifiable. Heyward's *Porgy*, with its human treatment of Catfish Row; the 1927 Broadway staging of the DuBose and Dorothy Heyward play version; and *Mamba's Daughters*, a second Charleston novel concerned with the relationship of black primitivism and folk culture to high art and changing times, all qualify Heyward for such consideration and won him recognition in his lifetime. Once he was mistakenly introduced as a "member of Harlem's intellectual colony" and "a Southern Negro of the old tradition," although he was of the Charleston white aristocracy and apparently did not meet any members of the Harlem "intellectual colony" until late 1926.[8] His relatively small place in histories of the Harlem Renaissance reflects a mistaken assessment.

Heyward's keenness of observation of the black man in Charleston and its surrounding environs—in his own community—is marked by an authority and freedom from the exotic and fake missing in both white and less gifted black writers. His largely successful escape from stereotypes was recognized by Davidson, who approved of the way Heyward's "Negro was allowed to stand forth as a human being in his own right" and by Countee Cullen, who called *Porgy* the "best novel by a white about Negroes he had read" and suggested that it "gives one the uncanny feeling that Negroes are human beings and that white and black southerners are brothers under the skin."[9]

At a time when much of the interest in Harlem focused on the black man's primitive innocence and freedom from inhibitions, Heyward was painfully aware that, in Charleston and Harlem, the black man was being forced to make a change that endangered those very qualities whites had come to admire. Such a burden of change marks all of Heyward's fiction as well as his three plays.

Still Heyward's intense interest in the black world of Charleston is contiguous with America's post–World War I disillusionment with civilization and turn from Puritan restraint to the primitive qualities found in African art and the uninhibited night world of Harlem. But Heyward's sense of the deadness of white southern culture and study of Catfish Row led him to see in simple folk not an escape into primitive exoticism but into the possibility of life, and the primitive life he admired and envied is observed and realized rather than thinly imagined. It is rooted in the earth, the past, and ordinary daily experience. The result is a responsibility and restraint in treatment notably missing from "The Congo," *Nigger Heaven*, *Dark Laughter*, and O'Neill's plays.

Finally, Heyward came to recognize, as others did not, what the essential rhythm of Negro life was. He appreciated the strength of the black man's faith, the reality of his community, and the essentiality of his race's suffering and long history of suffering. In 1959, a longtime leading Harlem writer summed up Heyward's accomplishment. Langston Hughes suggested that Negro writers could go to school to Heyward, the writer, who saw "with his white eyes, wonderful, poetic human qualities in the inhabitants of Catfish Row that makes them come alive in his book."[10]

After a survey of Heyward's life and career, this study offers an analysis and evaluation of his work, beginning with his poetry and then turning to the novels, plays, movie scenarios, and opera libretto of the fifteen-year period that began with Heyward's publication, at the age of forty, of *Porgy*.

Acknowledgments

Holt, Rinehart and Winston, Publishers—for permission to quote from the following selections:

From *Jasbo Brown and Selected Poems* by DuBose Heyward. Copyright 1924, 1931 by DuBose Heyward. Copyright 1952, (c) 1959 by Dorothy Heyward.

From *Skylines and Horizons* by DuBose Heyward. Copyright 1924 by DuBose Heyward. Copyright 1952 by Dorothy Heyward.

From *Carolina Chansons* by DuBose Heyward and Hervey Allen. Copyright 1922 by Holt, Rinehart and Winston. Copyright 1950 by Dorothy Heyward and Ann Andrews Allen. Reprinted by permission of Holt, Rinehart and Winston, Publishers

From *Peter Ashley* by DuBose Heyward. Copyright 1932 by Holt, Rinehart and Winston.

From *Lost Morning* by DuBose Heyward. Copyright 1936 by DuBose Heyward. Copyright (c) 1964 by Jenifer DuBose Heyward.

Studies in the Literary Imagination—for material adapted from my "Going to School to DuBose Heyward" in 7 (Fall 1974): 105–29; Jenifer Heyward Wood, John Bennett, and the Hervey Allen, Robert Frost, and George Gershwin estates—for permission to quote from the letters of DuBose Heyward, John Bennett, Hervey Allen, Robert Frost, and George Gershwin.

Charles Mathew, Henry Laurens, Jean Drake, Jeannie Heyward Haskell, Frank Durham, Laura Bragg, Kathleen Drayton Mayrant Simons, Jenifer Heyward Wood, Ralph Ellison, and Herbert Aptheker—for interviews.

Mrs. T. Grenville Pryor of the South Carolina Historical Society, Mrs. Clara Mae Jacobs of the South Caroliniana Library of the University of South Carolina, the research staff of the *Charleston News and Courier*, the staff of the Charleston Library Society, Miss Ruth Salisbury of the University of Pittsburgh Libraries—for research assistance; and the libraries of the University of Notre Dame, University of South Carolina, SUNY College at Geneseo, University of Wisconsin, Marquette University, Duke University, the University of North Carolina at Chapel Hill, the University of Southern Maine, the New York

Acknowledgments

State Library, and the public libraries of New York City, Rochester, Milwaukee, and Memphis—for use of holdings.

Leo Rockas, Rhea Miller, John Edward Hardy, Herbert Simpson, Ruth Nadelhaft, Gary Heim, Richard Sullivan, and Louis Hasley—for criticism of parts of the manuscript; Donald P. Costello—for his candid judgments and many suggestions regarding the earlier version of this manuscript; Sylvia Bowman—for her patience.

These and many friends in the profession and beyond—for encouragement when the groves of academe were infested with spruce budworm (or on fire), and so a distraction rather than a shelter.

Frank J. O'Malley, Ernest Sandeen, and John T. Frederick—for professing.

Elizabeth Shivers, James Griffin, and Bernice Anderson: they exemplified for me the nobility and the pathos of the lives of southern Negroes.

My parents—for their faith, and Ursula and the children—for various assistances, patience, sacrifices, and endurance.

Chronology

1885   Edwin DuBose Heyward born in Charleston, South Carolina, August 31, into an old Charleston family.

1887   Heyward's father, Edwin Watkins Heyward, killed in mill accident. Mrs. Heyward supports DuBose and his younger sister, Jeannie, by sewing.

1890–   Attends Susan Hayne's School and St. Philip's Church Sunday
1894   School.

1894   Delivers the *Charleston Evening Post*.

1894–   Attends Craft's School.
1898

1898   Boys' High School. Lacking interest, at fourteen begins work in a hardware store to support family.

1900   First of two summers at Hendersonville, North Carolina.

1902   Made general assistant at hardware store. Confirmed an Episcopalian but never communes.

1903   After a summer at Spartanburg, South Carolina, stricken with polio, which affects arm and hand muscles. Invalided three years; treatment in Philadelphia. Family takes boarders and operates a summer boarding house on Sullivan's Island.

1905   Suffers typhoid attack. Employed as checker on a steamship company wharf, among Negro stevedores. Company fails in 1906.

1906   Pleurisy attack. Recuperates for eighteen months in Arizona.

1908   Enters into insurance and real-estate partnership with Harry O'Neill. Reclaims Negro tenements of St. Michael Alley. The Heywards move to No. 9.

1913   One-act play, "An Artistic Triumph," produced at the South Carolina Hall.

1917   Second pleurisy attack. Recuperates at Tryon, North Carolina, where he takes up painting with Louis Rowell. Buys cottage property in Hendersonville.

1917–   World War I work among Charleston Negroes as chairman of
1918   Victory Liberty Loan "Four-Minute" speakers. In 1918, meets John Bennett.

1917– Writes seven short stories; only two are published. In 1919,
1920   meets Hervey Allen, poet and gassed war veteran.

1920   Turns to poetry. Discussions of poetry with Bennett and Allen
       lead to Heyward proposing a Poetry Society of South Caro-
       lina.

1921   First Yearbook of the Poetry Society, with Heyward-Allen fore-
       word. Heyward editor until 1924. Elected vice-president. First
       of several summers at MacDowell Colony. Contemporary Verse
       prize for "Gamesters All."

1922   First volume of poems, *Carolina Chansons*, with Hervey Allen.
       They also edit *Poetry* magazine Southern number.

1923   Marries Dorothy Hartzell Kuhns, thirty-three-year-old Mac-
       Dowell colonist and playwright, on September 22, in New York
       City. Her play, *Nancy Ann*, is produced that autumn. *Skylines
       and Horizons*. Moves with bride to 76 Church Street, across
       from courtyard identified as Catfish Row.

1924   Elected Poetry Society president. Gives up insurance business,
       moves to Hendersonville. Winter tour in the North.

1925   Writes *Porgy* at Hendersonville and MacDowell Colony. Pub-
       lished in October. Another winter of lectures. Absence prompts
       resignation as Poetry Society president.

1926   *Angel.*

1927   Play version of *Porgy*, in which Mrs. Heyward collaborates,
       produced in October on Broadway. The Heywards tour Europe
       and visit at Hugh Walpole home in Cornwall.

1928   First child stillborn. D.Litt., University of North Carolina.
       Builds Dawn Hill on Hendersonville property.

1929   Second trip abroad, to Mediterranean and Holy Land.
       Mamba's Daughters (Literary Guild selection) and book edi-
       tion of *Half Pint Flask*. Honorary Doctor of Letters, College of
       Charleston.

1930   Daughter Jenifer born in New York City. Stock-market collapse
       and local bond difficulty affect finances.

1931   *Jasbo Brown and Other Poems. Brass Ankle* has brief Broad-
       way run. Attends Southern Writers Conference at Charlottes-
       ville with Faulkner, Glasgow, and others.

1932   *Peter Ashley.*

1933   Movie scenario for O'Neill's *The Emperor Jones.*

1934   Hired by Irving Thalberg for Pearl Buck's *The Good Earth* scenario. Week in New York City and month on Folly Island with George Gershwin.

1935   *Porgy and Bess* produced. Major revivals 1942, 1952, 1965, 1970.

1936   *Lost Morning.* Buys home at 24 South Battery.

1937   First South Carolinian elected to National Institute of Arts and Letters. Honorary degree, University of South Carolina. Cruise with Huntington Hartford to Virgin Islands. *Fort Sumter*, with Herbert Ravenel Sass.

1939   *Star Spangled Virgin. The Country Bunny*, a children's story. Named resident director of Dock Street Theatre in Charleston. Play version of *Mamba's Daughters*, in collaboration with Mrs. Heyward, produced on Broadway.

1940   Dies at fifty-four in Tryon, North Carolina, June 16, and buried in St. Philip's churchyard near John C. Calhoun.

1948   Dorothy Heyward's *Set My People Free*, based on Denmark Vesey slave uprising, which Heyward had begun, produced on Broadway.

1952   Mrs. Heyward moves to secure Heyward's claim to equal billing with Gershwin as author of *Porgy and Bess*.

1961   Mrs. Heyward dies, November 19, in New York City.

CHAPTER 1

A Charleston Gentleman and the World of Letters

I Beginnings

IN 1924, at the age of thirty-nine, DuBose Heyward chose to make a career of belles-lettres—or at least give it a year's trial.[1] It was an audacious move for a newly married writer who had known poverty most of his life, had little profited from his publications, worked slowly, and lived in a part of the country where no serious writer had ever lived by his pen. His monthly check from the insurance partnership he had left no doubt eased his uncertainty; it was still a bold move.

Heyward had heard the romances of Cooper and Dickens at his grandmother's knee. His mother, a verse writer, "knew the history of South Carolina from A to Izard."[2] And Heyward had, over twenty years earlier, vowed to be a writer. But, except for occasional gestures, such as writing a one-act play in 1913, supporting his family from the age of fourteen had interfered with a writing career. In 1917, recovering from a pleurisy attack, he had taken up painting, with modest success, but upon return to Charleston he set about writing fiction in earnest. By 1920, two of seven short stories were published and his career was begun.

During this period, Heyward met Ohioan John Bennett, an older and published fiction writer and poet, and Hervey Allen, a returned war veteran who had published a volume of verse. Both provided him advice and criticism, and Allen influenced Heyward's turn to poetry.

Two other influences contributed significantly to Heyward's change in vocation at forty. H. L. Mencken's essay "The Sahara of the Bozart," published originally in 1917 and in a longer version in 1920, which heaped hyperbolic scorn on the lack of tolerance and culture in the South, stirred Carolinians as well as the Nashville Fugitives to anger and a determination to respond. Mencken had observed:

Down there a poet is now almost as rare as an oboe-player, a dry-point etcher or a metaphysician. It is, indeed, amazing to contemplate so vast a vacuity. One thinks of the interstellar spaces, of the colossal reaches of the now mythical ether. Nearly the whole of Europe could be lost in that stupendous region of worn-out farms, shoddy cities and paralyzed cerebrums: one could throw in France, Germany and Italy, and still have room for the British Isles. And yet, for all its size and all its wealth and all the "progress" it babbles of, it is almost as sterile, artistically, intellectually, culturally, as the Sahara Desert. There are single acres in Europe that house more first-rate men than all the states south of the Potomac; there are probably single square miles in America.[3]

The desire to disprove this essay contributed significantly both to the founding of the Poetry Society of South Carolina and to Heyward's commitment to writing.

Then there was Heyward's experience at MacDowell Colony, in Peterboro, New Hampshire, living and working among other writers— Edwin Arlington Robinson, Stephen Vincent Benét, Thornton Wilder, Elinor Wylie, Julia Peterkin, Frances Newman, and Constance Rourke, among others, as well as Dorothy Kuhns, an Ohio playwright who became his wife and encouraged him to pursue a writing career.

Heyward succeeded in his new career, not only by producing a number of publishable works but by using the same material again and again and by capturing something of a popular audience. Consequently, although his book sales were never large, with the exception of *Mamba's Daughters*, his writing supported his family for sixteen years.

II   *Charleston and the Literary Renascence*

Heyward brought to his art the experience of the mannered white aristocracy, fallen on hard times, and that class's burden, the still-exploited black man, a problem occasionally met with savage violence but generally with a stoic sympathy that altered neither the problem nor the guilt. Part of this legacy, too, was the insulated, uncritical, even anti-intellectual, cast of mind that stemmed in large part from the increasing isolation and defensiveness regarding slavery in the decades prior to the Civil War. Mencken was not, of course, far wrong. As Allen Tate observed, in 1932: "There was never a profession of letters in the South. There were, and perhaps here and there still are, ladies and gentlemen."[4]

In 1930 Howard Mumford Jones noted another dimension of this cultural handicap: the anti-intellectualism and emotionalism of Southern religion meant that a "significant interpretation of life" required for anything more than a businessman's civilization was sadly lacking.[5]

For several decades, one consequence of this situation for literature had been an exploitation of folklore and local color, from *Uncle Remus* and Mary Murfree's local color stories to the Gullah sketches of Ambrose Gonzales and the dialect readings of Heyward's mother. Another was the rejection of any serious cultural criticism between the time of George Washington Cable and William Faulkner. Any significant interpretation of life found in the local color and early regionalist tradition is either muted or well concealed. In Heyward's manhood, only the Virginians Ellen Glasgow and James Branch Cabell had challenged the conventional, and their criticism is concealed in irony or allegory. As Glasgow had noted of her own experience:

No hint of an outside revolution in ideas had ever penetrated the walls of our library. Only life had broken through these elegiac tones which were still the common chord in all Southern prose fiction. And as life broke into the surrounding gloom, I felt that I could not thrive or even breathe, as a novelist, in a funereal air.[6]

Before the First World War, as Julia Peterkin recalled in 1937, when the Southerner "set out to write he shut his eyes to what was because it failed to correspond to the pattern of life which he had been taught to regard as fitting for a superior people."[7]

But World War I reduced the old Reconstruction defensiveness and moral alienation, and southerners began to come into contact with modern art and thought, as Allen Tate observed, making possible a southern literature: "With the war of 1914–1918, the South re-entered the world—but gave a backward glance as it stepped over the border: that backward glance gave us the Southern renascence, a literature conscious of the past in the present."[8]

These new currents were one thing in Nashville, another in Charleston. As the outlander Hervey Allen observed: "Charleston is rather a state of mind with a name, than a familiar town, to persons living west of the Alleghanies and north of the Ohio River."[9] The complex fate of being a southerner in the 1920s is one thing; with Heyward we must understand also the unique and complex fate of being a Charlestonian.

The Charleston of the 1920s was little changed from a hundred years earlier, with its scores of old houses and public buildings, camellias, azaleas, live oaks, and the Battery. The same centuries-old family names were to be found in the crowded graveyards, on storefronts, and on social lists. The population was only 30,585, not quite double the 16,000 of 1790. The peninsula where, according to the Charleston saying, the Ashley and Cooper rivers meet to form the Atlantic Ocean continues to be the home of the old English dissenters, Scots, French Huguenots, and Jewish families—the Pinckneys, Manigaults, and Heywards—that had settled the city hundreds of years before.

The Heywards had come to Charleston late in the seventeenth century. Nathaniel owned 2,000 slaves and fourteen plantations. Daniel built the Heyward-Washington (slept there) mansion in 1770. His son, Thomas, a judge, signed the Declaration of Independence. DuBose's maternal grandfather, Edwin DuBose, had owned three plantations near Bonneau, but the family was reduced to modest circumstances by slave-purchase debts and an imprudent cotton-crop sale. His mother's maternal grandfather, Napoleon Bonaparte Screven, had become a missionary among the sandhill blacks. And the family's black retainers, Maum Sina, Daddy Spoon, and John, descended from the old slave society of the area.

Although Heyward was raised in poverty, his name established his social status and his heritage determined his perspective on the world. Heyward's first responsibility, then, was not to sustain his family but to become a gentleman, and, as one Charleston lady archly remarked, "DuBose is surely not a self-made man."[10]

In its early days as an international port, Charleston had been the most cosmopolitan city in the New World, but it had lost this status well before the Civil War. With Nullification, proslavery, and secession talk, perhaps more than the rest of the South, Charleston had closed its mind to outside views and with a determination to keep it closed.

The fiery zeal Charleston brought to Secession and the firing on Sumter invited the misfortunes that befell it—blockade, siege, shelling, and postwar poverty. Yet Charleston remained different in other ways. Its admirable traditions survived intact: good form was still enough to prevent lynchings in Charleston, although there were a hundred elsewhere in South Carolina during Heyward's lifetime. Now shabby, the city sustained its seventeenth-century way of life. The tragic posturing was left to Faulkner's Sutpens and Sartorises; Charleston had known the good life not for twenty years but for 200; it had only to curb its appetites and distinguish between the spirit and manners that remained and the material that was threadbare or gone. The stoicism it had learned from earlier vicissitudes now stood it in good stead. Stoicism and the mannered life closed off introspection. Unsurprisingly, Heyward's single philosophical expression was, "We're here because we're here because we're here."[11]

Now Charleston was a minor seaport, isolated, with no money for travel or education. Its politics was parochial: fear of upstate rednecks. As Hervey Allen observed, "Here God is dull, where all things stay the same."[12]

While Heyward could, as a Heyward, exercise considerable freedom, Charleston's literary taste was rigidly Victorian; its insistence upon traditional verse forms uncompromising. It scorned realism, even the moderate realism of *Porgy;* it acknowledged the Negro as a subject for art only in the most stereotyped roles. Heyward realized the Poetry Society could not succeed without the support of the city's bluebloods; the society unhesitatingly voted that one of its first guests, Carl Sandburg, was not a poet.[13] When Heyward had Saint Wentworth carry a Negro girl's suitcase in New York City, Charleston was displeased. The discreet silence of Heyward and Bennett, when they discovered that the mulatto author of *Cane,* Jean Toomer, had joined the society, prevented a major crisis.[14]

Charleston was probably never more closed than at the beginning of the First World War. But whether it was the war or one of the occasional conjunctions of noblesse oblige and courage, just a few years later it had produced a novelist who openly admired Negro culture and scored the injustice of Charleston justice to blacks.

Considerable for its time, Heyward's courage was not unqualified. As could other sincere southerners in the 1920s, Heyward could, to some extent, see the injustice and cultural shallowness that marked his region's life. But, like them, he had to cope with the rigid taboo of public discussion of race relations, and he did not address himself as openly to it as had Twain and Cable. He saw racism, but he could neither see the obvious alternative of social justice in his time nor had he a developed, coherent Christian or humanist view of life that would push him toward action. He was a part of that coincidence of eighteenth-century manners, tradition, Christian stoicism, and a measure of self-deception that defined the best of southerners. He could see the evil, but, because he could do little about it, he managed to live with himself by explaining it away, as Heyward does in "The Negro in the Low-Country," published in 1931 at the height of his career:

That the system of slavery by its very nature protected the sadist in the practice of cruelty cannot be denied, nor can it be doubted that there were individual instances of injustice. But we must remember that the Negro probably to a greater extent than any other living race is possessed of a genius for forming happy human relationships, for inspiring affection, for instinctively divining the mood of one with whom he comes in contact, and of accommodating his own mood to that of the other. He was temperamentally ideally suited to make his own way in a state of slavery. . . .[15]

Charleston had been living with things as they are since Stede Bonnet and his pirates occupied the city; so could Heyward, with a minimum of pain.

Writing about his world, as he could see it, Heyward's work stands somewhat apart from that of other Southern Renascence figures.[16] Place is very important to Heyward and he is conscious of a community, but there is hardly the pervading sense of community that Cleanth Brooks finds in *Light in August*. Heyward's mannered world is less sensitive to the concrete, at least to the dramatic or to a sacramental view of the physical world. He is too far from the revival sounds of the Bible Belt to have what Robert Heilman calls a sense of the elemental. He lacks the Greek and Latin and background in letters to be ornamental and elevated in style; instead, he adopts several of the decadent embellishments of Joseph Hergesheimer. As a memorialist, he is too modest to move an audience with the universality of his vision or to impress us with what Heilman calls a sense of the totality, particularly the dimension of time. Davidson is right in complaining that he does not speak with one voice, that of a traditional society, always a whole person, for he does not share Davidson's near-mystical sense of the order in the South's past; rather, he is wafted between a sterile past and a variety of contemporary experiences in which he finds little pattern. Again, the eighteenth-century Charleston heritage, his trust in the dollar for salvation, and his awareness of social constraints deny him that sense of the tragic dimension of life so often found in the Southern Renascence. And Charleston is one place in the South where the frontier folk tradition is too remote to have fathered a tall tale telling literature or one in which the speaker is heard behind the language, as in Faulkner. Students of Faulkner could conclude from this catalog that it was Heyward's misfortune not to have been raised in Oxford, Mississippi. The point is that he was a Charlestonian; it determined the kind of writer he would be.

III *Influences*

Perhaps it is only coincidental, but it is notable that in only two of his early poems did Heyward deal with black experience, yet after his trips north and summers at MacDowell Colony, he suddenly saw the story he would write in his dock experience. And it was a certain kind of story, reflecting little of the primitivists' exaggerations while revealing the rural southern black, only one remove from the woods and fields.

But *Porgy* came after a formative period in which other writers played a major part. John Bennett, whom Heyward met through a letter on growing apples and peaches in Hendersonville, was a journalist, author of a popular children's book, *Master Skylark*, a romantic novelist, and, later, an author of verse under the name of Alexander Findley McClintock of Jockey's Glen, North Carolina.[17] Pennsylvanian Hervey Allen had won acclaim for a war poem, "The Blindman," and would go on to publish three more volumes of poetry, a biography of Poe, and several romantic novels, including *Anthony Adverse*. For the half-dozen years before *Porgy* these two friends at once gave Heyward contact with writers who took their craft seriously and would give him counsel and criticize his efforts and, not always as fortunately, channeled Heyward's taste in the directions they were taking: traditional verse forms, local color, and popular romances.

Details are lacking concerning the Wednesday-evening discussions in Bennett's living room at 37 Legaré. We do know that Allen and Heyward called Bennett Mr. Hypercritic and his assaults on their work "fanging."[18] Heyward's correspondence indicates their debt to Bennett, and he was anxious to have Bennett's criticism of the *Carolina Chansons* and *Porgy* manuscripts.[19] But for help with *Porgy* he went to Allen, who assisted in arranging the sections and read proof.[20]

In leading Heyward to local materials, Bennett showed him a subject. Bennett's wider reading experience also offered Heyward some direction in how to treat it. In the summer of 1920 Heyward wrote Bennett: "I can not quite find the middle ground between the melodramatic and the strong, the realistic and the romantic, but some day, who knows."[21] Bennett replied:

What I want you to write, and what I feel you certainly can write, is honest, man-like, popular stuff, with general romance, real life, authentic feeling, true sentiment, and your own wit and humane analysis of men and motives. It is all very well to write high-brow literature which shall be read unwillingly

by school children of the third and fourth generations after we are dust; but
there is little in it; the real thing has as good a chance, or better; just be genuine, not too exaggerated, sympathetic, poignant, without false sentimentality; have a heart, and a good spirit. Find that happy hunting-ground between
Harold Bell Wright and J. M. Barrie, what you so exactly describe as the
middle ground . . . between the melodramatic and the strong. . . . though I
must not call Barrie "strong," rather is R. Kipling the man of strength and
power. Did you ever read any of Sarah Orne Jewett's down-east tales, "Century By-Ways," "The Queen's Twin," or the like? Look into her for quiet
truth, sympathy, suggestion, unexaggerated, honest sentiment . . . then Kipling for *power* and the intensely dramatic . . . and Barrie for quaint, sensitive
humor, Cable for feeling . . . O. Henry for the "popular," . . though often he
is false as – – – – and sham . . . . tish! tish! I grow pedantic . . . enough
. . but more anon.[22]

Such counsel may be questioned; what counted was Bennett's criticism
of Charleston's poor literary taste which led Heyward to ignore its genteel demands.[23]

Of particular value to Heyward was Allen's talent for narrative, a
chronic weakness in Heyward's fiction, which Allen later displayed in
his massive popular novels. But Allen also had a weakness for cosmic
philosophizing in his verse, which may explain the occasional, usually
nonfunctional, cosmic preoccupation in Heyward's work.

Bennett and Allen clearly shaped Heyward as a writer closer in technique to the late Victorians than to any of the major influences of modern English and American writing. Heyward complained sarcastically
of a Laura Bragg article on the new poetry that ignored Allen but
included "her little Chicago picked chicken verse of Winters."[24] But
Bennett and Allen redeemed themselves in bringing Heyward to see
that writing is a craft involving hard work and, through their contacts
with MacDowell Colony and literary people in New York City, opening doors for Heyward that made possible the play of other influences
and currents in his work.[25]

Heyward's Poetry Society involvement is more complex, as the studies of Frank Durham, Morris Cox, and Marjorie Elizabeth Peale have
shown. In one sense, it was merely an extension of the evenings at Bennett's to include Radcliffe-educated Josephine Pinckney, Helen Von
Kolnitz Hyer, Elizabeth Miles, Katherine Drayton Mayrant Simons,
and Laura Bragg (most accounts leave Beatrice Ravenel out of the
study group). However, that extension did focus Heyward's attention

on one genre, poetry, since the study group, prizes, yearbook, and speakers were concerned only with poetry.

But from the first the Poetry Society had an announced purpose other than an opportunity for writers to criticize one another's poetry. It would create hordes of poets, poetry being the "inevitable avenue through which the masses of people, untrained in the other arts, can find most ready and spontaneous expression."[26]

As the Poetry Society's first secretary, a large share of this mission initially fell to Heyward—writing for and editing the *Year Book*, serving as national salesman for southern writing, arranging for speakers, and organizing the prize contests. In the 1924 *Year Book*, Heyward boasts that while the society had not produced any poets, its lively activity had enlarged taste and so cleared the way for modern literature, a "foundation upon which a future art could build solidly," thus giving the region "a weapon with which to defend itself against the absurd and groundless charge that it was a region devoid of an inherent culture."[27] This assessment also comes close to being a valedictory. Within a year, Heyward, Allen, and Josephine Pinckney had left Charleston.

Precisely what the society had done for these writers may not be clear. Their creative energies were released; they discovered local materials and used them; they found publishers and an audience. But their failure to grow into literary figures of power and significance, explained by the limitations of their culture and the conception of the seriousness of art, is also explained by what seems to be the unconscious strategy of the Charleston group, one that developed out of these limitations: while they invited speakers and attracted poets from everywhere into their contests, what they were really trying to do was create from nothing a new literary tradition. They rejected almost everything modern and, except for some traditional forms, they also rejected or ignored literary tradition. Their talk of a literature of southern history, customs, and beauty and the organization of poets and audiences was directed toward making out of antique furniture, fanlights, broad verandas, and flower arrangement a taste that would produce a poetic literary culture all their own. Such a superficial effort was doomed, so that it is not surprising that by the early 1930s its leading writers had not only turned to prose but a number of them, most notably Allen, to popular fiction. Allen later claimed that Amy Lowell's criticism of the Charlestonians for trying to be minor lyric poets was the turning point in his career.[28] Louis Rubin's claim that they were all popularizers to

begin with is certainly true of Bennett, Allen, and Heyward in 1919.
And such an unprecedented effort—a literature innocent of
tradition—could hardly result in anything else. Although serious, they
were not serious enough. In every respect, they took the easy way. A
century and a quarter before the Poetry Society, William Gilmore
Simms wrote in his magazine of the necessity for intellectual "exer-
tions" to have a cultural flowering in the South.[29] The Poetry Society
of South Carolina did not believe it.

Within the limits of its real possibilities, the Poetry Society was a
success. It also spawned the Society for the Preservation of Spirituals in
1922 and renewed interest in drama in the city by producing *Deirdre
of the Sorrows* in 1922-1923. Such success does not, however, make
great poets.

For Heyward, the influences of Bennett, Allen, and the Poetry Society, along with summers in the shadow of Robinson at MacDowell Colony, largely explain his preoccupation with poetry between 1920 and
1924. Allen's new interest in fiction may also explain Heyward's shift
to fiction; it is unlikely that it was the direct influence of anyone at
MacDowell Colony. Rather, Chard Powers Smith writes of the efforts
of his fellow colonists to dissuade Heyward from the "atrocious" story
of the little crippled Negro, and Mrs. Heyward confirms this view.[30]
Constance Rourke had also severely criticized Heyward's handling of
point of view in *Porgy*.

The role MacDowell Colony played in Heyward's career was more
basic: it was not so much the camaraderie of poets and novelists; it was
the work regimen the studio hours established.[31]

The final literary influence on Heyward, of note here, was his wife,
Dorothy. Except for her superior education and rhetorical skill which,
according to his sister, Heyward drew upon, and her playwriting talent, Dorothy's known role was not appreciably different from that
played by Bennett and Allen. She, too, was a popularizer, from her
early and rather superficial plays to her later mystery novels, yet there
is no gainsaying the fact that Heyward's sudden maturing as a fiction
writer is coincident with their marriage.

IV *Apprenticeship in Fiction and Prose*

Two perspectives on Heyward's work other than the people and
forces that formed him as a poet, novelist, and playwright are provided
by his early stories and occasional nonfiction prose. Both show him

moving into his own *métier*, and the nonfiction reiterates several of his main concerns.

Heyward's short fiction efforts between 1917 and 1920 reveal both Heyward's need for criticism and Bennett's negative influence. The great emphasis is on plot, usually one dependent upon coincidence, as in "The Winning Loser," where "Brag" Calloway and Rayburn both stalk a mountain lion from opposite sides of a ridge and shoot it at the same instant. Unlike *Porgy*, their immediate fiction successor, there is little if any community chorus, so that, in most of these stories, two or three figures stand out starkly in the melodramatic actions. Their spare formal resources clearly identify them as apprentice work.

Perhaps their chief interest is their betrayal of John Bennett's enthusiasms. Bennett saw them as in the manner of Octavus Roy Cohen, but Bret Harte, O. Henry, and Kipling are there, too.[32]

"The Winning Loser" is a Bret Harte Western, with its characteristic ironic ending. Rayburn has left everything for a career, on his own, in the West. He comes to see that all he sought was adventure, but only the nobility of Belle Flavant, his new love, in going away with Calloway, sends him back to the East.

"The Quade Sense of Honor" has an insignificant coincidence plot in which a promoter traps himself in a tax-evasion scheme.

"A Man's Job" is a Jack London lumberjack story in which the hero must conquer man and nature to win his love.

"The Mayfield Miracle" is O. Henry sentimentality, focusing on a cripple whose walking movements are so ridiculous that he refuses to walk until a hospital fire occasions his "dance act" to avoid a riot.

The remaining three stories, however, show Heyward finding his native material. "The Ghost of the Helen of Troy" revolves around a ghost hoax. But here, before *Carolina Chansons*, Heyward is seen describing the Low Country to the accompaniment of Negro spirituals and folk songs.

In "Dorothy Grumpet, Graduate Lady," from its title to Dorothy's father counting the number of piano notes she could hit in a minute, there is something of the ironic eye for the pathetic encounters of the country hick with foreign experience that was to become so characteristic of Flannery O'Connor's people. But her irony is in the service of subtle themes; Heyward turns his characters' ignorance to a satiric attack on the corruption that follows upon industrialization, and he defends the primitive.

"The Brute," second of these stories to be published, is a mountain

triangle in which the brutish and suspicious husband is, finally, cuck-
olded and, in retaliation, gleefully drops several hundred tons of rock
on his wife and her lover with a dynamite charge: "Standing close with
heads high and breasts toward it, they waited; waited with that magnificent physical courage that is the heritage of all primitive people;
waited for a space during which a steady heart might beat ten—
THEN—"[33] "The Brute" is important, however, less for the melodrama that marks Heyward's later work, though nowhere as exces-
sively as here, or for the plot which is incorporated into *Angel*, than,
again, for Heyward's discovery of the local scene—his own experience.

In these stories, Heyward comes home to the Carolinas.

Before *Porgy*, Heyward's nonfiction prose had been largely limited
to a preface, an introductory essay, and several forewords to poetry
collections. In 1923 he did a brief biographical sketch of Beatrice Witte
Ravenel that spoofed the genteel approach to letters in the South.[34]

Also in 1923 came a herald of his fiction interest in the Charleston
Negro, an essay, "And Once Again—the Negro," published in the
Reviewer, a Richmond, Virginia, little magazine edited by Emily
Clark. This essay, which Frances Newman claimed revealed ironic
gifts that should lead Heyward from poetry to the essay form, discusses
distinctive customs of Charleston Negroes, wonders if the primitive
Negroes are an aeon ahead or behind, and sadly laments the Negro's
fate:[35]

But one thing is certain: the reformer will have them in the fullness of
time. They will surely be cleaned, married, conventionalized. They will be
taken from the fields, and given to machines, their instinctive feeling for the
way that leads to happiness, saved as it is from selfishness, by humour and
genuine kindness of heart, will be supplanted by a stifling straight-jacket.
They will languish, but they will submit, because they will be trained into a
habit of thought that makes blind submission a virtue.

And my stevedore, there out of the window I look at him again. I cannot
see him as a joke. Most certainly I cannot contort him into a menace. I can
only be profoundly sorry for him, for there he sits in the sunshine, unconscious, awaiting his supreme tragedy. He is about to be saved.[36]

Heyward returned to the topic of the Negro in a 1928 introduction
to the play version of *Porgy* and again in 1932 in the essay referred to
earlier, "The Negro in the Low-Country," which focuses once more on
the clash between the primitive Negro and change and suggests that

the Low Country Negro is ideally suited for the Uncle Tom role that pleases whites.[37]

The first of three articles on southern literature, "The New Note in Southern Literature," appeared in the *Bookman* just months before *Porgy's* publication. As in his early southern lecture, he is concerned with the interpretation of Negro life, here observing that it had been "caricatured beyond recognition."[38] Essentially a brief asking respect for art's own code, a plea for tolerance for the forthcoming *Porgy*, the essay celebrates the work of Lula Vollmer, Lawrence Stallings, Julia Peterkin, and John Crowe Ransom, among others.

A two-part essay on "Contemporary Southern Poetry" appeared in 1926. The first part argues that the southern aristocracy's "congenital feeling for beauty" sustains an atmosphere that can produce art and audiences. The remainder catalogs southern poets who have not left the South. This part follows closely Heyward's basic tour lecture, as probably do much of the other *Bookman* pieces.

As a half-dozen succeeding efforts show, Heyward was not an essayist. His articles and other prose pieces are slight, loosely organized, nondescript in style, and fuzzy when dealing with theory. He shows no gift for analysis or criticism. The only topic that seems to engage his deeper interests is the Carolina Negro. As in his fiction, he returns to this subject with obvious interest and passion, praising what he envies in the Negro and fearing its loss as the wheels of progress turn. He avoids the race question, implying that a clash between the Negro and progress is inevitable, and the white man can do little but stand stoically by. His two direct, published references to race relations in nonfiction prose are a note in the *Woman's Home Companion* in 1928 which cites his work with Negroes during World War I and his membership in the Interracial Committee "for the establishment of better relations between the races in the South" and the response to a National Association for the Advancement of Colored People questionnaire published in the *Crisis*.[39] In the latter, Heyward defends states rights but endorses a federal antilynching law in view of the failure of the states to deal effectively with the crime.

Heyward's letters, most of which are to Bennett, Allen, or George Gershwin, offer only an occasional insight into his work—or a solid sentence, as that in a letter to Kathyrn Bourne, on the Negro spiritual: "For the spiritual said everything for him that he could not say in the

new language that he found here—awe in the presence of death—his
racial terror of being left alone—his escape from bondage into the new
heaven—everything."[40]

V   *Accomplishments*

Heyward's essays, his fiction efforts, his ambitions, and his life all
came full circle, back to his first love, Charleston, back to fiction, and
even back to the theater, the genre of his first effort. The Heyward
name was reestablished among Charleston's leading as well as old families. Heyward did not, however, finally buy the Signer's mansion but
24 Battery, on the street of principal distinction, facing White Point
Gardens and the bay. Certainly by Charleston standards he had succeeded. He was a gentleman of impeccable manners, the first criterion.
As Edna Ferber observed, "He is incurably a Southern gentleman, and
he doesn't know it's not done."[41] A quarter of a century after his death,
Katharine Simons quickly summed up her memory of Heyward: "He
was a lovely gentleman."[42] Frank Durham, who knew him in the Dock
Street Theatre, described him as "sweet and keen."[43] Heyward had
survived poverty, illness, and lack of education to establish a business
and then a literary career. His first career undoubtedly exercised his
charm, as did his role in the Poetry Society; his second answered his
early desire to reflect in art his experience of his world and resulted in
Heyward memorializing Charleston in art. And, as Alfred Kreymbourg
wrote in 1929 of Heyward's success in promoting southern writing:
"From Colonial days onward, Southerners have been excellent publi-
cists. The work of the modest Heyward in the field of persuasion has
noble qualities."[44] Consequently, through his writing and the Poetry
Society he had jousted successfully with Mencken. The 1925 *Year Book*
quotes Mencken: "Perhaps the most significant phenomena to American literature today are the revival of the South, and the passing of the
Chicago School."[45] Heyward was gleeful upon selling "Jasbo Brown"
to the *American Mercury* editor for $75 in 1931, and he could claim
a significant share of the credit for Mencken's reversal, in 1935, of his
earlier judgment:[46]

No one can fail to note the great change that has come over Southern writers
during the past dozen years. At the turn of the century they were still com-
posing librettos for fairy operas, but of late they have been turning sharp eyes
to the actual Southern scene, and some of their reports have certainly not

lacked candor. That candor becomes contagious. There is a new spirit all over the South, and it begins to come to grips with reality.[47]

Heyward had also had his name in lights on Broadway.

Charleston was probably less impressed with his greater successes. He had courageously showed his audience the humanity and culture and point of view of the urban southern Negro as well as something of the inadequacy of his own white culture. His realism had also probed the effects of changes, particularly after World War I, on both. He had seen that life eluded his kind, and he pursued it into Catfish Row, the artist's garret, even as far as the Virgin Islands. He had, at a crucial moment for the South and its budding renascence, struck a quiet blow for truth in southern fiction.

CHAPTER 2

A Local Color Poet

I The Southern Poetry Scene

H EYWARD'S sudden prominence as a poet in the South of the early 1920s is largely explained by the absence of serious poetry there after the passing of Timrod, Hayne, and Lanier. The South had not figured in the poetry renascence that began at the turn of the century. Conrad Aiken, born in the South, became a New Englander. John Gould Fletcher left his southern home before he was twenty and in 1908, when twenty-two, left the country. After an apprentice volume in 1917, John Peale Bishop had gone abroad. Heyward came at the end of that line of minor and now almost forgotten southern poets extending from Father Ryan and John Banister Tabb to Lizette Reese, William Alexander Percy, James Weldon Johnson, Madison Cawein, and Cale Young Rice, who stand between the nineteenth-century Timrod and Lanier and the renascence of poetry in the South that began with the twenty numbers of the *Fugitive*. Heyward is particularly notable in relation to this group because while he was committed to the older southern poetry tradition, he was also original in his more realistic use of local materials. This was not the originality of the Fugitives or that of their friends Elizabeth Madox Roberts and John Peale Bishop, who were publishing elsewhere, so to call him a transitional figure between old and new would be something of a misnomer. Still, his work does fall between that of such traditional nature and landscape poets as Cawein, Reese, John Trotwood Moore, and Walter Malone and the distinctly modern Nashville poets.

II Charleston Poetics and Nashville Critics

Like his fellow Poetry Society of South Carolina members, Heyward was committed to the simple clear language and pathos of Legaré, to the reflection of the beauty and truth of the local landscape of Timrod and Lanier, and perhaps more than his fellow South Carolinians to the musical qualities of Lanier and Poe.

In their 1923 essay "Poetry South," Heyward and Allen make clear their commitment to their predecessors' kind of poetry: simple in theme and familiar in form.[1] They would be influenced by neither Imagism nor the highly allusive poetry of Eliot. Laura Bragg, the transplanted New Englander who became a Charleston museum curator, urged the fledgling Charleston talents to take the fresh winds of contemporary poetry seriously, but they would have none of it, and her influence, while significant, was largely negative. Allen inscribed her copy of *Carolina Chansons*, "You kept the artic [*sic*] teal and English skylark out of Carolina."[2] True, the Charlestonians abandoned the genteel rhetoric of earlier generations of southern poets, and updated their thematic concerns. Still, in their preoccupation with local color, the Carolina landscape, and the past, they are much more like Legaré, Timrod, and Lanier than the Nashville poets who began publishing the *Fugitive* only two years after Heyward, Allen, and Bennett organized the Poetry Society.

The second difficulty followed from the first. In the absence of any strong traditional influence, Heyward fashioned his poetics out of the few notions he had picked up from Bennett, Allen, and his fellow Charlestonians. In brief, he believed that taste is readily translated into poetry, so that poetry wells forth spontaneously from the cultured aristocracy when an audience commands. This poetry will echo in simple, clear, direct language—even dialect—the life, customs, history, and beauty of the locality. It will not be personal and subjective but classical, objective, and in form traditional, not experimental in the manner of the Imagists or T. S. Eliot. This is the essence of Heyward's four statements on poetry: the first *Year Book* foreword, published in 1921; the *Carolina Chansons* preface, written in 1921; the 1923 *Poetry* essay; and the two-part essay "Contemporary Southern Poetry," published in 1926.

In the first *Year Book* foreword, Heyward argues that the imminent southern literary expression will find "its most ready and spontaneous expression" in poetry, a prophecy that was dead wrong in that the literature of the Southern Renascence has been largely fiction and several of its notable poets are as well or better known for their fiction.[3] Although the Poetry Society leaders recognized that Mencken's metaphor was apt, the foreword also insists upon the viability of southern culture, presumably to stimulate the occasional poetic talent and to gather the audience Heyward had insisted was waiting to hear mature voices.

In the first installment of "Contemporary Southern Poetry," Heyward insisted that colonial architecture and the classics had produced a large audience whose tastes could be transferred to contemporary verse.[4] The founders of the Poetry Society quite obviously bought this argument, for they collected the first members by going to the Charleston telephone book and picking out the city's most socially prominent.[5] Right or wrong, the immediate popularity of the Poetry Society of South Carolina and of societies in other states that quickly followed did prove that there was some kind of audience for the muse.

The brief Heyward-Allen preface to *Carolina Chansons* is more clearly a statement of poetic theory. It declares the volume to be programmed: historical legends of the past in the "pensively melancholy" Low Country landscape.[6] "'You write the incidents; I'll take the atmosphere,'" Allen had said to Heyward.[7] It is to be local color poetry: the future lies with "local poets who can interpret their own sections to the rest of the country as Robinson and Frost have done so nobly for New England, rather than in the effort to yawp universally."[8] Heyward was listening to Mencken's call for regionalism; he would have none of Whitman.

The "Poetry South" essay develops the theme of that preface. It is actually a description of the kind of poetry he had written, but it also purports to be a survey of the poetry being written throughout the South and a program for contemporary Southern poets to follow—away from the plantation:[9]

If, in addition to the physical environment, we have also some grasp of the historical and ethnic background from which poets speak, some comprehension of the immediate social and local problems which surround them—in short, some knowledge of the poets themselves—we shall be able, to a large extent, to tell not only what subjects they will be most likely to select, but also, in a more limited sense, in what mood they will approach their theme. . . .[10]

It is to be a "poetry of and about places."[11] So southern poetry will be less intellectual and sophisticated and more "spontaneous and simple" because it rises from a rural rather than city environment, from the subtropics to the mountains.[12] It will reflect the "patriarchal life remnant" about the poet and "the spontaneously lyrical and primarily rhythmic melodies of the Negro."[13] While white prejudice and the white South's "intimate mood of memory and contemplation" may stop the white poet short of the syncopated rhythms of jazz, it will not, as Heyward knew from practice, stop attempts at "unauthentic dialect."[14] Southern poetry, then, will concern itself with the grotesque and primitive in Negro life and culture, as use of the spirituals already suggests; with rugged mountains and their folk culture, suffering, and religious sects; with the flora and fauna, lagoons, gardens, and turbaned blacks of the Low Country; the labor exploitation and race tensions of the Piedmont; the old cities and centuries of history. It will be a poetry marked by the eighteenth-century classical tradition more than by Puritanism or Romanticism, and indebted to its forerunners who "overcame literary taboos and tradition, and dared to have a personality; with them poetry was not simply polite."[15]

According to Heyward and Allen, there were several things southern poetry would be. First, impersonal: "And it is also to be hoped that the cleverly inane, or the small accidental dream-life of the individual, so seldom worth uttering—tiny loves and smaller hates, and the baldly phrased usual; above all, the banal echo and the purely sentimental—will be left unsaid."[16] Second, it would not be experimental in form or more concerned with form than content. This was the same stance Heyward took in his first lecture and was the substance of his poetics.

Heyward's correspondence with Allen and Bennett reveals what a poetically immature audience the aristocracy in whom he places so much hope really was. Because of its irreligious theme, when Ransom's "Armageddon" won the society's main award, the editors cautiously published it separately from the *Year Book,* available to those who asked for it, undisturbing to those who did not.[17] Another crisis came with the appearance of Edna St. Vincent Millay, whose reputation for unladylike manners had preceded her. She justified their fears by explaining to a party that in Europe menstruating women were not allowed to get into the tubs to press grapes.[18]

Nowhere does Heyward recognize that poetry is born of richly textured language, of a complex and harmonious vision of being, of a high degree of consciousness which, of course, transcends region and is poetry first and regional only incidentally or as a point of departure. Heyward's poems do better than his theory, although most can be classified as largely local color expressions. Heyward never explains, in his attention to place and time, what it is that makes Frost and Robinson *great* New England poets.

Heyward was not alone in his overemphasis on local color. In introducing the Southern Number of *Poetry* in 1928, Harriet Monroe notes her efforts to encourage "a strongly localized indigenous art," and goes on to echo Heyward's and Allen's view of the art the South would produce.[19]

The emphasis of the Charleston poets on landscape and history produced a reaction in Nashville: it initiates a series of statements by the Fugitives and those associated with them that constitutes a poetic unlike Heyward's, one which contradicts his notions, occasionally criticizes his poems, and taken with his own notions on art, serves to introduce us to Heyward's poetry and the fiction and drama that follow. Many of the important questions about his work are raised here. How was Heyward's work unlike that of the writers generally identified with the Southern Renascence and like that of those—Peterkin, Stuart, Ravenel, and Stribling—who are not? Is his work sentimental? Is the difference the burden of Charleston? Does Heyward's handling of the Negro transcend local color? Does Heyward make any notable contribution to the forms he employs?

An editorial comment in an early number of the *Fugitive* rejects Miss Monroe's insistence upon the Old South as the proper material for southern poets.[20] However, an editorial note in the next issue distinguishes between the Charlestonians' successful use of the local scene and its misuse by others and between recent southern poetry and that of the Fugitives:

. . . Of Southerners writing in late years of the local scene they [Heyward and Allen] alone are distinguished: not least of all for their awareness of the difference between versified provincialism and indigneous poetry, for they have done as all good poets do in setting about to locate the emotion of art definitely in space and time. Unfortunately, however, a review of the literature recording some of atavism and more of sentimentality may have much to do with rendering a "jewel-weighted" tradition inaccessible to many of the present Southern poets; and if a considerable bulk of our poetry should be discovered to sound a new note, while it would be within the province of criticism to account it the less "southern," it would not be within the province of criticism to account it any the less southern. Whether the limitation be in the poets, or whether there is something fatally oppressive about these materials most readily obtainable from the past, we do not know. At any rate, we fear to have too much stress laid on a tradition that may be called a tradition only when looked at through the haze of a generous imagination.[21]

Working from these distinctions, Donald Davidson's criticism over the next ten years makes two further ones that all but complete a Fugitive aesthetic regarding local color. The first is his subordination of place to the integrity of the poem:

Frost has written of New England, Sandburg of Chicago, but whatever is good in their poetry is good not merely because they wrote of specific places. Place is incidental. . . . The poem, not the "scene" or the business of interpreting the "scene," must be uppermost in his consciousness.[22]

To Davidson, Heyward's Charleston towers, unlike Frost's pasture lots, lack universality and so do not make good poetry. Heyward is too often merely place-conscious, so could as well be "a Californian apostrophizing the climate and the Golden Gate."[23] Surface impressions of place and time make slight poetry.[24] Too often, in Davidson's view, the southern writer immersed in the local scene behaves "like a fool" in his empty though accurate handling of local references.[25]

Davidson's second distinction is between the atavistic and sentimental southern poetry of the past and a poetry rising out of the southern experience of defeat, poverty, belief, and conviction.[26] Here Davidson's concern is that the Charlestonians and others do not reflect the distinctive inner dimension of the South that became Davidson's major subject as a poet.

But it was left to Ransom to develop this distinction in his 1935 essay "Modern with the Southern Accent." Ransom's argument is that the Charlestonians "are producing a literature, but it is irrelevant to what Charleston stands for, and it is not Southern."[27] Southern writing, such as Heyward's fiction, may be vigorously written, even overwritten, but it is not truly southern if it reflects romantic primitivism or a popular viewpoint. For it then lacks a distinctively southern "fixed basis of judgment, and a conventional way of talking about things."[28] In Ransom's choice of Heyward's fiction rather than his poetry for discussion and his reference to the Charleston poets as "less subtle," there is a strong suggestion that, like Davidson, he considers the Heyward-Allen poetics oversimplified.[29]

The Fugitives argue for a literature southern in spirit: concern with what Robert Penn Warren called the "romantic possibilities" of local color and the legend of the South does not necessarily make significant literature or southern literature.[30] More importantly, the Fugitives recognized that serious art requires critical intelligence, an intensity of experience, and a healthy attitude toward language. And by all of these criteria the Fugitives find Heyward's work wanting. Identifying Heyward's poetry as regional, Davidson writes: "It exploits the Negro, the mountaineer, the picturesque ways of Charleston. It reflects fine feelings and good taste and has a gentle lyrical charm. But it never shows great strength or originality."[31]

Allen Tate demurred from this view in observing that Heyward's "honest transcript of phases of the local scene, unsentimentalized, unwept, but not unsung" makes poems, if "intensely local" ones.[32] Singling out the Skyline portraits of mountain people in prisons of their "own dumb suffering," Tate praises Heyward's use of significant detail and realization of the essential emotion of their blindly protesting Hardy stoicism.[33]

A final, crucial distinction was left to one of the later Vanderbilt academicians. Heyward and the other Charleston poets were not, in Cleanth Brooks's view, simply victims of a cultural lag, local color addicts, or reformers in a low key, satisfied to prune away Victorian dead wood. Like the Fugitives, they were in revolt, he observes in a notable 1935 essay, "The Modern Southern Poet and Tradition." It is a revolt in favor of originality, realism, and local color.[34] One aspect of their reaction against Victorianism, Brooks argues, is a preoccupation with materials and an option for new materials. But that revolution can take several forms. It can rest in the objective description of things, in what Ransom calls physical poetry, which would appear to include Imagist practice as well as the handling of "new and unworked materials" in the poetry of local color, for example, Jesse Stuart's "The Man with the Bull-Tongued Plow."[35] Notably, Brooks observes, the more local color there is, the less sense of the past, from the many southern local colorists such as Heyward to some of Frost's landscape and character poems. But where Ransom and Tate, poets with a strong sense of tradition, use accurate detail of place as background or example in poems where the critical intelligence synthesizes past and present, thought and feeling, and the discordant and contradictory into a poetry of inclusion, like that of the Metaphysicals, they move toward universal statement.[36] In Brooks's view, Robert Penn Warren's "Kentucky Mountain Farm" opens to the universal, but Heyward's "Mountain Woman" is interested in the local color setting for its own sake and reveals only the "crudeness" and "pathos" of the mountain people.[37]

While Heyward and the Charlestonians found their own materials, like their Victorian counterparts they remained poets of "sharp exclusion," Brooks explains.[38] They rejected the introspective. They clung to simple lyrical forms. And looking upon place or the past without critical intelligence, they did not achieve the tension between incongruities that Tate talked about, but, in Brooks's view, sentimentality:

Sentimentality always involves the posing of the sentimentalized experiences in a favorable light. Artists, of course, always select and exclude, but sentimentality involves an illegitimate exclusion of elements because they are apparently inimical to the particular mood. To put it another way, the sentimentalist takes a short cut to intensity by carefully removing all tendencies which seem to conflict with the favored mood. Needless to say, the totality of the poet's vision is sacrificed, and the intensity for the mature mind is felt to be the result of a trick. The intensity of the poetry of inclusion is won by more difficulty, and because of this is genuine.[39]

Brooks compares "Mountain Woman" unfavorably with Tate's "Last Days of Alice," where two emotions are viewed simultaneously in a state of tension.[40] Between Heyward and Tate stands Davidson's "The Tall Men," where past and present are in tension, but Davidson has come to terms with tradition in too "personal" and "mystical" a way for the tension to be "intimate" and "active" enough.[41] But in general, the achievement of the Fugitives is that they unite the past of Bayard Taylor's poems and the present of Carl Sandburg's.[42] The weakness of the Charlestonians as poets is not that they fail to write southern poetry according to the Fugitives' definition but that in settling for a poetry of exclusion they fail to write great poetry.

So it was left to Brooks to make a critical distinction based on something more than proportions of local color and southern values and a general claim for the poem as poem.

Davidson's 1957 judgment of the southern poets of his generation outside the Fugitives' circle sums up the Nashville critics' argument:

That the other Southern poets of this period did not practice this serious, exclusive devotion to their art seems clear from the record. Either they were caught up in the superficial excitement that attended the "New Poetry" and practiced facile imitations of its merely rhetorical features without asking themselves any very hard critical questions or submitting to the discipline of high art, or else they were in equally uncritical revolt against modernism and were imitating the rhetoric of nineteenth century poetry without any questions as to its artistic premises. Thus, whether rebels or reactionaries, they slid into a false kind of self-consciousness that put them into a wrong relation both

to the present and their past, and so lost the inherited advantages that, as
Southern poets, they should have enjoyed.[43]

More critically oriented and more contemporary in theme and technique, the Fugitives did not publish the Charlestonians. But they did
come back to Heyward and the Carolina group again and again in
discussing the uses of the southern experience and the local scene in
poetry. All of this was lost on Heyward and the Charlestonians—and
their art. For that matter, so was just about everything else that might
have contributed to a fuller development of Heyward's poetic. Heyward traveled widely, meeting other writers, and the society played
host to Davidson, Ransom, Frost, Æ(George William Russell), and others. Charleston had many writers and painters, bookstores, and Miss
Bragg's library of contemporary poetry. But Charleston's insularity had
apparently so shaped Heyward's mind and taste that travel and association with other writers would not enlarge his perspective, as study
in the East did for Josephine Pinckney and Beatrice Ravenel.

As Louis Rubin observes, the Nashville Fugitives, in contrast to the
Charlestonians, were all university men and several were sons of clergymen, and as students and teachers of literature, they had a "highly
literate intellectual attitude toward language" and a deep interest in
criticism unshared in Charleston.[44] This interest is clearly revealed in
the occasional short statements on critical theory and reviews in the
Fugitive regarding the Imagists, T. S. Eliot, and the changing form of
contemporary poetry. For example, a review of Hervey Allen's *Earth
Moods* shows a fine discrimination between Allen's cliché-free use of
old forms, "modern sonority and color," skilled use of rhetorical and
declamatory devices, and, on the debit side, the overload of picture
and panorama and a paucity of "fine thoughts."[45]

The Charlestonians were also committed to just the opposite view of
language. As Rubin observes, to them the Chicago writers took words
too seriously; they demanded a poetry simple, obvious, immediately
intelligible, about a familiar world.[46] It was the language of popular
writing.

Instead of developing the small circle of serious writers which had
preceded it into something approximating the kind of group that met
at Sidney Hirsh's in Nashville, where the Fugitives argued about
words, ideas, and their own poems, the South Carolina Poetry Society
gathered the socially acceptable.[47] By comparison to the Fugitives'

poetry, the Charleston poetry, as Morris Cox's summary indicates, appears mindless of changing times, ideas, or literary fashions:

> Indeed, the poetry of the Charleston renaissance seems peculiarly insulated from the streams of fashion, even from the passing events of the outer world. In it one finds no "postwar disillusion," no burden of satire, no sense of disgust or intimation that living is futile or life hollow. It reflects little painful sense of social dilemma or of insecurity, or of a world ravaged and exhausted by war or cheapened by commercialism, little irony, anger, frustration, emotional conflict, or maladjustment. Charleston poets seemed strangely satisfied with life as it was and had been, and showed little desire to improve it or even to examine it critically. At a time when poetry elsewhere seemed to be turning inward to man, Charleston poetry turned outward, to locale. In the poetry they wished to read and the poetry they tried to write, highest value was set upon directness and lucidity, and violations were given short shrift in the formal discussions of the Poetry Society.[48]

They were Charlestonians, and Charleston had substituted manners for education and art—particularly in its view of language. It rejected the new or foreign. It had not experienced the clash of values World War I, the New South, and the Scopes trial in nearby Dayton, Tennessee, had provided the Vanderbilt community. Nothing changed so precipitously in Charleston as to become a crisis; nothing was so serious, complicated, or profound as what Faulkner saw in Yoknapatawpha Tate in the Confederate dead, and Ransom in the passage of life.

III Carolina Chansons: Legends of the Low Country

As early as 1936, Edd Winfield Parks published only two of Heyward's poems in *Southern Poets*, and none appears in the 1967 edition of the Young, Watkins, and Beatty anthology, *The Literature of the the South.*[49] Still, *Carolina Chansons: Legends of the Low Country* (with Hervey Allen), *Skylines and Horizons*, and *Jasbo Brown and Other Poems* include many poems and parts of others worth remembering.

Carolina Chansons, published in 1922, generally alternates Heyward's and Allen's poems. Allen's poems are easily categorized as exercises in historical imagination (LaFayette's landing, Osceola's Indians canoeing toward Europe, a Civil War blockade runner's voyage, the history of the Marsh Tackies left by DeSoto), local color description, and Poesque ghost-story writing, sometimes lapsing into popular, even glib, versifying. One exception is "Beyond Debate," a wryly humorous commentary on Mrs. Perdue, an old Charleston blueblood. Allen's poems have been compared with Heyward's numerically fewer contributions to *Carolina Chansons*, but the comparison sheds no important light on Heyward's work.

In "Silences" Heyward celebrates tradition by explaining to the traveler who hears in the bells of St. Matthew's and St. Michael's the song "Of lyric youth with voice unschooled by pain" what he finds missing: he does not hear the sound of St. Philip's bells that imaged the city before the war.

> Then from the soaring lyric of the spire,
> Like the composite voice of all the town,
> The bells burst swiftly into singing fire
> That wrapped the building, and which showered down
> Bright cadences to flash along the ways
> Loud with the splendid gladness of the days.
>
> The rhythmic seasons chill and burn and chill,
> Cooling old angers, warming hearts again.
> The ancient building quickens to the thrill
> Of lilting feet; but only singing rain
> Flutters old echoes in the portico;
> Those who can still remember love it so.

But the poem is marred by strained personification, awkward diction at the end, and the awkward joining of the visitor and the past. It also leans heavily on the poignancy of Charleston history.

"The Pirates," Heyward's second-longest poem—202 lines—is more historical than "Silences." It is an interesting experiment with narrative verse, from the viewpoint of a present voice recalling his witness of Charleston's distant past. The narrator begins with a description of the early town but focuses on the events of an era of pirate ascendancy and ends with their defeat and hanging. What strength the poem has is in the tension achieved by recovery of the past and in its description, as of the old mud flats:

> Yes, I have seen them sprawling nude
> While an Autumn noon hung chill
> And the tide came shuddering in from sea,
> Lift by lift, until

> It held them under a silver mesh,
> Responsive to its will.

"The Last Crew" is a Civil War poem, Heyward's longest, about the fifth "fish-boat" submarine crew to sacrifice itself in an effort to sink the Union *Housatonic* and the first successfully to complete the mission. After an opening strongly reminiscent of Henry Timrod's "Charleston" and "Spring" in its description of the coming of spring to the war-weary city, on one of those "rare nights" the narrator sees "the last crew go/Out of a world too beautiful to leave." The poem ends with a crowd, including the eight mourning widows, at the river. "These sunny islands were not meant for wars," the narrator says, observing that "They laugh like happy bathers, while the seas/Break in their open arms." Particularly impressive is the disappearance of the crew into the unidentified craft and its merging with the shadows and sounds of marsh life and the scene of the straining men and fetid air of the hand-cranked submarine.

The poem's rhythm is so subdued until the last section that the poem has much of the quality of a tale. Only the compression of events and emotions, the vivid detail, and the rhyme insist otherwise. Again, however, there are faults. The vocabulary in the first stanza of Part II is overwrought, as is the melodrama of the last crew, en route to its doom, passing the coffins of the next-to-last crew and the widows' faces that "hallow the town."

After a metrically smooth imitation of Masefield, "Landbound," Heyward makes his first overt statement about the Negro in "Modern Philosopher," later titled "Philosopher."

> They fight your battles for you every day,
> The zealous ones, who sorrow in your life.
> Undaunted by a century of strife,
> With urgent fingers still they point the way
> To drawing rooms, in decorous array,
> And moral Heavens where no casual wife
> May share your lot; where dice and ready knife
> Are barred; and feet are silent when you pray.
>
> But you have music in your shuffling feet,
> And spirituals for a lenient Lord,
> Who lets you sing your promises away.
> You hold your sunny corner of the street,

> And pluck deep beauty from a banjo chord:
> Philosopher whose future is today!

Heyward employs the sonnet form well here. In the octave the black voice wearily notes the paternalistic white effort to bring his race into conformity with staid white ways, which he answers in the sestet with a confident expression of his own philosophy: joy in life and trust that God's mercy will care for tomorrow. The contrast is reinforced by diction and the shift from predominant plosives to nasals, repeated in all but the last line of the sestet. Heyward also uses alliteration effectively for emphasis in lines five and ten and especially in "And pluck deep beauty from a banjo chord," where six plosives, alliteration, assonance, and three nasals create an onomatopoetic penultimate line. The paradox of the last line rounds off the enigmatic happiness of the Negroes very neatly.

The earliest of Heyward's expressions on southern race relations, however, in poetry or prose, written before "Philosopher," is "Gamesters All."

In the succinct opening description, before the narrator intrudes himself in lines 11–14, Heyward uses alliteration of c's and d's (lines 2–4); strong, fresh verbs in "loitered," "cupped," and "sucked"; an effective simile in likening the bay and day; personification of "cruel noon"; and relatively few adjectives to establish a languid atmosphere for the violent action to follow:

> The river boat had loitered down its way;
> The ropes were coiled, and business for the day
> Was done. The cruel noon closed down
> And cupped the town.
> Stray voices called across the blinding head,
> Then drifted off to shadowy retreat
> Among the sheds.
> The waters of the bay
> Sucked away
> In tepid swirls, as listless as the day.
> Silence closed about me, like a wall,
> Final and obstinate as death.
> Until I longed to break it with a call,
> Or barter life for one deep, windy breath.

Then, in a quick-moving, increasingly jazzlike tempo, the "mellow laugh" that begins the second stanza turns into the alternating lines of a spiritual and crap-game talk which, together, express again the theme of "Philosopher": "'Oh, nobody knows when de Lord is goin ter call,/*Roll dem bones.*'"

The movement is slowed by ten lines that do no more than reemphasize this fatalism and fearlessness. Then the police arrive: "'Now, Joe, don't be a fool!/I've got you cool.'"

The central action quickly reaches its climax and denouement in the clash between the sharply realized protagonist and antagonist. In choosing flight and freedom over slavery in prison, Joe sees this his "stiffest hand." "His laughter flashed" and he flees on "spurning feet." In turn, the Marshal is "Aflame with the excitement of the chase" and, "honest sportsman, as they go," he would "wait until he had a yard to go" before firing. The irony is immediately evident, the advantage being distinctly with the marksman shooting protected game out of season. Again ironically, the Marshal sees Joe only as game: "'Just once, at fifty feet,/A moving target too.'"

That the Marshal's view of the act is inadequate is evident in the four lines after his speech which, but for the final line, end the poem:

> He mopped his head, and started down the road.
> The silence eddied round him, turned and flowed
> Slowly back and pressed against the ears.
> Until unnumbered flies set it to droning . . .

There was silence in the beginning and now it returns, but only to change into the droning sound of the flies.

The poem is flawed, however, by the narrator's intrusions. He serves an essential purpose, yet he interrupts at the end of the first stanza, breathless in the heat; again to discuss the players' fatalism; again to describe Joe's physique as he ran; even to observe the Marshal's gun barrel; to comment hopefully after the shot; and, finally, to hear "a woman moaning." The moaning woman may counterbalance the Marshal's callousness, but she is really no more necessary than the rest of this. What remains speaks well enough for itself. On such a day, what does one do with his leisure? If he is black, he does not shoot craps or, arrested, flee. The animal thing to do, the Marshal suggests ironically, is to seek freedom, and the human response is to deny it, because Joe is, of course, no more than an animal to him. Once more Heyward is

seen to capture the race relationship in traditional terms that go much
further toward universality than local color.

"Dusk" is anthologized in *The Lyric South* as a local color poem;
Beatrice Ravenel called it Heyward's best.[50] It is, however, generally
a failure, for while Heyward's sincerity in recognizing his debt to
Charleston need not be questioned, the substance of that debt is not
communicated, as if the poet could count on his peers to understand
his abstract references, general labelings, indefinite pointings, and pro-
testations of identification and love. There are a few good lines of
description:

> Her chimes that shimmer from St. Michael steeple
> Across the deep maturity of June,
> Like sunlight slanting over open water
> Under a high, blue, listless afternoon.

But then the poet tells us he communes with Charleston by night—in
its "thrill," "Glamor," "memories," and the "faith" of those who tend
the "calling lights." Charleston is, in fact, "the stir/Of hidden music
shaping all my songs." But if grass, trees, night, water, fog, and harbor
bells make it so, there is no hint. Instead, "her cheek is on *my* cheek."

Along with "Landbound" and the unfocused "Edgar Allan Poe,"
"Dusk" offers some proof that the *Fugitive* was right in pointing to the
danger of programmatic local color poetry. By contrast, "Gamesters
All" and "Philosopher" move to the universal from unmistakably
southern settings.

IV   Skylines and Horizons

Heyward's reputation as a poet was secured in 1924 with the publication of *Skylines and Horizons*. The volume begins unimpressively
with "Your Gifts," a frankly sentimental dedicatory paean to his
mother's ability, in their poverty, to substitute her stories and dignity
for the toys and servants provided other children. But the group of
eleven mountain poems that follow made him, in the eyes of some, the
leading poet of the South.

"A Yoke of Steers" is best in its first five lines, where the fresh noun
"heave," the adjectives describing heads and horns, and the verb for
the darkness create the animals in the perspective of the landscape:[51]

> A heave of mighty shoulders to the yoke,
> Square, patient heads, and flaring sweep of horn;
> The darkness swirling down beneath their feet
> Where sleeping valleys stir, and feel the dawn;
> Uncouth and primal, on and up they sway . . .

But then Heyward gets into trouble with straining language and images—and editorializing: if the steers are the *"Unconquerable spirit of these hills,"* we fail to see how the vehicle relates to the tenor.

Robert Frost wrote Heyward in praise of "The Mountain Woman." But, Frost added, "Poetry societies are a more doubtful good."[52] "The Women" (in *Jasbo Brown* Heyward removed "Mountain" from the titles of the Skyline poems) may well be the most powerful of his poems:

> Among the sullen peaks she stood at bay
> And paid life's hard account from her small store
> Knowing the code of mountain wives, she bore
> The burden of the days without a sigh;
> And, sharp against the somber winter sky,
> I saw her drive her steers afield each day.
>
> Here was the hand that sunk the furrows deep
> Across the rocky, grudging southern slope.
> At first youth left her face, and later, hope;
> Yet through each mocking spring and barren fall,
> She reared her lusty brood, and gave them all
> That gladder wives and mothers love to keep.
>
> And when the sheriff shot her eldest son
> Beside his still, so well she knew her part,
> She gave no healing tears to ease her heart;
> But took the blow upstanding, with her eyes
> As drear and bitter as the winter skies.
> Seeing her then, I thought that she had won.
>
> But yesterday her man returned too soon
> And found her tending, with a reverent touch,
> One scarlet bloom; and, having drunk too much,
> He snatched its flame and quenched it in the dirt.
> Then, like a creature with a mortal hurt,
> She fell, and wept away the afternoon.

"The Woman" is a tragedy, for hardship, loneliness, isolation, loss, and rejection are compressed in these few lines. "The sullen peaks" yield slowly to a little cultivation. The "code of mountain wives" requires her to do the housekeeping, farming, and animal husbandry while her man logs or engages in whatever cash crop employ he can find. Spring may appear to come, then a frost destroys her planting. The harvest will be disappointing. Life is so hard that she is forced into a stoic denial of emotion, even when her own son is cut down by the needless violence of Prohibition law. Moreover, each farm is so isolated that there are no neighbors; she must face this life with "her small store." There is no developed imagination, and her religion offers little help in facing the pains of this world. The only thing in the poem that possibly stands against the pressures of her environment is her personality, her "small store" of individuality as a woman. But she yields to her fate passively when her drunken husband scorns a symbol of her love, the only one left.

The weight of pressure in this stark, simple drama is finally measured by the austerity of the poem in terms of other poetic techniques: one symbol, one figure (line 17), fewer than Heyward's usual number of adjectives, and nothing in the way of original use of diction.

"The Mountain Woman" is powerful and moving in its starkness. "The Mountain Girl" sings in an elevated style a mountain variation of the universal theme of passing youth. The variation, the narrator sees, is that the hard life "Here where the mountains shoulder to the sky" speeds the maturing process and then, too quickly, their lives are "burned out," and life "hangs long-withered on the bough."[53] The narrator's perspective is essential here, the tension in the poem being between the beauty and spontaneity of the Dorotheas and the narrator's long-range fears.

"The Mountain Preacher" is a compressed characterization of another mountain type, but seen more in narrative terms than "The Woman" or "The Girl." The scenes in the preacher's work are juxtaposed. The first two stanzas draw the congregation through the wild beauty of the laurel and rhododendron to the "ugly blot" of the church where the preacher, "Raw-boned and thunder-voiced, with brandished fist," wakes in them "sullen fear/Of the all-seeing Foe they worshipped there." In the third stanza, a mountain freshet, with a "slow shudder, hurtled like a tawny beast,/Froth-lipped and baying," tumbling home "on yellow chaos, and the sky's hard slate," killing Tom Garvin's boy. In the fourth stanza, the preacher staggers in at Garvin's, after crossing flooded streams, and his silent presence, holding the broken form, shows them "There was a God, and He was very kind." It is the God of Justice and of Love, if of the latter he "said no word." The preacher's hellfire sermon is in sharp contrast both to the beauty of the mountains and the consolation his visit brings the grieving Garvins.

"Black Christmas" is a farm wife's mountain-idiom monologue, extraordinarily compressed, just before her husband's funeral; he had been killed in the continuation of a feud he had thought ended, while cutting a Christmas tree.

In "The Mountain Graveyard," again the outsider views the scene, a barren graveyard that denies the beauty beyond the patch of raw earth because the congregation, living and dead, failed to appreciate that beauty. Instead, those who use the cemetery look for beauty elsewhere; the graves are decorated with symbols of distant hopes, shells from the seashore and "bits of broken glass/Which speak the foreign glories of the town—" The viewer's understanding fails here, however, for while he sees well that the bleakness of the place symbolizes their lives and that its "troubled clay" offers all they ask of it, rest, his regret that they failed to "know/The beauty that is theirs to breathe and touch" falls short. He attributes their failure of sensitivity to their preoccupation with distant dreams. Yet, as Heyward has already shown in "The Woman" and "The Preacher," it is the very hardness of their life that denies them a sense of beauty, and certainly an ability to appreciate the beauty of their daily antagonist: the hills the narrator finds so impressive.

As Allen Tate notes, the poet's regrets in the last stanza nullify the poem's "capacity for excitement."[54] Several personifications and weak images also reduce the effective realization of the pathos of the paradox—barrenness in the midst of such beauty.

"The Blockader," "The Mountain Town: Spring," "The Mountain Town: Summer," and "I Stumbled Upon Happiness" complete this group of poems.

Heyward's sympathetic observations of the mountaineers are among his strongest poems. A group called "Other Poems" includes "Spring Mood," in which a "callous wind" provides a cosmic vision of the cycle of youth and death that turns the square into "a charnel cage." Imagery and dramatic tension contribute to its success.

"New England Landscape," Heyward's one Imagist poem, may lack the concreteness of the Imagists, but the colors and spatial arrangements create a design.

"Suffrage" is a Robinsonian tale of a spinster who would not marry beneath herself or live by her art, a woman stifled by mores and codes, but it lacks Robinson's ironic characterization.

"Aftermath," in its portrayal of "Revenge and greed" emerging to claim their victory, after a war victim's sacrifice, provides Heyward's most bitter overt social commentary before his next-to-last novel, *Lost Morning*.

The first of the six Horizon poems is "Horizon":

> This sun-drugged land of ours,
> Huge, tawny-limbed, low-breasted like a man,
> Sprawling in indolence among sea-nurtured flowers,

holds the poet, and his effort to free himself meets only the enslavement of its beauty:

> Across the low-hung moon
> Late curlews sway
> The trailing pennant
> Of their silent flight.
> Slowly they curve,
> And then come streaming back
> Across the yellow disc,
> Low on the water like a riding-light,
> Then out to sea along the copper track.

"The Return" may be read as a companion to "Horizon" in its image of sleep settling over the sandy shore.

Louis Rubin compares "Buzzard Island" to Ransom's "Conrad in Twilight," both melancholic southern evening landscapes, as an illustration of how the Charleston School tends towards abstraction where Ransom's poem is a concrete and colloquial evocation.[55] Rubin is right, but the naked limbs, flooding streams, and sunset in Heyward's poem do suddenly become, with the settling of the buzzards until "Awaiting trees blossom and leaf with death," a special place, a macabre, almost apocalyptic assembling site for all kinds of carrion: "stillborn dreams," "old faiths," "outlived despairs," and "bitter memories." The abstractions that gather are also not altogether abstract. In the first stanza the description of the island notes the "blind canals," "empty fields," and "fallen dikes." Once, the island was cultivated; it embodied long-shattered hopes. Fittingly, death inhabits it now, a place remote from the "white cities" where "young voices ring." The abstraction is history's making—southern history's, and while its concrete events are outside the poem, that history can be seen and touched and remembered in the relics it has left. Ransom, however, would never have yielded to an abstraction like "sanguine anguish of the west" or been guilty of the overdone opening picture.

"The Equinox" is a remarkable description of a hurricane and its effects, likening it to a "wrestler's body/ Muscled under its sweat," seeing a dwarfed sea-oak "drunken,/ Brandishing terrible arms" and the palmettoes that "batter the winds with great hands." The effective use of adjectives, similes, onomatopoeia, and paradox all realize the storm's power and terror.

"Chant for an Old Town," the longest of this group, a sonnet plea to modern builders to recognize the grace and magic of the old town and not destroy it, followed by five long sections in which a group of pirates leave a treasure, time passes and the city grows, modern engines come to destroy in order to build anew, Negro workers find the old chest, but during the night the pirates return for their treasure, and the city awakes to the renewed sounds of progress.

Narration and description are often effective here, but the pirate story is not the appropriate illustration of the architectural beauty of the past. It is only temporal and the old town's beauty is spatial and temporal, primarily spatial, and not even incidentally tied to Black-beard's treasure burial, which is not even intended at the time to con-tribute to the permanent splendor of the city. There is a contrast between the romance, mystery, and echoes of the past in the pirate story and the passionless, timeless movement of the engines of progress. Heyward's intention appears to be allegorical: the pirate treasure is Beauty, and this Beauty is more temporal than spatial. Because the forces of progress are blind to Beauty, there is no contest for the uncov-ered treasure as it is carried away. But the allegory is forced.

The final poem of *Skylines and Horizons* is "Epitaph for a Poet," which celebrates the "spendthrift" who "scattered seeds" for strangers "to reap," who sang of the freedom of failure, who makes the most of the "dazzling nearer sky," and "never flinched" until the "last silences were shaken/With songs too lovely for his pen." The stanza on the prison of success and freedom of failure is an uncanny prophecy of Heyward's novels where successful middle-class white sterility is at the opposite extreme from the life of Catfish Row. And the third stanza foreshadows the recurrent motif in Heyward's work of the beloved local scene changing with time and industrialization.

V   Jasbo Brown and Other Poems

Jasbo Brown and Other Poems, published in 1931 after Heyward had stopped writing poetry, may be viewed as his selected poems, though his concern about Macmillan's charges for the use of *Carolina Chansons* and *Skylines and Horizons* poems may mean that it is something less that that.[56] Only four poems from his first volume are included, and it adds only four new poems, three of which require attention.

The title poem may have been chosen with the view of gaining it wide popularity. After first appearing in a four-page spread in Mencken's *American Mercury,* then in this collection, the situation was adapted for the beginning of *Porgy and Bess* and the poem was broadcast twice over a national radio network with George Gershwin's "Rhapsody in Blue" as background music.[57] It is, however, far from a complete success, chiefly because Heyward is unclear just what he wants to do.

Jasbo is the center of the poem, from his lonely night arrival by steamboat, through the command all-night performance in a local tavern, to the next morning, when he tells an admiring woman that he must go where his song takes him. But Jasbo is not mentioned until line 50 of 175 lines, and the first 49 lines include little requisite to his experience. The first three stanzas are largely a vivid description of the steamboat's arrival, particularly virile in its verbs. Neither is it clear why Heyward's imagination sees such cosmic implications in the steamboat's arrival. With Jasbo's entry, the cosmic nonsense disappears. Jasbo is immediately seen as tired and alone. Once off the boat, the other passengers forget him. And he is alienated from the town, religion, and the music of the spirituals. Hearing the spiritual, he "would yearn to shout/Queer broken measures" instead.[58] The river, a screech owl, the spirituals, and the memory of a New Orleans girl who rejected him for his addiction to music add to his loneliness.

Heyward's restraint in giving Jasbo no individuality or past, only his weariness and his song, properly emphasizes that he has no life of his own and can have none. He is the poet of his people, their property. The weakness of an undeveloped action is also, in a way, proper:

Jasbo's fate does not have real narrative possibilities. He is moved by the hand of fate. His life is process, not drama.

As "Porgy" and the novel with which it appeared indicate, "Jasbo Brown" was not Heyward's only sign of interest in black rhythms. Nor does "Jasbo" take those rhythms as seriously as Heyward does in *Porgy*, where he says in more intelligible form what is most important in "Jasbo," or in *Mamba's Daughters*. For Jasbo is unique in his vocation; he is not Jasbo because "They sho' got rhythm." He is simply a born musician; as such he reflects his experience in his song. Nor is he obliged to learn the white man's song or discipline his own. His improvisations serve to express his woes; insofar as they are representative of the Negro, his songs serve.

"Dusk in the Low Country" is Heyward's last description in poetry of that locale.

And a sonnet, "Prodigal," is the last new poem in the volume. The octet neatly balances three failed aspirations with the candor of humility; the sestet catalogs three unusual expectations for his passing:

> Some day when the stern seeker in my brain
> Has ceased to drive me stumbling through the dark
> Dropping dead cinders for each faint new spark,
> Only to see the new one wax and wane.
> When all my dreams are numbered with the slain,
> And Wisdom, that egregious Patriarch,
> Has told his last half truth, and left me stark,
> I shall go home. I shall go home again.
>
> Friendship will greet me in the panelled hall,
> And Laughter will enfold me on the stairs
> Sweet as old rose leaves wrinkled in a jar.
> Battles and loves will move me not at all.
> There will be juleps, billiards, family prayers,
> And a calm crossing to another star.

Parks considers this the one Heyward poem with "the stamp of durability."[59]

VI *A Poetry of Place*

Heyward's poetry received considerable attention when it appeared. "Gamesters All" won a Contemporary Verse prize in 1921. Heyward was invited to MacDowell Colony in 1921 and 1922. Anthologies reprinted his poems. But even contemporary criticism was restrained and studies of American poetry have largely ignored Heyward's verse.

Still, he makes his notion of local color poetry work, and many of his best poems are strongly local in theme and surface. If he lacks the southern voice Ransom defines, in "Philosophy" and "Gamesters All" his perception of the southern scene is nonetheless impressive. He can and does make poetry out of his extreme sensibility to place, his strong interest and feeling for local history, his sense of the patina of time and of change in his spatial world, his understanding of blacks and mountaineers, and his sympathy for those who suffer in their environment. Physical poetry or poetry of exclusion, it is poetry. And some, "The Woman" and "Horizons," for example, realize a dramatic tension that is more than what one expects in poetry of exclusion. Some, too, including the better mountain poems and "Gamesters All," do move from the local scene to universal statement. On the other hand, such notable poems as "Suffrage" and "Prodigal" resist any local color label and could qualify as modern.

Second, while Heyward's poems reveal a deep interest in the local scene, they do not show the narrative talent he was to develop as a novelist. His narrative poems are usually dependent upon a ready-made historical incident or legend. The dramatic moments of great pathos in "The Woman," "The Preacher," and "Black Christmas" are end moments of lifetimes of suffering.

Third, although at least a dozen of his poems and parts of more than another dozen should not be forgotten, Heyward's short and modest career as a poet did not promise greatness. Poetry requires a conception of art, a subtlety and complexity of mind, and an intensity of experience he lacked. Poetry also requires a sensitivity to words and their rich possibilities he did not often appear to have. And it requires a respect for and mastery of the craft largely lacking in the whole Charleston circle. Heyward was particularly sensitive to criticism, even that of his Charleston friends, and impatient with it. Some of his verse is unclear, some private in reference, some all too sentimental. Some of his local color poems stop at description or assume historical knowledge unshared by anyone outside Charleston, as in "Dusk." He could use fresh images and words, sounds effects, and metrical variation, yet the fine lines are relatively few.

Still, we are in his debt, however ironic that debt, that he took his subject, the local scene, so seriously. He made what he could of it.

CHAPTER 3

The Irony of Freedom
in Charleston: Porgy

I *"Beautifully Rich Orchestration"*

DUBOSE Heyward's first significant fiction publication is his best
known, *Porgy*. The story is simple, of a summer in a Negro quarter in Charleston at the turn of the century. It is novella length and
seemingly little more than a series of vignettes in structure. But *Porgy*
is generally considered Heyward's most accomplished work and it is,
with Jean Toomer's *Cane*, the most successful fiction associated with
the Negro or Harlem Renaissance of the 1920s. It was also the first
longer work of fiction with predominantly Negro characters to appeal
to the whole country. Its publication in 1925 made Heyward one of
the most promising new fiction talents in the South.

Yet, in the forty-odd years since James Southall Wilson wrote, "No
more beautiful or authentic novel has been published in America for
a decade," asserting that Heyward has "given freedom to the negro
soul in the region of art" as Lincoln had given freedom to his body,
Porgy has received little serious critical attention.[1]

Porgy did receive notable praise in the 1920s. Heyward's fellow
southern writer Frances Newman, a notoriously acerbic critic, scolded
Heyward for trying to enter the feelings of a Negro—he should "leave
the souls of black folks to black folks"—but then observed, "It is
undoubtedly the most admirable book about Southern Negroes that I
have ever read, and it is the only one I can remember which substitutes
beautifully rich orchestration for a thin line of melody."[2]

Heyward's biographer, Frank Durham, discusses *Porgy* at length
but largely from an historical perspective. Only in 1970, just after I
had completed for publication an extensive critical study of *Porgy* and
shortly before Durham's death, did Durham begin to explore Hey-

ward's interest in Porgy's humanity and the obstacles that blocked his happiness.[3]

Popular interest in the novel and the play that followed in 1927 has been only slightly greater than scholarly interest, for almost two generations now have met Heyward's Porgy and Bess only in the Heyward-Gershwin folk opera or the little-shown movie version of the opera. If there is more to the novella than the simplified opera themes of love, weakness, violence, and pathos in a summer of easy living, few have read *Porgy* to see. The last printing of the novel was in 1953, following a triumphant revival of the opera.

The novella's appeal is one of literature's most certain ones: Porgy's heroic but doomed effort to find contentment. Surviving the hurricane, Porgy experiences a sense of worth: " 'You an' me, Bess,' he said with conviction. 'We *sho*' is a little somet'ing attuh all.' "[4] But in the end, when the threat of Crown is gone but Bess has left, the Row leaves "Porgy and the goat alone in an irony of morning sunlight" (196). His superstitious fear of Crown's corpse, the white world's interference, and Bess's weakness to men and drugs in Porgy's absence bring defeat.

II   *Catfish Row's Antagonists*

The weaknesses of Porgy and Bess are representative of Catfish Row. The Negroes of the Row are unready for the world in which they must live. In outwitting Archdale and old Frasier and overcoming Crown, Porgy is more intelligent and courageous than most but, like Crown, Clara, and Jake, Bess, and Sportin' Life, his hopes and self-discipline are insufficient. Primitive instincts, innocence, lack of self-discipline, and Sportin' Life's irresponsibility; the forces of the white world surrounding them; and fate are formidable antagonists and their undoing. Jake and his comrades foolishly go to sea despite storm warnings and at the height of the storm Clara mindlessly joins them in the killing waters. Whites tax the Row for its failings, demand of it civilized conduct, and then, in the sanctuary of their caste world, are indifferent to the Row's needs. The Row meets fate—death and the hurricane—with elemental human resignation, a passive response. But the Row's inhabitants are undone by the demand for action, for social conduct, which all too often brings them to grief at their own hands or those of the white world.

The movement of the summer toward Porgy's defeat is really a choral movement in which all move from life and hope and love toward death, resignation, and loneliness. The thematic movement is from innocence to experience, from spring to fall, from hope to defeat.

The one notable strength the protagonists bring to the struggle is a community spirit. Catfish Row has its own inner rhythm and style; its own code, especially in dealing with the white world; and its rituals of joy and defeat, as the saucer burial, parade, and picnic scenes illustrate. The single enveloping conflict, then, is the struggle of Catfish Row— never on even terms—with the snares of life. Handicapped in so many ways, they seek dignity—in a white and alien world. The effect of the story is pathos, the unmerited sorrow that is almost certain to be Porgy's fate, from the moment he first takes Bess in and dares to love and hope, a sorrow also shared by the Row. Heyward's genius is his ability to explore the operation of this complexity of forces in the modest space of *Porgy.*

Only when the everyday vignettes are seen in this pattern of community and representative conflict—the Row's and the central characters' struggle—is *Porgy*'s unity recognized. Porgy's dealing with Archdale is representative, the Row dealing with the Man in the only way it can. This is one of those few but essential excursions in the course of the story beyond the Row and the adjacent wharf. Likewise, the storm is a community experience, the meaning of which is finally expressed by Porgy, whose leadership of the prayers in that scene suggests that he is a kind of priest among men in the Row. The initial gambling scene shows the Row at play—and suggests the shape of life there: the future is contingent upon the chance occurrences of the next moment or dice roll. It may be lucky; it is certain to be full of passion and grief. And here, of course, Porgy is most alive, as a person, and in full communion with his brothers.

That Heyward's intention is to embrace both the Row and Porgy's personal drama is supported, too, by external evidence. First, Heyward identifies the subject of *Porgy* in the poem-prayer that stands as a prelude:

> Porgy, Maria, and Bess,
> Robbins, and Peter, and Crown;
> Life was a three-stringed harp
> Brought from the woods to town.
>
> Marvelous tunes you rang
> From passion, and death, and birth,

You who had laughed and wept
On the warm, brown lap of the earth.

Now in your untried hands
An instrument, terrible, new,
Is thrust by a master who frowns,
Demanding strange songs of you.

God of the White and Black,
Grant us great hearts on the way
That we may understand
Until you have learned to play.

In the musical imagery of the first two stanzas, Heyward emphasizes the harmony of Negro life in the "woods." But the occasion is the passage of the chief actors in *Porgy*, whom the poem addresses, from the jungle and the elemental life of the plantation to freedom and responsibility in white society. Now he petitions God to see to it that the white race is understanding as Negroes learn to use this freedom, foreshadowing society's need to reckon with Crown's cotton-hook, Bess's weaknesses, and Porgy's murder of Crown and subsequent flight. It is a "strange" and "new" instrument, one which takes learning.

Second, Porgy's central role in the drama of the Row that the poem defines is clearly reflected in the story's genesis. One morning, while Heyward was visiting his sister at 98 Church Street, coincidentally only a few doors from the setting that Heyward transferred in the story to nearby Vanderhorst's Wharf, he read in a local newspaper of a local court proceeding involving a familiar Negro beggar:

Samuel Smalls, who is a cripple and is familiar to King Street, with his goat and cart, was held for the June term of court of sessions on an aggravated assault charge. It is alleged that on Saturday night he attempted to shoot Maggie Barnes at number four Romney Street. His shots went wide of the mark. Smalls was up on a similar charge some months ago and was given a suspended sentence. Smalls had attempted to escape in his wagon, and had been run down and captured by the police patrol.[5]

Heyward noted that the story had "great dramatic possibilities" and put the clipping in his wallet, where it remained until mid-1924, when he began to write *Porgy*. As he remarked later, the story made him realize that he "had concluded that such a life could never lift above the dead level of the commonplace."[6] Yet, Heyward observed, "Into the brief paragraph one could read passion, hate, despair."

(Years later, it was learned that Sam, who had disappeared from his usual haunts with the publication of *Porgy*, had "fell sick of de jail house fever" and gone off to "Jim"—James—Island, a refuge since the days of slavery for blacks who would live unbothered by whites. He was identified as one of Mrs. Elvira Gibbs's twenty-seven children; she had said of his missing legs and feet, "He had what you might call little images of feet." When Sam's wife, a woman of stature and dignity and a face of great sweetness, was located in 1959, she pointed to his child-length grave, decorated with utensils in the old Gullah fashion. He had died in 1924.[7])

Heyward begins with Porgy and the setting: "Porgy lived in a Golden Age" (11). As Heyward characterizes it, Charleston in 1900 is a cul-de-sac in time and space, just before the modern world intrudes upon the somnolence in which the Civil War left the city. If Jim Crow has come to town, Heyward has not noticed. Living, in an agricultural and fishing economy, is easy—comparatively, seasonally, economically, barely. As the narrator, looking back some years, says at the end of the paragraph in a series of tranquilizing anapests, it is a Golden Age "when men, not yet old, were boys in an ancient beautiful city that time had forgotten before it destroyed" (11).

But Porgy, silent, patient, listening, is not alone in the Golden Age. He lives in Catfish Row, and as the antagonistic forces reveal themselves, the definition and careful joining of Porgy and the other black inhabitants of the Row are everywhere evident.

The initial scene, the crap game that ends in Crown's murder of Robbins, immediately joins Porgy's life with the Row's and begins the orchestration of the antagonistic forces of the story. The murder is enacted before "shadowy watchers" who "wailed eerily" (20). Porgy, who "shivered violently, whimpered in the gloom, then threw himself across his threshold," is a focal witness (21). Heyward's imagery turns the scene into an atavistic ritual: Crown exhibits "gleaming teeth," "thrusting jaw," "sloping brow," and the "prehensile claw" of a cotton hook, and he emits a "low snarl." "Down, down, down the centuries they slid," the narrator tells us, until "a heady, bestial stench absorbed all other odors" (19–20). Since Robbins most aspires to white ways, Crown's conquest is a victory for the jungle.

In the remaining scenes of Part I the identification of Porgy and the Row is completed. Still, within these scenes, Porgy is something more

than a mere representative of the Row or a member of the Row community. He wails "long and quiveringly" at Robbins's wake (26). He
expresses, with finality, the reality of Robbins's going: "'Dat's all right
now fer Robbins,' commented Porgy. 'Gawd done sen' he rain already
fuh wash he feet-steps offen dis eart" (33). When Peter yields to the
police threat, Porgy stands implacable. Of the Row, Porgy is its poet
as well, experiencing most fully its suffering.

The following saucer burial is a community ritual of identification
with Robbins, difficulty in resignation, common cause in financing the
burial, and, finally, triumphant song in consignment of Robbins to
heaven as the chorus sings, "'An' I'll meet um in the primus lan''"
(27). The burial spirituals, one providing a catharsis of grief and the
other an act of faith, are separated by the human cry of grief at the
funeral, "'Death, ain't yuh gots no shame?'" and followed by the panic
of superstition as all flee the graveyard: the second hymn has not qui-
eted primitive fears of death (30).

The episode had begun with a growling thunderhead that left "the
air hot, vitiated, and moist" and the Row irritable, as Crown's "moody
silence" illustrates (16). It ends with the police taking Peter away as a
material witness and a creditor repossessing his things—and Porgy
reflecting on the inadequacies of Providence in allowing the death of
the good Robbins while letting Crown go free to kill again.

In Part I, the setting becomes characters, the characters a community, and the community an action, with the Row as protagonist and
nature, primitivism, and the white police as antagonists.

Heyward's command of the enveloping action is cause for wonder.
We know, from the play's Introduction, of Heyward's imposition of his
own "conception of a summer of aspiration, devotion, and heartbreak
across the colour wall" and of Hervey Allen's assistance in arranging
the scenes.[8] Wherever Heyward's skill came from, the pattern of Part
I is a recurrent one, as the other tragedies of love in the book demon-
strate. In another powerful Row scene, the conjure-ridden Clara abandons herself in the storm in a futile effort to save Jake. The separation
of Porgy and Bess involves Crown's bestiality, Bess's wildness, and
Porgy's "aboriginal" laugh; the jailing of Bess and then Porgy; and
Porgy's superstitious fears (172). The Porgy-Bess relationship is emphasized by the space given it and by its centrality. It is also marked by
strong suggestions of a mythic-moral dimension: a snakelike Sportin'
Life tempts the repentant Bess, and Bess, who passes a rattler in search
of a fan-shaped leaf in the Kittiwar wilderness, meets a seducer,

Crown, whose "small wicked eyes burned" (119). But whether agents or principals, the antagonists remain the same.

The structure of the novella is itself an illustration of Heyward's subtle shifts of attention between Porgy and the Row and among the forces—the primitive, the white world, and fate—opposed to the Row's good fortune. After the wild fight and emotional outpouring of Part I, the second part is a quiet interlude between encounters with primitive power and white power—a season for the good things of life except that Porgy, without Peter's wagon for transportation, is disconsolate until, encouraged to have faith, he contrives his own freedom. Part III involves both Porgy's conquest of Archdale with his odorous goat cart and Bess's conquest by life in the white man's jail. Apart from Bess's encounter with Crown and the consequent apprehension regarding Crown's return, the primitive parade and picnic in Part IV show the Row in command of its fate. But then, in Part V, the storm confronts the Row with Destiny personified; it also shows Porgy and Bess their worth and gives them a child. In Part VI, the Row saves Porgy from discovery after his murder of Crown, and he seeks assurance from Bess of her fidelity, but then a solitary buzzard settling on the roof of his room sends him in flight from a primitive sense of doom toward the woods of his origin and into the casual hands of white justice—and Bess is lost.

But *Porgy* does not end with Bess's departure. If Porgy's defeat is to be truly representative, it must be shared by Catfish Row. So it falls to a shaking, sobbing Maria, as the Row's spokesman, to disillusion him and witness his defeat. Her empathy speaks for all, and their silence and retreat behind closed doors reveal the return of that dimension of life which the summer, despite its tragedies, had largely banished from the Row: suffering, present and extending into the future. Porgy's fears, the laws of white society, and Bess's weakness have all conspired to frustrate the aspirations to a human life of the most promising citizen of Catfish Row. For this, the Row has no liturgy, only silence.

Each of the major characters in the novel is, the action suggests, a distinctive battlefield of the forces that defeat Porgy. Porgy is shrewd, sensitive, hopeful, and patient. But his shriveled legs mean that he cannot escape the basest agents of white society or compete with the "hot han'" of Crown and his kind. His primitive laugh upon killing Crown and his fear of Crown's corpse indicate that he remains divided. Bess recognizes Porgy's humanity and love, but her honesty and sense of values reside in a vessel too weak to withstand the pressures upon it.

Serena's straitlaced Puritan religion and determination to be a "white folks' nigger" lead her to reject the life of the Row and send her husband to his death, just as Crown's violence exiles him from society to the woods. As an emancipated Harlem black, Sportin' Life is an example of the tragedy and corruption Heyward sees awaiting Negroes divorced from their roots and values and cast loose in the modern world. Maria, who presides over the island of humanity that is the Catfish Row chorus—as surrogate mother, moral arbiter and symbol of order, judge and jury in exiling Sportin' Life, is herself caught between her dependence on the conjuring she brought from the woods and her grudging respect for Christianity while authoritatively upholding the Row's basic law of survival.

Heyward's characters are all very much subject to the determining forces of history, nature, and society. On the first page it is Porgy's fate to come in time just when he does. It is Clara's to step out into the storm just a moment before it strikes with its greatest fury. When Porgy gets his cart, he is in "the grip of new forces," as if he has no will of his own (48). And, of course, it is the Row's fate to be subject to the white man's law in all of its direct and indirect manifestations. The Negro's effort to "learn to play" is beset with great difficulties or obstacles: the past, which has made the Row what it is; the present, in which, slavery gone, the Negro must struggle from day to day for survival and suffer second-class citizenship; and the future, which answers the basic questions with graveyards and storms and winter.

III   *Primitive Weaknesses*

The initial characterization of the primitive influence operative in Heyward's world is in the poem prelude reference to the journey of Row inhabitants from "woods to town." The primitive traits and acts of the Row are traceable less to atavistic memory than to the isolated, elemental, largely undisciplined life—the free, natural life (real or a fancied antecedent of the Golden Age)—of Negro cabins hidden away from plantation houses and the demands of white society. In that world, the black man had his own relaxed code and way of life, Heyward posits, which help explain Crown's conduct, Porgy's violent defense of Bess, and the characters' sundry superstitions. The separation from that natural state and its simple gratifications of emotional need, rather than some African susceptibility to drugs, better explains

Bess's lapses. Heyward's characters are, first of all, Americans, and their conduct is rooted in their American experience.

Heyward is not altogether unambiguous in defining the primitives encountered in Catfish Row. The African note is struck in the initial description of Porgy's "unadultered Congo blood" and his "pleasant atavistic calm" (13–14). He remembers "strange things and places," which the manuscript identifies as "elephants crashing through a forest" (23).[9] And when Bess is ill, he turns "to the beginning of things" for a cure (155). The lapses into wildness are frequent. Crown turns beast in the fight with Robbins. Under the influence of dope, Bess "whirled like a dervish and called horribly upon her God, striking and clawing wildly" (86). The parade strikes a "wild, barbaric chord" (113). And Bess abandons herself to Crown with a "wild laugh" (121). Animal imagery extends from the atavism of the crap-game fight to Maria's characterization of Sportin' Life as "dat yelluh snake wrigglin in de do' way" (127). However, Heyward also associates certain traits he admires—Porgy's "infinite patience" and "unrealized, but terrific, energy" and the marchers' abandon in the parade—with the Row's primitive character (13). Yet, the repeated falls, which Eric Bentley sees as unrelieved, and the often violent note—the deaths, fights, and Bess's abduction—suggest as well Heyward's somewhat condescending participation in the common southern belief of the time that it might take centuries to civilize the Negro.[10]

In several instances, though, the narrator goes beyond the observable and plausible "wilderness" influences and primitive imagery to identify Negro conduct with ancient racial memory, an identification neither observable by the narrator nor really functional in emphasizing the links with the wilderness. Porgy's "atavistic calm," full-blooded dozing ability, the racial memory pictures that pass before him, and the "aboriginal" quality of his laugh after killing Crown add nothing to the reader's appreciation of the fragile bond between Porgy and civilization. The line during the fight between Crown and Robbins, "Down, down, down the centuries they slid," is a good line—for any such fight. But in the context of these other lines, it suggests that Crown and Robbins revert to savage Africa in a way different from everyman's reversion to animality when his brute nature takes over.

By contrast, the narrator's envy and condescension mark his view of the Negro community's freedom as the parade passes:

For its one brief moment out of the year the pageant had lasted. Out of its
fetters of civilization this people had risen, suddenly, amazingly. Exotic as
the Congo, and still able to abandon themselves utterly to the wild joy of
fantastic play, they had taken the reticent, old Anglo-Saxon town and
stamped their mood swiftly and indelibly into its heart. Then they passed,
leaving behind them a wistful envy among those who had watched them
go,—those whom the ages had rendered old and wise. (114–15)

These ambiguities remain unresolved in *Porgy*, but in its totality,
particularly in the narrative perspective, Heyward's attitude is sufficiently clear. The lapses of Porgy, Bess, Crown, and even Clara and
Jake are, first of all, lapses in the learning process such as might be
found following from the frustrations of virtually any simple rural folk
thrust into a modern industrial society. But their frequency and seriousness indicate a level of difficulty that contributes greatly to the
effect of pathos. At the same time, in such major scenes as the saucer
burial, the parade and picnic, the hurricane, and the choral exchange
of silences with Porgy in his loss of Bess, Heyward recognizes a primitive dimension, a culture, a rhythm of life, that he clearly admires and
would not see disappear in the adjustment to "town."

The absence of atavistic motivation, the narrator's civilized view of
the Row's failings, and the restraint and the understatement in the
treatment of primitivism indicate a notable movement toward genuine
realism. Thus Heyward's primitivism—the "woods" influence and the
black man's sense of the rhythm of life—must be clearly distinguished
from the pseudo-realism that Alain Locke called the "last serious
majority cliche, that of blood atavism and inherited Negro primitivism," of which Locke began complaining in the year *Porgy* appeared.[11]
Where an inhibited Van Vechten character wallows in self-pity at her
lack of the primitive passions she sees in other blacks, Heyward evokes
a largely indefinite sense of atavistic influences but focuses on the lack
of discipline and the depth and quality of human feeling in the Row's
and Porgy's expressions. While Heyward identified such primitive
traits as savagery and strange rhythms as relics of a heritage quite
unlike white Anglo-Saxon Protestantism, he also saw them as expressions of the elemental life southern blacks experienced. And he knew
very well that the song and dance of Catfish Row were the simple black
man's ritual response to his frustrations and suffering in a white world
and in no significant sense atavistic in origin or a continuance of African tradition.

Heyward's fidelity to his experience of black life meant a restraint in the handling of primitivism that stands in sharp contrast with the strongly lyrical and mystical qualities in Toomer's Georgia scenes and the haunting world of Julia Peterkin's superstitious and passionate rural folk. But the important distinction here is its distance from Van Vechten's and Claude McKay's primitive characters. When Van Vechten says, "She watched Lasca and Byron glide softly, dangerously, like panthers," it is something else than Heyward's big stevedore crossing the court, "his body moving easily with the pantherlike flow of enormous muscular power under absolute control" (44).[12] Heyward's simile is only a simile, fitting for the muscular stevedore. Van Vechten's is coupled with "dangerously" and follows an observation that Lasca and Byron are more animal than Mary is or whites are in general.

McKay's leopard—or panther—even more clearly denotes the Harlem identification of primitivism with sexual license which aroused Locke's ire. In *Home to Harlem,* Rose is likened to "a lean lazy leopard" and then "moves down on him like a panther, swinging her hips in wonderful, rhythmical motions."[13] And at a party, jungle imagery prevails as, "like some shameless wild animals hungry for raw meat, the females savagely searched the eyes of the males."[14] As Anritjit Singh has observed, Locke's condemnation of the cult of primitivism was not always heard: the popular images of the Negro as the noble savage, carefree, and sexually uninhibited was supported by the popular misreading of Freud and the interest in African art in reaction to the mechanized and fit in with the positive reaction against Puritanism.[15] McKay was catering to what his audience expected, and he was not alone. During the 1920s, Gertrude Stein, Sherwood Anderson, Vachel Lindsay, Eugene O'Neill, and E. E. Cummings all celebrated the black man's primitivism.

In shedding their inhibitions for a parade, Heyward's blacks never forget, as does Lindsay in "The Congo," the 200 years between the jungle of the imagination and 1900. Nor does Heyward ever, as Countee Cullen does in "Heritage," have his contemporary characters hear great African drums beating. Thus *Porgy* comes much closer to honesty about Negroes, closer to squaring with reality, than does what Ralph Ellison calls the "Paul Robeson and silver bullet in the jungle bill of goods" of *Emperor Jones* and many other works of the Negro Renaissance.[16] Crown's primitive brutality is constant and motivated; Brutus Jones moves inexorably backward to the jungle. As Harlan Hatcher observed long ago, Heyward succeeds in "giving to the prim-

itive life the illusion of complete realism without losing the sense of
awe and wonder and pathos which belong to romance."[17] It might be
added that Heyward does so without sacrificing or ignoring what
Locke calls the disciplined, sophisticated, laconic, and fatalistic qualities of African expression.[18] Porgy manifests all of these qualities in an
environment of exuberance and emotional upheaval, among a people
whose art is equally emotional.

One reservation, however, must be entered, which stems from Heyward's tolerance of Porgy's violence. In a 1952 review of *Porgy and
Bess*, Eric Bentley sees Heyward's view of the Negro as "close to the
traditional and dangerous image of the Negro as primitive, the primitive as savage," and faults him for excessive kindliness toward Porgy
after he "commits murder": "His people are not quite human beings—
they are likeable, if not housebroken, animals, among whom killing is
not murder."[19] Bentley fails to see the pathetic struggle of the Row
with its antagonists, a struggle in which the narrator is sympathetic and
not merely fascinated. He also fails to understand that Porgy's claim
to Bess entitles him, according to the code of the Row, to fight for her.
Nor does he notice that Crown is breaking and entering. But he is right
that the "ambush" knifing of Crown is not clearly warranted by
Crown's past brutality, his intrusion, or his intention to take Bess away.
Heyward glosses it over by skipping the scene in which Maria helps
dispose of the body, then offering, immediately, the investigation scene
in which the reader's sympathy is with Porgy and the Row against the
detectives and coroner.

But it is Bentley's remark about the lack of humanity in Heyward's
characters that is telling. Heyward makes their primitive qualities convincing, but there is no relief from Crown's hostility, Bess's helplessness, even Jake's recklessness, save Porgy's sensitivity, and then Porgy
kills without scruple. All remain susceptible, therefore, to the worst in
their racial past. And what is that? Contrary to the "Porgy" poem,
which speaks of "Marvelous times you rang/From passion, and death,
and birth," those times now seem invariably to have included violent,
inhuman notes. What appears in the poem a human harmony with the
earth, in the fiction is tainted with savagery that lacks convincing
motivation, whatever the tune, and also lacks probability: it is, of
course, only the white racist myth in America that makes all Africans
savages—in Africa—and in America still savages at heart. Thus,

despite his fidelity to experience, realism, and moderation, Heyward hesitates to recognize the essential humanity of the primitive Negro, past or present.

IV   *The White Man*

Where primitive forces and nature do not bring trouble to the Row, the white man does. On the other hand, whites make no positive contribution to the Row beyond occasional partial ameliorization of the suffering other whites have caused. In this sense, the story becomes Heyward's ironic response to his prayer in the prelude poem: it is a story of the nonunderstanding of the Negro until he has "learned to play," for the understanding the Row receives from the white community is invariably a parody of understanding. The whites laugh as Robbins's funeral passes. The "vile-mouthed bearded Teuton" merchant leaves Peter only a chrome of "The Great Emancipator," which makes the reference to Porgy's "new emancipation" ironic (33, 48). Peter well understands the white man's readiness to start him again on his weekly furniture installments: "'De buckra sho got nigger figgered out tuh a cent'" (62).

Archdale's assistance to Peter and to Frasier, who sells divorces outside the law, and his relations with Porgy are pure paternalism. And the whites go on laughing—at the colorful parade, which masks for a moment the black world's ghetto life, as well as at Porgy's futile goat-cart flight from the police. Beyond this pervasive irony, Heyward's comments on race relations are largely concentrated in a few pages where Bess appears before the magistrate and the jail and jailers' attitudes are described. The scene begins with a description of the judge:

> Behind a high desk sat a man well past middle age. His florid complexion caused his long grey mustache to appear very white. His eyes were far apart and suggested a kindness that was born of indolence, rather than of wide compassion. His hands were slender and beautifully made, and he sat with elbows on desk, and fingertips touching. When he spoke it was in a drawl that suggested weariness. (87)

Turning to the jail, Heyward notices that "When life reaches a certain level of misery, it envelopes [*sic*] itself in a protective anesthesia which deadens the senses to extremes" (92).

Frank Durham notes that there is no "conscious cruelty, no sadistic malignancy on the part of the judges or the jailers" but "merely apathy, indifference, and an occasional flash of the affection one might display while punishing a wayward child."[20] But the irony in the jailers' indifference and the judge's hands, mustache, power, and impatience with crime's inconvenience to him is evident: the jailers' indifference is inhumanity, and the judge's indifference is insensitivity to the consequences of his casual use of unlimited power.

This account also reveals another side of Heyward's handling of this antagonist, however: Heyward's comment about the Negro being anesthetized against further suffering, though the further suffering may be fatal, appears to be only accidentally ironic. It is also Heyward's commonplace excuse for white indolence; his narrator knows of the white man's complicity in the black man's situation.

Archdale is a white bridge to the Row, but less so than the police are an instrument and symbol of the Row's isolation from the white community. This isolation of the Row from the white world is further emphasized by the narrator's lack of omniscience. He sees only what a southern gentleman of his time would. While Heyward's narrator stations himself inside the Row, no inner thoughts of the Row's inhabitants serve to contradict the white narrator's perspective. They *appear* resigned. Still, Maria's warning to Sportin' Life, the observation that it is "hahd tu be er nigger," and the song about the sleeping lumber-yard worker who marches to a different drummer make clear that Heyward sees (84). No white character in the book, however, appreciates that living is *not* all that easy in the Row.

The Row's isolation is an element in Heyward's realism and allows him to focus narrowly on the Row, more closely than any previous white American writer had ever focused on an urban Negro community. But it is also part of a narrative strategy by which Heyward finds the white community inadequate in meeting its responsibility to the Row while stopping well short of a full exploration of the realities of racism in South Carolina in the "Golden Age." Although this is the era in which Jim Crow came to South Carolina, lynchings in the state were frequent, and Walter Hines Page observed that he would rather be "an imp in Hades than a Negro in South Carolina," there are no black-white confrontations.[21] As Samuel W. Allen has noted, the crippled hero is no threat to the white community, and the one Negro of stature is kept altogether away from whites.[22] Except for that one revealing moment of attention to the courtroom and jail, the Row's difficulties are attributed not to a faulty social order but to a few unscrupulous merchants and insensitive police officers.

The Row's inhabitants are themselves largely uncomplaining and resigned to incarceration, exploitation, and the harshness of the elements. The very brevity of the quickly shifting vignette scenes cloaks the absence of any penetration of the Row's consciousness and allows great freedom in choice of moments to treat or ignore. Finally, the white aristocratic narrator condescends: while he respects primitive virtues and the Row's community spirit, his emphasis is on primitive failings, social immaturity, resignation, and, always, defeat. As James Southall Wilson observed, "Heyward's darkies have the distilled honey of the Old South's sweetness in their mouths."[23]

This limited perspective means that Heyward's dedication to realism is not complete. But in a deeper sense *Porgy* is more authentically realistic than such omissions might suggest. For Heyward is historically quite accurate—and, therefore, implicitly critical—in placing the Row squarely in that southern order which recognizes for the Negro no past or future or real place in the present. The Row is a place apart, an enigma, and no real white communication with it is possible—despite the relaxed view of life, the same sense of life's immediacy, of community, the same stoicism, and other qualities its citizens share with the other Charleston.

V *Fate*

Life in the Row has a timeless quality; only Porgy seems to sense that life is passing unfulfilled. But the Row is repeatedly forced—in such experiences of terror and death as the Robbins-Crown fight, the saucer burial, the resort to conjurers, and the unnatural power of the hurricane—to contemplate fate, the primacy of the future. After death in the Row, life reasserts itself, as in the adoption of Clara's baby. But the working of Destiny is not only another adversary; it effects a resignation and humility before life shared by all.

The storm is the central experience of fate in the novella:

There was something utterly terrifying about the studied manner in which the hurricane proceeded about its business. It clicked off its moves like an automaton. It was destiny working nakedly for the eyes of men to see. The watchers knew that for at least twenty-four hours it would stay, moving its tides and winds here and there with that invincible precision, crushing the life from those whom its preconceived plan had seemed to mark for death. (143–44)

Porgy responds in fear and wonder and soon all turn to the "Sabior" who offers a "home in de rock" (152). In each scene, Heyward employs the spiritual, a choral folk expression, to provide a powerful articulation of the inner life of the Row. As Heyward observed in 1931: "The spiritual said everything for him that he could not say in the new language that he found here—awe in the presence of death—his racial terror of being left alone—his escape from bondage into the new heaven—everything."[24]

The events of *Porgy* call forth the Negro's profound response— primitive, human, Christian—to the workings of fate. Heyward also employs sun imagery skillfully to indicate the movement of fate, a sun causal, indifferent, benevolent, comforting, concealing, and, finally, mockingly benevolent:

The keen autumn sun flooded boldly through the entrance and bathed the drooping form of the goat, the ridiculous wagon, and the bent figure of the man in hard, satirical radiance. In its revealing light, Maria saw that Porgy was an old man. The early tension that had characterized him, the mellow mood that he had known for one eventful summer, both had gone; and in their place she saw a face that sagged wearily, and the eyes of age lit only by a faint reminiscent glow from suns and moons that had looked into them, and had already dropped down the west.

She looked until she could bear the sight no longer; then she stumbled into her shop and closed the door, leaving Porgy and the goat alone in an irony of morning sunlight. (196)

Fate overwhelms all, and its ways are as whimsical, as merciless, and as harsh as the weather. Nature, sun, time, the cosmos are beyond man's power, and Christianity, Heyward implies, has not reduced their awesomeness to human size for the Row. Humbled, the Row does not challenge fate. Time future in the Row is always fate, never social change.

VI   *Structure and Voice*

Heyward's exploration of the array of forces confronting Catfish Row authenticates the Row's reality. The reader sees Porgy, crippled and alone, and Bess, alone and desperate, as representatives of that back-alley community, seeking to reconcile past, present, and future, at least to accept their meeting, and to survive in the face of the obstacles they afford. In accounting for so much, Heyward largely compensates for the sentimentality found in the simplifications of white supremacy, the cosmic, and primitivism.

Porgy's unity is subtly, deceptively realized, its dozens of vignette sections ultimately falling, as we have seen, into an order embracing plot, theme, character, point of view, and imagery. Because they appear to be fragments and only sketching out an action, however, the vignette structure has provoked critical judgments that do less than full justice to the novella form. Frederick J. Hoffman observes that "one almost feels that the novel deliberately anticipated the play."[25] Leo Rockas has noted that *Porgy* is really a cinema scenario.[26] The complex fictional development of *Porgy* suggests, however, that Heyward was preoccupied with the fictional realization of his story. The vignettes are, in fact, mostly dramatic scenes, rendered with such economy because Heyward could, like other southern writers, once they established a setting and a social order, dispense with stage directions and transitional passages to focus on the action.

This technique also accounts partly for the book's brevity—only 39,000 words. How Heyward has done so much in so little space is explained chiefly by his handling of the novella genre. Despite its number of characters, isn't *Porgy* a novella because the important characters are all intimately involved as a single community—Catfish Row; a single, traditional society—Charleston; in a single action of often tightly interwoven conflicts? Isn't *Porgy* essentially one character, the Charleston back-alley Negro of 1900, fragmented into several parts, trying to reconcile his past, present, and future, at least to accept their meeting? Isn't *Porgy* one character trying to survive in face of the obstacles afforded by the past, present, and future?

Porgy has faults. One, as Ransom observed in 1935, is overwriting: "Heyward writes vigorously, if in fact he slightly overwrites, like an energetic novelist on a flying trapeze, doing full justice to all the functions of narrative, being very pictorial when it is scenery, and very dramatic when it is action, and more sympathetic than patronizing when it is characters."[27] This is, in good part, a matter of language. Heyward likes polysyllabic and unfamiliar words, however they sound together: "Tangibles and intangibles alike were whirled in a mad, inextricable nebula" (145). He is overfond of certain words, such as "utter," and he occasionally misuses words: "The rain was utter" (151). He

would have ornamention serve for profundity, as in his occasional
cosmic references. James Southall Wilson calls it "exquisitely poetic
prose," but it is not always exquisite or poetic.[28]

The problem is really Heyward's handling of point of view. The
narrator's self-conscious prose, by contrast with his handling of the
uninflected and syntactically eccentric Low Country Gullah dialect,
sometimes sounds like a poor man's Henry James telling Huck Finn's
story. Heyward creates the world of Catfish Row, but he will not let it
speak for itself, so that the customs, which become integral to the
action, obtrude from the pattern of the story as local color, and the
whole is seen with a certain condescension. Hoffman complains of
Heyward's being "too much the white-man master of ceremonies,"
whose tone, in introducing characters, is "slick and artificial."[29] Constance Rourke faulted the manuscript, when she saw it at MacDowell
Colony, for the confusion of the personal narrator and the impersonal
observer, the outside and inside points of view.[30] Heyward sought to
heed her counsel, but straddled. The narrator's frequent shifts of scene,
attention, and distance from the action would seem designed to com-
pensate for the lack of any inner perspective upon any character's
experience. But Heyward compensates also by surmising what is going
on within his characters.

VII   A Failure of Irony

A further inadequacy of point of view is Heyward's near-complete
denial of the ironic perspective his material invited. Upon hearing that
Heyward was writing about Charleston, Beatrice Ravenel insisted that
it would have to be satirical.[31] But it is not satirical and the irony is
muted by the use of a very limited omniscience, omission of ugly social
dimensions, emphasis on primitivism and fate as motivation, and omission of major white characters, scenes in white society, and clashes
between the races.

Heyward blames the ill-breeding of the police, the greed of merchants, and even the heat for racial injustice. Archdale, who in his stoic
irresponsibility pays the system blackmail, would appear to be Heyward's surrogate. Heyward's emphasis on primitive sensuality, violence, and folk superstition suggests that the black man may not be
ready for change. No black expressions of real bitterness about the
race's lot are heard. Heyward would have no quarrel with Charleston
society. As Hervey Allen observed, Heyward "did not pity, patronize,

suggest, assume the white-man's burden, or try to add to or lighten that of the colored man."[32] In truth, in order not to assume the white man's burden, he does pity, patronize, and add to the black man's burden by making his situation either more hopeless or helpless. Coming several years before Faulkner addressed the American Negro's agony of identity—and his suffering and the white man's responsibility for it, Heyward's limited understanding and lack of a sense of immediacy allows him to strike a gentleman's bargain with his fellow Charlestonians. He will content himself to insist upon Porgy's humanity and reveal it.

VIII   *"Wonderful, Poetic, Human Qualities"*

Overbalancing such failings, however, are those very "wonderful, poetic, human qualities" Langston Hughes saw in the book.[33] Heyward's characters are sometimes dismissed as stereotypes, but they are not. None of his characters fits James Weldon Johnson's 1928 characterization:

What is the Negro in the artistic conception of white America? In the brighter light, he is a simple, indolent, docile, improvident peasant; a singing, dancing, laughing, weeping child, picturesque beside his log cabin and in the snowy fields of cotton; naively charming with his banjo and his songs in the moonlight and along the lazy Southern rivers; a faithful, ever-smiling and genuflecting old servitor to the white folks of quality; a pathetic and pitiable figure. In a darker light, he is an impulsive, irrational, passionate savage, reluctantly wearing a thin coat of culture, sullenly hating the white man, but holding an innate and inescapable belief in the white man's superiority; an everlasting alien and irredeemable element in the nation; a menace to Southern civilization; a threat to Nordic race purity; a figure casting a sinister shadow across the future of the country.[34]

And while all of the adjectives John Hope Franklin sees characterizing the magazine and press depictions of the Negro during Heyward's formative years are in some ways applicable to Catfish Row—ignorant, lazy, improvident, clownish, irresponsible, childish, criminal,—the Row is not a composite reflection of these images.[35] These elements are played down. Sportin' Life clowns, but not for white audiences. Porgy's clowning is deliberate frustration of white power. Porgy also plays Uncle Tom, but he is never servile and lives for no white master. Heyward's erotic primitive, Crown, is quickly exiled to the nearest facsimile of Africa.

Porgy represents, instead, Heyward's view of the Negro at his best. He is sensitive to rhythm and color, better attuned than whites to the elemental rhythms and mysteries of life, committed to justice, and desirous of a human life of love and peace. His weaknesses are a primitive legacy of fear he has yet to overcome, his loneliness, and the readiness to kill to secure himself from that loneliness. He is, finally, only human; he would survive and escape loneliness in love. Porgy is not the complex Negro character Ellison calls for in his essay on "Twentieth Century Fiction and the Black Mask of Humanity" and offers in *Invisible Man*. But Porgy is, in his time and setting and role as central representative, the first among several members of a society complex and human enough to transcend the stereotypes.

Moreover, although it shackles him to fear, Porgy's primitivism provides him many good qualities. As Heywood Broun's review observed, Heyward grants Porgy's, the Negro's, superiority over the white man, at least in sensitivity, rhythm, and emotion.[36] As Heyward himself observed, "I saw the primitive Negro as the inheritor of a source of delight that I would have given much to possess."[37]

The book's worth is here, in Heyward's revelation of Porgy's humanity. In *Porgy*, the "instrument" of freedom requires "strange songs" from the Row, songs the past, the white community, and an uncertainty about the future make it difficult to play. Yet, despite the irony that accompanies this freedom, for such freedom requires conformity, there is a poignancy and pathos about the Row's affirmation of life in the face of great odds. James Southall Wilson said of *Porgy*, "DuBose Heyward's poetic 'Porgy' is to me the most beautiful book about a Negro."[38] When Ellen Glasgow says, "Nothing finer has occurred in American literature since Uncle Remus, and with these two works of genius, the South will challenge any other part of the country," this affirmation must be what she means.[39]

Such affirmation is made possible only by the book's substantial realism. The search for life in *Porgy* is never overstated, perhaps because it is less consciously pursued by the characters than observed as a way of life lived in the Row. What Heyward envies in the Row is that it confronts the elemental forces of life without the inhibitions and repressed feelings of the mannered white aristocracy and that it is a living community of mutual interests, affections, and cares. Heyward sees in Porgy a sensitive man who finds identity and dignity in a summer of love and accepts his loss as summer ends. The failure of any of Heyward's white characters to achieve as much makes *Porgy*'s affirmation all the more notable.

IX   *The Staging of Porgy*

As everyone knows, the career of Porgy did not end with publication of the novella in 1925. The novella became a play in 1927, *Porgy and Bess* the opera in 1935, and the popular opera was turned into a movie in 1959.

DuBose Heyward had tinkered with the stage in 1913 when his one-act farce, "An Artistic Triumph," was presented at the South Carolina Hall and again on the occasion of the 150th anniversary of the Charleston Museum when he contributed a witty eighteenth-century scene, "1773, An Historical Interlude."[40] But it was not until his wife, Dorothy, showed him her scenario for a play version of *Porgy* that he again took the idea of playwriting seriously.

The play version of *Porgy* is a collaborative effort of Heyward and his wife—his story and characters and her solid technical playwriting experience; her Harvard Prize play, *Nancy Ann*, had been produced on Broadway and she had published a one-act situation comedy.[41] Mrs. Heyward's role, however, was minor; according to her, the play versions of both *Porgy* and *Mamba's Daughters* were nine-tenths DuBose's.[42]

The novel offers a fully realized black world and a fully realized black hero of unmistakable humanity. The play's value is less its literary achievement than the initial access to the serious Broadway stage it and a small number of other plays in the 1920s gave black actors. But the changes for the stage result in a fuller appreciation of the role of Negro folk expression and a richer understanding of the inner spirit—the rhythm—of the black community. For by 1927 Heyward felt that he had identified the "unique characteristic" in Negro life, a source of delight that made him the white man's envy. It was the "secret law" of "rhythm," which he defined as "a sort of race personality that dominated and swayed the mass, making of it a sum vastly greater than the total of its individual entities." So the dramatization of *Porgy* became a challenge to "give the flow of life . . . its proper place in the canvas":[43]

That it was bigger than the individual who moved upon it was evident, for it had driven its dark stream on under our civilization, while generations came, were swept forward by it, and vanished. As with singing, where the Negro seldom excels as a soloist and yet with three or four friends picked up almost at random creates a successful chorus, so in their work and play it is the mass rhythms, the concerted movements, the crowd laughter, the communal interrelationships of the Negro quarter that differentiate it most sharply from its white slum neighbor. We felt that the play in order to possess any degree of verisimilitude must show its people moving in response to the deep undertow of this tide. . . . (xiii–xiv)

Heyward attributed their success in expressing what Stark Young called the "glow" and "rhythm of life" to the cast's involvement in the unconscious rhythms of the primitive Negro in becoming "a living representation" of Catfish Row (iv).[44] And to the play's techniques:

We used the spiritual as they actually occur to express emotional stress when the limited spoken vocabulary becomes inadequate. We employed the rhythmic, spontaneous prayer with which the primitive Negro makes his supplications; the unfaltering rhythm of time, expressed in the ebb and flow of day and night, and the chiming of St. Michael's bells; and the crowd movements, with their shifting pattern of colour and sound. (xvii–xviii)

But the Heywards also place more emphasis upon the community, where rhythm is generated, than does the novella. There is more song and group movement. And, as Frank Durham points out, the scene structure is usually a mass effect, then a dramatic dialogue, followed by a mass effect.[45]

Thematically, primitive superstition and fate are subordinated to the central conflict in the play, that between Christian faith and morals and disbelief, sin, and natural evil—death and the hurricane. In the eyes of the Row, Bess and Crown are sinners, not victims of cultural lag. Crown blasphemes and murders. Serena prays to "Jedus who done trouble de Sea ob Gallerie" to "cas' de debil out ob de afflicted" when Bess is ill (111). Maria considers Sportin' Life sold to the devil.

The play's theme is most clearly revealed in the scenes of death and fear of death, especially in the spirituals. The plaintive query of death, "Deat', ain't yuh gots no shame?" is given greater emphasis and followed by another spiritual anticipating heaven (28).

A final exchange focuses the moral conflict in the play. Serena says of the departing Bess, "'Dat gal ain't neber had Gawd in she heart, an' de debil get um at last.'" Maria replies, "'Tain't de debil. De happy dus' done for um'" (201). The two views, religious and secular, are balanced, but Maria does not explicitly reject Serena's view of Bess; her quarrel is only with Serena's Christian spirits. In the Row's ready resort to spirituals and prayer, it is clearly not ready to abandon the Christian view for the superstitious or the secular.

Notably, the evil the Row faces in the play is only that found in nature and themselves. The evil of the white world recedes to minor proportions. And in moral and spiritual crises, the Row shows itself to consist of essentially simple people in an essentially simple world, clever only in frustrating whites.

While a number of scenes are heightened in the play, the focus is so much on the group that individual characters are reduced to secondary roles. The novella triangle, now a quadrangle with Sportin' Life's involvement, is out of harmony with the rhythms of the Row. And the characters are correspondingly at odds with themselves. Bess resists Crown and happy dus' but then, fated, succumbs to the depravity of Sportin' Life's promise that they will make a "swell team"—her body and his friends (25). Maria, a deposed matriarch, is only a shadow of her old self.

Maria's loss of influence has one explanation that accounts for the apparent wrenching of everything, especially characters, out of the novella's focus. The time is moved thirty years forward. Porgy, the contemplative and seer, becomes more realistic about his fate in the 1920s, which is to be a clown. As a minstrel figure in a story that has lost most of its pathos, his pursuit of Bess in the end, "'Up Nort'— past de Custom House,'" is less pathetic than comic (203). Bess knows from the first scene what Sportin' Life has to offer. "'I ain't come to dat yet,'" she tells him, but the simple sex of her relationship with the primitive Crown is past (25). She despairs and retreats from reality in dope. Even Crown in his brutality is mentally more complicated, as the storm scene shows. Nor can Bess be faithful or wait patiently for the more intelligent, sensitive, living, successful invader of the white world, Porgy. While more honored, Serena's "Christian" alternative is strident and less human. Sportin' Life is more immoral than amoral. Maria's simple, practical authority, bridging woods and town, no longer recognized, she sounds more like Serena in her righteous indignation toward Bess. The "golden age" is past. Primitive innocence and resignation to fate are fading as the corruption of change sets in. But

Heyward does not fully shift gears, so the elements of past and present are left at odds in the play.

While the heightened dramatic effects make the play a lively folk drama, the proportion and harmony between community and main characters are sacrificed. Primitivism fades as theme but balloons as atmosphere in the pervasive Negro rhythms. The moral theme becomes central, so the race conflict is soft-pedaled, lest it now have to be faced directly in moral terms. To accomplish this obscuration, Heyward makes the Row a minstrel world and shifts the primary focus to the next world. Several new incidents, involving new minor characters, pander to a white audience's demand for minstrel conduct from Negro entertainers.

Disjointed, too, is Heyward's pursuit of life in the play. While individual characters move toward 1920s racial stereotypes—clown, loose woman, brute, and bad (Harlem) nigger, Heyward is identifying life as the ability to experience rhythm, secular and Christian.

The effect is that the conflict is too slight and unconcentrated. Characters seldom confront one another. Important scenes cease to be functional. Porgy is too unchanging.

On the other hand, the excessive primitive weakness, white patronizing, and stoic acceptance of fate in the novel largely disappear, and the obtrusive narrator vanishes, an immediate consequence of which is stronger dramatic scenes.

The most notable addition is the secret "rhythm" Heyward had discovered and expressed in music and group expression. It saves—and makes—the play and sweeps almost all objections before it. As Oliver M. Sayler observed: "No one can sit through 'Porgy' in the theatre and deny that his eye, ear, and mind have been played on like so many instruments by the various hands of rhythm. No one can read 'Porgy,' the novel or the play, and report half so vivid an experience."[46] The price Heyward pays in the adaptation is considerable, though, especially the sacrifice of the novel's subtle unity and some of the elements comprising it. As one reviewer observed, the play lacks the energy and strength of the book and, despite its dramatic heightening as a folk play, is weak in plot development, ordering of scenes to climaxes, and curtains.[47]

To the extent that the play succeeds, much of the credit would appear to go not to the Heywards but to the spirituals; to other indigenous group expressions of the South Carolina Low Country Negro—the crap game, vending chants, shouts, and parading; and to the cast's

ability to express freely something of that rhythm of life a southern
white admirer of the Low Country Negro had determined to transfer
to the stage.[48]

Ironically, it was the courtly and reserved white aristocrat, Heyward, whose play, *Porgy*, forced Harlem to begin to recognize and
appreciate the American black folk culture and experience it was so
studiously ignoring.

X   *The Gershwins and* Porgy and Bess

Reportedly, in 1836 Fanny Kemble, the young English actress who
triumphantly toured America in 1832 and two years later married a
Georgian, Pierce Butler, suggested an opera of southern Negroes sing-
ing.[49] Ninety-nine years later and eight years after *Porgy* appeared on
Broadway, *Porgy and Bess,* the first American folk opera, with George
Gershwin's music, Ira Gershwin and DuBose Heyward's lyrics, and
Heyward's libretto opened in New York.

Gershwin had taken an early interest in *Porgy*, but Al Jolson's desire
to do it and Gershwin's other commitments accounted for the long
delay.[50] When they finally set to work, following Gershwin's stay on
Sullivan's Island, South Carolina, Heyward's was the initial task, to
abbreviate the play scenes for opera. Then, with Ira Gershwin's help,
words—George insisted on recitative—and lyrics were fit to the music.
Heyward had a major role in the lyrics, both in selecting spirituals for
the opera and as author of "Summertime"; the six-part prayer, "Oh,
Doctor Jesus"; and, with perhaps some help from Ira, "It Takes a Long
Pull," "I'm On My Way," and "The Buzzard Song." Ira Gershwin also
credits Heyward with "A Woman Is a Sometime Thing." "I Got Plenty
O' Nuttin'" began with a Heyward version and ended with Ira's.[51]

The responsibility for the libretto was Heyward's alone, and the
changes in scenes, dialogue, lyrics, characters, and the overall dramatic
effect cast another light on his story.

The songs themselves return the Row to the Golden Age, make Bess
fickle and doomed rather than comic or tragic, and give her greater
motivation for leaving. Porgy's final song, "Where's My Bess?" leaves
him not in an "irony of morning sunlight" but en route to New York
to pursue Bess—as if New York is " 'a Heav'nly Lan'.' "[52]

As Stark Young observed of the play, "the progression of its plot suits
the simplification and widening that music entails."[53] (He goes on to
praise Heyward's libretto.) And the opera profits both by its escape

from the play's clutter and the opportunity its songs provided for the characters to express their personal feeling. Certain songs, such as Clara's "Summertime," serve as a counterpoint, in their repetition, for successive events—the crap game, the hurricane, and Bess's "new life," holding Clara's baby. Through song, Heyward and the Gershwins move inside Catfish Row; the songs become interior monologues revealing both inner hearts and communal attitudes and rhythms of life.

Choral words, crowd movements, repeated songs and refrains, the Honey Man's chant, and recurrent expressions of the motifs of Catfish Row all serve to define theme, season, and place better than in the play. Porgy becomes more contemplative and human again. Reuben Mamoulian, the director, largely achieves the figure he describes as wanting Sidney Poitier to project in the movie Porgy: "To me he's a Charleston, South Carolina, version of Don Quixote. In his way he's a deeply religious man of great faith. He's naive, but he's capable of tremendous love and devotion and a man like Don Quixote in courage."[54]

Virtually all of the argument about *Porgy and Bess* has to do not with Heyward's libretto but the Gershwins' contributions—Ira's lyrics and a music which, while indebted to Negro rhythms, is not Jones Island but New York jazz. Some feel that neither the music nor Ira's sophisticated lyrics is compatible with the simple world of Porgy.

The Gershwins have defenders, too. Stark Young praises the opera's "pressure, glow, and rhythm of life."[55] William Youngren defends the fittingness of the music that accompanies the recitative as "inventive, intelligent, and wonderfully contrived to project and clarify the dramatic action," and he praises the "carefully shaped musical and dramatic sequences" and the strength of the songs in the dramatic action.[56] In answer to the many critics of "I Got Plenty O' Nuttin'" as inappropriate, Youngren observes:

The song's harmonic pattern is first heard, played softly by the strings, behind Porgy's strangely moving invocation to the dice during the crap game in Act I. The song itself appears fully formed in Act II, as Porgy's carefree response to the fisherman Jake's declaration that he must take his boat out, even in the face of hurricane warnings, if he is to earn the money to give his children a college education. We recall Porgy's luck in the crap game, and his song seems the celebration of the far more significant stroke of the same luck that has, in the interim, brought him Bess. Jake will die in the storm, but at the end of the opera. After Bess has abandoned him, Porgy has, precisely, nothing—except for his goat-cart and the pathetic hope that drives him to leave for New York in search of Bess. The opera offers no simple endorsement of either man's attitude, and it is made clear at the time of the song that Porgy has not always felt this way: immediately after it, the women comment on how much he has changed since Bess has come to live with him.[57]

Another view is Joseph Wood Krutch's disappointment with the opera as music and drama; the conflict and the characters' roles are so reduced and the thematic conflict is so oversimplified as to patronize the sober and simple folk experience of the novella.[58]

Carried to the extreme, that view becomes Eric Bentley's:

It is worth stressing that *Porgy and Bess* is a musical, not an opera, because the work of Heyward was to be salvaged by exploitation for "lower" not "higher" purposes. A musical is, *per se* a kind of fairy tale in which the Arcadia of Heyward's imagination could find its form. Even the pleasant nonsense of musical comedy comes in useful. It purges *Porgy* of a nonsense that was unpleasant both as style and meaning.

I do not want to carry my inverted snobbery (if that's what it is) too far, and pretend that *Porgy and Bess* is beyond criticism. Heyward and Gershwin created a world, not an action; an idyll, not a drama; a series of numbers, not a tragic or comic whole. The tradition of the musical is not that of music drama but that of operetta, vaudeville, and revue, it has the defects of its qualities, and toward the end of *Porgy and Bess*—as I judge from three different productions—the cumulative effect is not more impressive than it is exhausting.[59]

A dissenting opinion is required here. As literature, *Porgy and Bess* certainly has more merit than vaudeville. What Heyward's audience encounters is a novella turned into a play and then into an opera. The qualities each realizes are not all found in any one form—the subtle, poignant, and realistic experience in the novel; the race rhythms and moral drama of the stage; and the rhythms, color, music, movement, and passion the opera realizes. Still, the opera reenacts, with great feeling and the power of song, the summer of Porgy's happiness and its loss.

The productions of *Porgy and Bess* won it acclaim that the critics cannot ignore. Todd Duncan, as the first Porgy—he played the role over a thousand times—was complemented in 1935 by John Bubbles as Sportin' Life. The 1952–1954 production, the most celebrated, starred Leontyne Price, William Warfield, Lester Scott (who replaced

Warfield as Porgy), John McCurry, and Cab Calloway.[60] (Scenes from this production were recorded, using Price, Warfield, McHenry Boatwright, McCurry, and Bubbles.)

Ironically, every effort to stage the play or the opera in Charleston failed, including one with all-white performers, until a South Carolina Tricentennial production of *Porgy and Bess* opened in June 1970. For years it was thought Charleston Negroes would feel they were being ridiculed, but in 1956 it was sometime Mayor, Governor, and Senator Burnett Maybank who had decided it gave "too much attention to the Negro."[61] The screen version of the opera, including Sidney Poitier and Sammy Davis, Jr., along with a weeping Bess with a lifeless voice and a more brutal and pathetic Crown, had, at last report, made it only as far as the Charleston suburbs.[62]

CHAPTER 4

Eden, Exile, and the Highway: Angel

I *The Apple of Experience*

GROWING up among Charleston gentility, Heyward focused in *Porgy* upon another part of Charleston that he had studied closely, the Negro community of Catfish Row. In his next novel, published a year later, he turned to the only other world he knew at all well, the folk of the North Carolina Blue Ridge Mountains foothills.

Several of Heyward's Skyline poems and the ending of the early story "The Brute" suggest the main characters as well as several scenes of *Angel*. It is, then, the story of a young mountain girl ("The Girl"), Angel Thornley, daughter of a gaunt, severe backwoods clergyman ("The Preacher"), Gabriel Thornley. Her mother ("The Woman") could not survive the hard life, leaving Angel with nature and her uncommunicative father. She falls in love with Buck Merritt, member of a family of moonshiners ("The Blockader"). When Gabriel learns that Angel is pregnant, he informs on Buck, who is arrested at the still. After preaching a revival, Gabriel tricks Angel into marriage to ne'er-do-well Stan Galloway.

An account of Angel's determined resistance to Stan and her struggle against defeat by mountain hardship ("Black Christmas") follows. The coming of progress to the valley and the prospect of victory over Stan and the mountains mark the transition to the final part. With progress comes Buck, a trusty working on the new road with a chain gang. Jealously trying to blow up Buck, Stan is killed. Unscathed by their harsh experiences, Buck and Angel head for the city with little Buck to make their future.

The first part traces Angel's fall from innocence and her exile from the beautiful Eden of her childhood. In the second part, Angel suffers in exile, working by the sweat of her brow, hoping for deliverance from her bondage to Stan. In the final part, Buck returns with a halo and astride a machine of progress, the new dispensation.

85

The novel begins with the isolated Cove, "so utterly Earth's"—"like a child without its first definitions."[1] Thunder Falls is a "small, impotent thunder," which has no power over the "wild creature" abandoning herself to the current (9). Accidentally discovering Angel bathing, Buck leaves, the flame azaleas "a tangle of fire about his feet" (12). If there is any doubt of the passing of innocence, Angel is accused of "idlin'" and responds to her father's insistence that she study the Commandments with curiosity about the meaning of adultery (14). After meeting Buck and dancing with him, Angel feels shame as she disrobes for her next swim—"and fear at her heart" (40).

The limited "moral vocabulary" of Gabriel Thornley answers none of the riddles Angel encounters (43). The very name Gabriel has given her suggests his rejection of the flesh. His "mouth was a wide, thin-lipped symbol of suppression, and the eyes let inward upon steel walls" (35). In his view, the only way to evade evil is to evade the world itself, to isolate himself and his daughter on the mountainside and seek no pleasure, yield to no emotion, experience no joy.

Angel has been taught to view the moonshiners as "fiends incarnate" and the sin of dancing as the herald of doom (30). As her father denies exit from the moral innocence of Eden, he also bars entrance to life. He reveals no shadow of feeling for the daughter with whom he lives alone. Nor can he share her sensitivity to the beauty of the falls.

By contrast, Buck seeks a balance, a union of body and soul: "'Dancin' an' revivalin's just two different ways o' sayin' the same thing,'" Buck says (26). Both are emotional releases and fulfillment, one secular, one spiritual.

When Gabriel announces a revival down in the valley, the prospect of Buck's evening visits "opened up for Angel that brief period in the springtime of every woman that sees the swift rush of life up through the sleeping bud into the open flower" (52).

So the battle lines are drawn between Gabriel's claim for God and those of earth and man, between coldness and warmth, repression and the freedom of nature, will in the service of the abstract and the will to concrete life—her father's terrible singleness of purpose as against "the almost audible beat of life," the escape from the Cove's monotony, and the rationalization that her August repentance would make it "all right" (53–54).

Initially, Angel spurns Buck's proposal of marriage, wanting time to "laugh and play" (56). But one Saturday night of full moon Angel feels an "intolerable hunger for Buck" and moves in an "atmosphere of unreality" with him through the sounds of nature to the Falls where she responds to his cry that they have to get back into the light with "a low, entirely feminine laugh of victory" and the smells and sounds of the "ancient Earth" cloak her fall (59, 60, 65, 67). Angel has partaken of the Tree of Knowledge.

A pattern of light-dark imagery, reinforcing this theme, pervades these chapters. Angel is a "flash of gold and ivory" diving in the pool (10). Her hair escapes her fingers "to float about her face in a mist of silver-gold" (19). She builds castles in Spain when the valley is "brimmed with golden haze" (20). Buck sees her "almost luminous" in white "against the black square of the open door" (45). Angel is clearly "trailing clouds of glory"—golden glory. But when Buck tells her they are sweethearts, "the apple trees wove a black net between them and the moon" (46–47). Again, the apple is the vehicle for the descent of darkness. In the day world, she is Gabriel's angelic daughter; in the light of the gradually filling moon, she is Buck's.

When Angel leads Buck to the falls, images of descent and darkness converge, and there is no light:

He followed her in silence, wondering. Down they went, and the white world of the hilltops flickered for a moment between the columns of the pines, then died out as they plunged into the tunnelled way under the interlacing laurel and rhododendron. She led him with unhesitating sureness down the steep trail. The darkness was more than that of night. It seemed the very stuff of which blindness is made, pressing impenetrably against the open eyes. As used as Buck was to night travel and the ways of the woods, he realized that he would be lost without the guiding pressure of the little hand that extended back to him from the blankness into which he plunged. (63–64)

Notably, they go open-eyed, with Buck, the proper Adam, following and wondering.

Their movement is also away from reality and out of time, Heyward insists. The roar of the falls "was a barrier of impenetrable sound reared between them and the world of actualities" (64). Their erotic bliss isolates them from the world beyond themselves. But it is still the Fall, and Gabriel is the self-appointed God of judgment. When he catches Angel and Buck together, his eyes are "as menacing and as impersonal as two blue-steel revolver muzzles" (70).

When Buck is jailed for ten years, Angel's heart "seemed quite dead within her" (77). She goes into a heavily laden apple orchard to weep.

For Thornley, the world is a snare of thorns, and Gabriel rejects the Merritts' creativity and Buck's maleness and sexuality. Originally, Angel notices his gaunt frame and stoop in contrast to Buck's beauty; now she sees her father's evil in informing on Buck and in protecting his reputation and the revival's success by marrying her off rather than responding to her agony of spirit. In her innocence, Angel had thought that there was "love, naked and pleading," if mute (18). Now his voice was "tremendous, terrible, with the call of a trumpet in it" (98). If flawed, he is still the harsh Calvinist Jehovah.

Heyward's narrator patronizes Thornley's revival, seeing his success as a transitory response to a lonely folk's need for companionship, confidants, and excitement, which the mountains view with irony, waiting "with the indifference of certitude for their children to come straggling home" (96).

Angel's ambivalence comes to focus when she imagines Thornley's followers driving the whores whom they patronize "into an unknown world, under the vast taciturnity of the mountain night"; she senses the contradiction between nature's tolerance and man's hypocritical intolerance (107). Also, as quickly as the revival ends, the reader sees the world resume its worldly way, with heated trading of animals, fighting, and Gabriel's own betrayal of his daughter. Nonetheless, Angel accepts her biblical fate, a life of emptiness and exile, passively.

As a conflict between Calvinist fanaticism and humanity and as a journey from youth to maturity, from spring to a first winter, and from Eden into the timelands to be followed by a period of exile and trial, the thematic pattern of the first part is clear enough. But these conflicts are not fully sustained thereafter. Angel's moral code at Beartown is more pragmatic than primitive, Calvinist, or a continuation of her old conflict with Gabriel. The single reminder of her fall is that she lives, literally, by the sweat of her brow.

II   *The Barren Life and Redemption*

Besides difficulties in sustaining his themes, Heyward also has difficulty with his characters in the first part which continue throughout the novel. Angel is more a figure of primitive innocence than human. Gabriel's religious fanaticism turns out to be self-serving, and now he virtually disappears. Buck, barely sketched, reappears again only near the end. Galloway is a wraith.

The second part does reflect man's experience in time. In Beartown,

Angel must "bear" her child and the burden of her labor—all "barren" of love. It is cold; there are no neighbors, and Stan's gaze is "vacuous" (120). She nears despair and panic, only to find nostalgia "for the lost and gone things of the spirit" sustaining and the sun of early spring warming (132). She can break, as had Galloway's first wife, or harden. She chooses the latter. Myra Kent offers a momentary communication, but that passes; she makes a fine crop and declares her independence from Stan, but her future continues bleak. The Kents leave, and Myra's gift, a box of snuff, rests on the mantel "as a symbol of defeat" (167). The Kents' return for a visit reveals that they are sickly, mechanical, thoroughly corrupted by life in town.

Heyward's purpose here seems to be not dramatic action realizing theme but the rhetorical mode of process: this is the way life goes— success or failure—in the mountains. The scenes are momentary or seen in retrospect, through reverie, except for the Dixon cabin death-bed and the Kents' visit, and they, too, signify the pattern of defeat of the mountaineers. Only the ravages of time—Angel's aging and the autumnal death signaled in the flame color of the sourwood leaves— and Angel's loneliness sustain the larger theme. And again the characters are unconvincing: Little Buck is largely ignored, and no notice is taken of any sexual tension between the brutish Galloway and the wife who spurns him. The five years is handled with largely remote narrative. And if the mountains are "the ultimate rampart of a tottering, primitive world, beset by a devastating civilization," in the narrator's abstract and cosmic view, Angel is quite passive about the coming change, even as the railroad approaches Misty Valley (120). Likewise, the past has lost meaning: her passion for Buck appears dead and her father's visit has no meaning for her.

Progress comes to Misty Valley in the third part of the novel, with its worldly miracles and, in Thornley's view, "emissaries of the Devil" (212). The road-building frightens Angel; Galloway's sinister power, derived from the dynamite he uses, is disquieting. The mountain folk and the chain gang view each other's worlds contemptuously—as prisons. A drought occurs. And then, in the coolness of an evening, as Angel looks into the sun, a huge truck, a "fabulous denizen of another world," bears down on her, and the sun behind the driver "aureoled him with intolerable light" (245). It is, of course, Buck.

The next twenty pages are an orchestration of light and darkness, cold and heat, drought and rain. Buck's smile turns up "a light behind

steel bars" (252). The night grows darker but the old passion returns
"like the stirring of a sleeper in a shadowed room" (256).

The denouement is all melodrama. A cloud appears in the August
sky. Galloway's explosion kills him. And where Buck and Angel had
"walled each other out" in their separation, "some strange spiritual
communion" now renews the love between Angel and the unconscious
Buck (247, 274). Angel fears the city of man, to which Buck intends to
take her, but we are to believe that a sunny day and their dignity and
strength mean that they will prevail. In the end, "The great vehicle
gathered speed and plunged eastward. Two lofty hills opened to
receive it, then drew together after it had passed" (287). The mountains have released two of their own.

The logic of the conclusion is right. Gabriel Thornley's code cannot
account for the world and time. Man must fall to be redeemed; he
must live and love. Buck—humanity—twice rescues Angel. But we are
asked to take it all on faith—and melodrama. We are denied a sensitive portrayal of the clash between cultures as Angel experiences and
anticipates it. To live is to leave Thunder Cove. Frances Newman said
she had an idea it was written for motion pictures.[2] Since Angel and
Buck remain types, it would require a lot of background—or foreground—music. In a letter to John Bennett, Heyward expresses relief
that the critics were not more harsh regarding his hurried effort.[3]

III   *Alien Material*

The novel is seriously flawed in its lack of unity, moving from allegory to types to a rushed melodramatic ending. Angel's preternatural
innocence and type-role compare poorly with Porgy's primitivism and
humanity. Nor does change provide any dramatic tension here. Buck
and Angel never reach town.

One difficulty Heyward meets is the result of his choice of a group
of characters whose lives are so barren and repressed and who are so
inarticulate that only crabbed gestures or allegorical role-playing
reveal at all what their experience means to them. A similar clash of
southern Appalachian life with progress occurs in Peter Taylor's play
A Stand in the Mountains.[4] But the play includes newcomers, longtime residents with a wider perspective, as well as a few "indigens or
autochthons" who can articulate the dramatic yielding of the old to the
new and the pathos consequent upon that change.[5] None of Heyward's
characters approaches such a role.

In praising Elizabeth Madox Roberts's "lovely thing," *The Time of Man*, which appeared the same year, Heyward recognized its superiority to *Angel*.[6] Both books celebrate the beauty of the land and recognize man as wedded to the cycle of nature, enduring, season by season. But Angel is not committed to the land. She fears the loss of youth, struggles against rather than in harmony with her fate. The soil is a means, but it lacks the significance that it has for Ellen Chesser, whose self-respect and wisdom grow out of a poetic contemplation of life and nature Angel seldom experiences. Ellen's movement is from youth and deprivation to maturity and richness of life, to a profound sense of its order and mystery at the end, and she has the lyrical voice to express it. Angel moves from youthful nature to self-discipline to a blind gamble on life in the city. Ellen is seen from within, quite deliberately in her youthful years, Angel largely from without, skimmingly. Ellen's journey is inward, Angel's outward, along the line of time and space. As Heyward probably saw, *The Time of Man* becomes an epic of man's struggle with the soil as he journeys through life toward meaning, while *Angel* remains, like the more effective Skyline poems, local color testimony to the bleak fortitude of the southern mountaineer types, overlaid with an Eden-exile-life journey theme that Heyward cannot sustain adequately.

When *Porgy* appeared, Frances Newman advised Heyward to stay away from the inner life of Negroes; she was on better ground in suggesting that his summers were not enough to know the mountaineers as he knew Charlestonians—at least well enough to give their experience the breath of life.[7]

CHAPTER 5

Excursions into the Primitive

I "The Half Pint Flask"

DESPITE his early work in the short-story form and his compressed narratives of the pathetic Negro or mountaineer in his poems and in *Porgy*, Heyward published only one serious short story during his fifteen years as a professional writer, "The Half Pint Flask," written in 1926. And even its 5,000 words or so he agreed to have decked out in book form—100 words to the page.

Heyward's choice of genres is not surprising. He wished to be a memorialist—of settings, customs, character types, of representative incidents, themes, and fates—and that required a larger canvas than the short story. Also, slow writer that he was, Heyward could not make a living from occasional short stories, although, ironically, the book publication of *The Half Pint Flask* sold 5,086 copies.[1] The *Saturday Evening Post*'s rejection of it as "too highbrow," before *Bookman* took it, points to the story's weakness as a story: although it is almost entirely straightforward narrative, it goes nowhere; nobody learns anything; and nothing changes.

The story involves a scientist's visit to Ediwander Island to study "'Negroid Primates.'"[2] His study is interrupted, however, when he is subjected to the evil spirit Plat-eye's torture. The torture ends only when the rare old South Carolina Dispensary medicine bottle Barksdale has removed from a gravesite a few minutes after his arrival is found by the superstitious Negroes and returned to the plot. The center of reader interest is Barksdale's inner experience in coping with the eerie sounds and sensations of the African spirit, but Heyward does not enter Barksdale's mind and so neglects this almost altogether. At the beginning of the story, the narrator, Courtney, a writer and manager of the Ediwander duck club, is flipping through Barksdale's book on his Ediwander study, in which, Courtney is surprised to discover, Barksdale attributes his nightmare experience to insomnia and a swamp fever resulting in extreme delirium. Courtney then recalls the incident, finally noting why Barksdale honors only the scientifically proven. But neither the book nor the past explains how, short of pathological obsession, Barksdale can continue in his trust in scientific fact alone, after being driven to the brink of death by the voodoo spirit.

On the surface, Barksdale's experience reminds one of Poe, but Roderick Usher's disintegration is an action, the disintegration of a psyche in its self-absorption. Stubbornly resisting any influences upon his rigid view of life, Barksdale does not subject the intrusion of Plat-eye to scientific analysis or substantiate the statements about Negro superstition in his book, asserting instead that the Negro "'unreservedly espoused the doctrine of Christianity'" (2). He is simply a fanatic whose truth is shaped altogether from within rather than by experience. Spencer's explanation, when he comes to take Barksdale away, that Barksdale got that way when his one love, Celia, rejected him as a boor, shattering his trust in emotion, is convenient and neat. But Barksdale's bruised heart, noted when the story is nine-tenths over, comes awkwardly late to explain his narrowness and obstinacy or his dedication to facts and insensitivity to beauty. In Courtney's account, Barksdale simply resists Plat-eye with his usual stubborn refusal to recognize the immaterial phenomenon until he is thoroughly exhausted and hypnotized by the spirit. Barksdale's motivation, his inner struggle, is simply too sketchily and tardily seen—and irrational.

While Courtney, who serves as narrator and shares part of Barksdale's experience, serves also as a counterpoint to Barksdale's myopia, it is never clear why Courtney is so passive before Barksdale's stubbornness about the bottle: he quite fails to serve as an antagonist. Nor are there any Negro characters to fill that role. Courtney's narrative assumes to a considerable extent that he, a southerner familiar with the Ediwander Negroes, is talking to other southerners at least half as familiar as he with the inscrutability of the half-pagan and anonymous islanders and their sinister powers.

The result is that "The Half Pint Flask" is more an incident than a story, an incident revealing the double world of the Ediwander Negro community, placid by day and possessed by primitive rhythms and powers by night. Second, we meet the opposite world of dispassionate reason, and Heyward again finds reason alone inadequate in dealing with the rhythms of experience. As in *Porgy* and *Angel*, old ways encounter new; here black mystery is pitted against white science. But Barksdale is a psychically wounded automaton of science who never becomes a real threat to the natives' order of things, an order still untouched at the end of the story, even by their first sight of an automobile.

For all his deficiencies as narrator, Courtney is nonetheless essential. He responds to nature, which is seen to be peacefully indifferent to Barksdale's acquisitive spirit: "The sunset was going quickly, dragging its color from the sky and sea, rolling up leagues of delicately tinted gauze into tight little bales of primary color, then draping these with dark covers for the night" (10). He conveys the reality of Plat-eye:

The wave of movement lasted for several minutes, then it abated slowly. But this was the strange thing about it; the agitation was not dissipated into the air; rather it seemed to settle slowly, heavily, about my body, and to move upon my skin like the multitudinous crawling of invisible and indescribably loathsome vermin. (30)

Courtney's sympathy with the primitive Negroes who are more in harmony with the rhythm of nature than the ordinary civilized white becomes evident, setting in even sharper relief Barksdale's exaggeration of rationality. As Courtney's name suggests, he is a courtier, on his knee to the occult Negro community in which he lives alone. Distant though the Negro antagonists are and compressed as Courtney's narrative is, we sense a fullness of life in their huts that encompasses the "flaming calico," beat of drums, and occult powers they conjure up in an attempt to drive Barksdale to self-destruction. Courtney takes in stride their occult response to Barksdale's desecration of the grave; the strange rhythm of the beating sticks that precedes the first experience of the Plat-eye agitation; the warm, deep laughter of the Negroes when he and Spencer seek help in finding Barksdale; and the traditional greeting when the Negroes pass on the way to work the morning after the bottle is restored. The Negroes may take to the trees or the water at sight of Spencer's automobile, but Courtney's spare narrative sketches clearly the formidable resistance of their primitive culture to serious white interference.

Courtney also serves as Barksdale's judge, noticing his inhumanity toward Negroes and his blindness to beauty, criticizing his disregard of the local moral code in taking the flask for his selfish ends. Barksdale is not, however, simply a man ruled by science or the past or self-interest. His arrogance in not respecting the grave and what is not his is also an arrogance regarding anything distinctively Negro. Ironically, for such a rationalist, he finds no contradictions in attributing to the Negro a "'deeply religious'" Christian commitment while characterizing him as "'primitive'" and a "'Negroid Primate'" in the same breath (1, 7). Barksdale is a white supremacist. He judges the Ediwander Negroes before he sees them: "'Simple souls, I fancy'" (8). Courtney has to remind him of the development of Congo art and the Negro's cultural past, to which Barksdale's response is "his mocking, intolerable smile" (17).

With the writer's eye for structural, symbolic, and verbal techniques of narrative, Courtney employs several. Barksdale faces Courtney "truculently" after asserting his ownership of the bottle (13). Courtney describes the Negro curs the next day as "truculent" (24). The curs' attitude is one way of discovering, he notes, "how you stand with a Negro." Barks are the most significant communication from the Negro community the whole time Barksdale defiantly keeps the bottle.

The story is framed by the passing columns of Negroes, laughing and speaking softly, giving a greeting and then disappearing silently over the hill. Another structural element is the appearance of the moon, full when Barksdale sees Plat-eye, absent when he lights a flare in terror of Plat-eye's coming, a "high white moon" when Courtney and Spencer search for Barksdale, and a low moon at dawn when they find him in the water, facing east (47). Plat-eye is associated with the darkness and the moon; Barksdale is rescued in a "forest, dark even in the summer noon" (54). The island has its own rhythmic life, timeless, rooted in nature and the past. When the bottle is returned, life can go on quietly.

Another symbol is Barksdale's glass collection, a hobby in several ways appropriate for one "wounded by something elusive, intangible" (48). This symbol, like the book and the information about Barksdale's lost love, is handled badly. The early appearance of the book denies the reader any suspense about Barksdale's fate; denial of early knowledge about his love and the hobby denies the story a genuine conflict— between fact and feeling. Courtney questioning his own experience, on receipt of Barksdale's book, is unbelievable, and his rehashing of the story to Spencer at the end makes wearisome an already overexplicit tale. Courtney also fails to find a way to let the reader see what Barksdale sees.

The self-conscious first-person narrative is also pitted with lapses in style, from the inane first sentence about picking up the book. Courtney "commences to rehearse" rather than "recalls" (3); he tries to "embody the abstract into something" (14); it is a "tenuous little wharf" (4); the moon rises into "the immeasurable tranquility" (38); and, at dawn, the "east was a swinging nebula" (52).

But in showing us the world of Ediwander Island, Heyward, more clearly than before, uses nature symbolically and realizes in the terror of Ediwander a level of Negro experience he only touches on in *Porgy*.

II A *Movie Scenario for* Emperor Jones

One of the two movie scripts on which Heyward worked, an adaptation of Eugene O'Neill's *Emperor Jones*, is consistent with the emerging pattern in Heyward's work—the black man's encounter with change in white society.[3]

Heyward himself describes the shape of his contribution of Brutus Jones's early life to the scenario for the Krimsky-Cochran film as providing the encounter with the "disintegrating power of our white civilization" that changes him from a rather simple Southern Negro to the shrewd, grafting Negro of the play."[4] The initial scene dissolves from an African ceremonial dance with barefoot Negroes beating tom-toms and the dancers' bodies swaying "in barbaric rhythm" into a Negro church scene with "shod feet moving in similar rhythms."[5] This scene clearly embodies all of the distinctive contributions Heyward makes to the scenario: pictorial variety, careful attention to locale and dialect, character motivation (including the close link between the Negro's primitive past and his Christian present), Negro rhythms, and the shift in the film's focus from the Island experience to Jones's whole career.

The scenario moves from the southern church to Harlem and the president's private railway car to Savannah and a Georgia chain gang. Although heroic in helping an exhausted Negro boy, Jones's travels have taught him that survival is for the fittest, cleverest, and most ruthless, black or white, and that the white man's ways are available to all. So when he finds himself a slave, it is only a matter of time before he gambles his way to a partnership, replaces his owner in the chief's favor, and turns himself into a magical god and emperor. Now the unshiftless boy of the opening scene can be shif'less, vain, puffed up, and prodigal with impunity. He is a black Horatio Alger hero.

The "tragic life story" the film became is the reverse of the pattern of "The Half Pint Flask," as Jones exports the vices of white society, craps, corrupt power, and master-servant class relationships.[6] The difference was not at all lost on Heyward's home folk, either. When Heyward suggested that the movie be filmed on Folly Island, a Charleston resort area, the residents threatened to leave in a body if it was.[7]

It was, in the end, all Hollywood, as Robert Stebbins observed of Paul Robeson's portrayal of Jones: "And when finally they rise against him his false front falls away. He is revealed for what he and by extension, what all Negroes are supposed to be, creatures who stand trembling in a murky land of shadow, peopled with the ghosts that rise up out of the swamps and jungles of the primitive mind."[8]

III *Dorothy's* Set My People Free

Heyward's interest in the long Negro journey from African spirits to freedom in white America continued to his death. A year before he died, it was reported that the Heywards were working on a new, original play.[9] Inasmuch as Heyward had devoted several pages to an account of the Denmark Vesey (Telemaque) slave uprising of 1820 in "The Negro in the Low-Country" essay published in 1931, and *Set My People Free* (later titled *Charleston, 1820*) was, according to Dorothy, completed shortly after her husband's death, it is quite probable that Heyward played the major role at its inception.[10]

Set My People Free, produced in 1948, traces Vesey from his refusal to be bought by Rose's owner in order to marry her to the visions in which God tells him to free his people, the abortive uprising, and his betrayal by George Wilson, another slave.

Mrs. Heyward is sympathetic toward Vesey, but dramatic interest focuses too favorably on the uprising's Uncle Tom betrayer, Wilson. Consequently, both Paul Robeson and Canada Lee, than a Communist, refused parts in the play.[11]

The play is also an interesting part of the Heyward-Heyward canon in another respect. As Joseph Wood Krutch observed, it offered the most impressive display of surviving Negro primitivism since *Emperor Jones*.[12] This is particularly evident in a lonely island night scene which moves, as the drums beat, from primitive ecstasy and voodoo to Old Testament messianism. Vesey identifies himself as the descendant of the "head of we people," his grandfather, victim of a white man's broken promises.[13] In the second scene, at a wake, although Vesey does not believe in the Duppy (ghost), he makes a deal with Gullah Jack, a witch doctor who would exorcise the ha'nt, to become Vesey's first disciple. At an island meeting in Act II, Scene 3, Vesey says, reminiscent of "The Half Pint Flask," "There are things the drums and the moon

can say that can't—" Bishop, one of Vesey's followers who is highly
regarded by the whites, replies: "Remember how it was on Eddistow—
They got to dancing, beating the drums, and we couldn't quiet them
before morning." Vesey, the disbeliever, then asserts: "Now you can
beat your drums! Now you can raise your voices to the Gods of your
fathers. Now you can sing your praises to Nyankopon." The same
drums echo through all of the Heywards' Negro fiction and plays—if
much more softly.

IV   The Country Bunny and the Little Gold Shoes

DuBose Heyward published only one short story, besides "The Half
Pint Flask" after his first volume of poems, *The Country Bunny and
the Little Gold Shoes,* which appeared in book form in 1939. It is a
children's story about domestic order, competition, the underdog's victory, a great challenge, and the handicap of injury, replete with a magical happy ending. It contributes nothing but a demonstration of simple, clear prose to Heyward's achievement as a serious artist.

CHAPTER 6

The Rhythms of Charleston:
Mamba's Daughters

I *The Acceleration of Change*

IN *Porgy* DuBose Heyward celebrates the humanity of Catfish Row, caught between Africa and the demanding discipline of white society. After *Angel's* delivery of a mountain woman into the clutches of industrial civilization, Heyward returns to the Charleston Negro quarter, for, by 1928, when *Mamba's Daughters* was serialized in the *Woman's Home Companion,* Heyward was ready to look directly at the Negro's effort, in the 1920s, to "learn to play."

Catfish Row is the point of departure, unchanged from *Porgy* except in its blatant amorality. Mamba, a lively grandmother, emerges from that world of color, song, and crime to work at the Wentworths', where we see her in long conversations with passing hucksters and vendors and hear her complaining to her daughter, Hagar, that her work makes her " 'belly ache from de pure polite' " (30).

The great difference here is that Mamba leaves the timeless order of the Row, that community of freedom and common cause that is her home and in which she finds her being. " 'But time is changin',' " Mamba tells the poor but aristocratic Wentworth family: " 'Nigger gots tuh git diff'ent kind ob sense now tuh git long. Ah gots daughtuh, an' she gots daughtuh, an' all-two dem female is born fuh trouble. Ah gots tuh be ready when de time come' " (36).[1] Her anxiety proves well founded because much of the novel concerns the simple, overgrown Hagar's career of staying out of jail in order to finance Mamba's ambition for Hagar's daughter, Lissa—and Lissa's for herself. Finally, it concerns Lissa who must survive to escape Carolina and become a successful opera singer in New York.

Mamba's anxiety sets the story in motion. The near-static world of *Porgy* becomes dynamic and the clash inevitable between change in both black and white Charleston and the traditional roles and social codes that bind both races to the past. It is particularly a clash between change and a rigid, established pattern for racial relationships that profoundly limits or influences the courses which change may take on either side of the color barrier. Most significantly and ironically, this racial distinction appears to close off for one race, in Saint Wentworth, the very possibility of the pursuit of art, of creative expression, that is Lissa's route to success.

The second great difference from *Porgy* is, of course, that the white world is not peripheral. For *Mamba's Daughters* is also the story of Saint Julien de Chatigny Wentworth's movement from a dreamy desire to paint to a successful business career. His success, in turn, makes it possible for him to support his widowed mother in the manner to which she was by birth but not fortune accustomed (the family's "worth" has "went") and to take a wife, Valerie, and father a son. He is also able to help Mamba, Hagar, and Lissa, as well as Davey and other blacks, in the best paternalistic tradition or better.

Heyward's longest novel, *Mamba's Daughters*, is a cluttered, episodic story, carrying the two families through more than twenty years in three locales and involving numerous minor characters: Gilly Bluton, political boss Proc Baggart's mulatto henchman whom Hagar saves from bleeding to death and later kills when he tries to rape Lissa; Davey, Saint's helper at the store; Maum Netta at the Wentworths'; Maum Vina at the mine; the Atkinsons from the North, neighbors of the Wentworths, and Valerie, their relative; Saint's mother and Polly, his sister; and the backwoods and New York Negro clergymen, Whaley and Grayson. One result of the clutter is hurried leaping from time to time, town to country, white to black, group to group. To the reader, motivation appears weak and after the fact for the episode where Mamba incorporates the Judge's lost teeth into her scheme to invade the "Four Hundred" and become "'quality cullud folks'" (5, 9). The combat between Grayson and Whaley for the congregation at the mines has no strong plot role at all. The day by day, year by year, development of Saint as a businessman is hardly exciting, apart from the fact that Heyward holds the Wentworths at arm's length. One notable omission is any report of Saint's face to face encounter with the unscrupulous Proc Baggart, leaving Baggart's shadowy presence shadowy and evidence of Saint's ability to get through the unpleasantness of compromise hidden from the reader's examination. A glaring excess in the author's omnibus approach is the series of stream of consciousness passages at the end, as the Wentworths hear Lissa singing at the Met, which one reviewer would completely excise.[2]

This is not to say the story is lacking in interest or value. Mamba and Hagar's determination to give Lissa a chance requires that they negotiate all the obstacles that the energetically defended codes of black and white Charleston society place in their way. And Saint Wentworth's relation to that effort as well as his pursuit of his own destiny makes for a far more complex and intense story than Porgy's hope possibly could.

Generally, the struggle is again with the alien forces met in *Porgy*. But the concern here is not survival; it is what of the primitive past can be taken into the future, in how the black man can change without losing his identity, how he can escape the role assigned him by whites, and how he can control his fate. Moreover, in *Mamba's Daughters* a greater force than the Row's united front appears to make victory possible: love.

Primitivism shows itself here as animality and a native sense of rhythm. The animality of the physical scene is evidenced when, after leaving Gilly's corpse in the swamp, Hagar broke "savagely" through the tangle until she found high ground: "Crouched over almost on all fours, with prehensile hands tearing her way through the undergrowth, the great woman emerged like a prehistoric creature quitting its primal slime, and climbed out upon the knoll" (274). Hagar is a sort of driven animal from the start, massive and powerful but lacking the intelligence to avoid trouble or to control her simple instincts. Earlier, Lissa has leaped upon Gilly with a "strange savage utterance," clawing his face (255). The difference with *Porgy* here is that the wildness of Mamba's daughters is an unpremeditated burst of feeling, not deliberate violence, as with Porgy, or a brutal way of life, as Crown's, or the cunning bestiality of Gilly Bluton. Moreover, strong racial feeling is important as a critical element Lissa must not lose in her transformation into a Metropolitan Opera star. On the other hand, Lissa's mother, Hagar, is too simple—and good-hearted—to survive in white society. Drink is to her what happy dus' is to Bess: "Hagar would drink with the rest, and her enormous body, released from its slight control, would become one of the gesticulating, whooping dervishes in the ensuing orgy that inevitably resulted in a riot call" (52). Again, her righteous anger at the cheating stevedores and her rage at Gilly's attempted rape of Lissa turn her into a murderous combatant.

As in Porgy, primitivism moves in two directions, toward trouble

and toward life. Mamba can employ the wiles of the Row to survive.
Hagar cannot, and when Atkinson sees her in court, the court is like
the Greek gods "looming sudden and inexorably against the gaiety of
life" (68). Mamba's daughters can survive the whim of the Greek gods
only by accommodation, channeling and controlling their strong feelings and gaining the protection of one of the gods. Unfortunately, this
is not enough to save Hagar from exile and an overpowering fear of
Proc Baggart.

Accommodation is also required in channeling those powerful feelings Hagar and Lissa experience. Hagar must accept exile from her
beloved child. Lissa must find the proper art form for her feelings.
Hagar's accommodation is seen to be, in a sense, easier, for Lissa finds
such accommodation as the leading forces in the cultured Negroes'
Monday Night Music Club make, aping white manners, tastes, and
styles, impossibly sterile and alien. She can discipline her art, can meet
the Music Club's technical standards, but no more than her mother or
grandmother can Lissa abandon for their Victorian mode the "gaiety
of life" or the other strong feelings of life that she recognizes as part of
her racial identity and which seek expression in her song (68). It is for
Lissa to discover the answer implicit in Saint's African woodcarving,
primitive in its disproportion but given form in the expression of feeling the kneeling position conveys.

II   *"The Secret Law"*

In an "Introduction on the American Negro in Art," published with
the play version of *Porgy*, Heyward had tried to identify what he
called "the secret law of rhythm" that he had recognized as a "sort of
race personality that dominated and swayed the mass, making of it a
scene vastly greater than the total of its individual activities" (x). This
evasive definition and the example of Sam Smalls's desperate act of
passion that follows are less helpful than Heyward's indication in
Mamba's Daughters of what lies behind that faculty or ability Lissa
shares with her mother and with other Negroes of "giving her whole
being to an emotion" (208). Passing the jail with North, who has just
dismissed a revival service as " 'a lot of dirty negroes,' " Lissa finds the
"night suddenly dark with the suffering of the thousands who had lain
there in the cages—slaves, freemen, her own people" (218). And the
following Sunday, she "let herself go into the music" (219). This quality is again reflected in the preference of the congregation for Rev.

Whaley's God, "who wanted them to pour their sorrow out in a flood of song . . ." (188). As Heyward defines it and illustrates it, rhythm would seem to be the Negro's unique expression, with his whole being, of the strong experience of suffering and longing and joy common to the race, an expression that communicates truth and infects those of the race who join the expression.

In *Mamba's Daughters*, the vehicle of expression, which may also be a vehicle of persuasion, is music—spirituals, shouts, or jazz. For Mamba and her daughters, it is primarily song, and in song that racial rhythm or feeling appears to reach its most subtle, profound expression. So we meet song, from the doorway harmony of Maum Netta and Mamba's "longing throb" to Lissa's New York triumph (12). Mamba even seals Saint's and Valerie's love by taking them on an adventure that speaks tongues of wildness and rhythm:

Over them, like the crash of breakers, swept the terrific, cumulative intensity of the worship, now throbbing with an old terror of jungle gods, again lifting suddenly into rapt adoration of the new Christ. This, and the pounding rhythms of the spirituals, the amazing emotional release wrought by the music, so fascinated and yet frightened the white girl that she sat huddled against Saint, clinging to his hand with tense fingers, her head pressed against his shoulder. (164)

Mamba and her daughters all express themselves in song, culminating in Lissa's disciplined Met performance: "The song lifted and hovered .above the shadowed figures in a repressed agony of yearning and supplication" (301).

The rhythm of the Row and race seen at the beginning extends from the swaying bodies singing spirituals at the mining camp to the church near the Charleston jail where the "air rocked to a deep solid chorus . . . shaving harmonies with fractional notes so fine and so spontaneous that no written page could ever capture and prison the sound" (217). At the dance hall, the ragtime "Under the Bamboo Tree" hypnotizes Lissa.

As the authentic vehicle by which the essence of racial integrity is expressed and transmitted to the future, Lissa must somehow honor and reconcile rhythm with her musical training. This reconciliation is, moreover, her avenue to social and economic success in a white world. The story of Mamba and her daughters is, then, the stories of three women, each a story of struggle and sacrifice toward Lissa's achieve-

ment of this goal, the consistent vehicle of which is song. Mamba leaves
the Row and sings to win Mrs. Wentworth's favor. The lonely, inarticulate, slaving Hagar finds voice only in song. Lissa's voice is to be
trained, although she is fearful that it may mean sacrificing the heart
of her music—the soulful spontaneity of the church choir and the loneliness of the suffering Negroes in the jail.

Lissa is tempted to emulate her friend Gardinia, who manages to
satisfy the Monday Night snobs with only the slightest sacrifice of her
"sheer animal spirits," and, in New York, to give way to the "alien
syncopation of laughter and song" in the lazy rhythms of Harlem (228,
300). Lissa resolves the conflict—between racial spirit and art—only
when she fully appreciates the sacrifices that have brought her to New
York, a resolution her final Met song reflects:

The music caught the mood of the sky. The arresting dissonances, the sharp
syncopations of the early acts, were no longer individually evident but
seemed to merge into a broader irresistible current of sound. The rhythm,
too, was no longer a thing separate. It became a force as indistinguishable
and pervasive as the life current. It was a fundamental law that moved light,
music, the sway of the crowd, the passage of time, in a concerted and inevitable progression. The artificial declamations of operatic convention were
gone. The cast was reduced to two elemental forces. The crowd with its heavy
mass rhythms and reiterated choruses was the body, and the single transcen-
dent mezzo-soprano that soared above it was the spirit, aspiring, daring,
despairing, lifting again. (306)

Lissa has mastered the art and poured herself into her voice, as the
Monday Night performers, the Broadens and Whitmores, in their
desire to be white could not. When she sings the "National Anthem of
the American Negro" for an encore, Wentworth feels something
reaching back to claim "its heritage of beauty from the past" (308).

Lissa's accomplishment represents the kind of victory over change—
perhaps of Heyward's wishful thinking—that Heyward hoped for but
had appeared to despair could come. In his first essay, "And Once
Again—the Negro," published in 1923, he wonders if the Negro is "an
aeon behind, or an aeon ahead of us."[3] His main concern in this essay,
however, is that the old Negro ways that led to happiness will succumb,
with urbanization, to a "stifling moral straitjacket," because the Negro
is blindly submissive. "He is about to be saved," Heyward observes
with sorrow and fear. Such salvation meant the disappearance of the
Negro's soul, of his integrity as a race, of what he described in 1931 as

"his spontaneous abandonment to emotion, his faith in his simple destiny."[4] Lissa's success constitutes Heyward's response to those black voices of the Harlem Renaissance that ignored black music and saw the white race's high art as the proper objective for black expression. But Heyward's sense of the fullness of Negro humanity as reflected in Lissa directs his attention as well, perhaps more credibly, to the still stronger force that stands against an excessive and self-destructive primitivism and that conquers change: Mamba's and Hagar's love, which becomes a testament to all their kind.

Mamba runs some risk of becoming a stereotyped Uncle Tom figure, but her clearly stated distaste for the white world and her tremendous hope, recognized by the dentist who explains his acquiescence in the conversion of the Judge's teeth for Mamba's use as chivalry, along with her single-mindedness, save her. She waits three years for her chance at the Atkinsons', as she had waited for the unlikely chance at the set of teeth she needs. She sees the great chance for Lissa, then must stand helplessly as the fading tail light of Prince's scarlet roadster signals possible failure. If Mamba has a flaw it is that her single-mindedness makes her oblivious to the pain of Hagar's separation from Lissa.

Hagar, like Mamba, is seen sketchily, but she emerges as a combination of great physical strength, great simplicity, and great virtue—and as doomed in town as Billy Budd is in the world. She has risked jail to save the worthless Bluton from bleeding to death so that when her efforts for Lissa are completed and she deems her suicide necessary to secure Lissa her chance, she quite deliberately ends her long loneliness. Her violence, then, is a matter of simplicity and strength, moral outrage, and maternal concern. And it is always balanced by humility. Her sacrifice of her daughter, her years of hard work to make Lissa's escape possible, and her suicide attest to her commitment to Mamba's design and to her great generosity. When she is gone, Lissa "imagined her as vast inarticulate power—encompassing love, possessing her all the more now because of her silence" (294).

Hagar's suicide to save Lissa from implication in Gilly's murder may be unconvincing, but Hagar has long since realized her helplessness in the hands of the police and Proc Baggart is wilier than most. Her entire life has been a sacrifice; even her life is dispensable. Moreover, she has been so much separated from Lissa that her daughter has become more a figment of imagination than a reality, and she can have no place in Lissa's future either. Still, there is great poignancy in her death as the culmination of her exile. Her maternal yearning had prompted her to

befriend Daddy Drayton. Her years of loneliness let her understand
Grayson's fate and led her to help Gilly as her starved maternity led
her to kill him.

As Mamba bears a pure African name, Hagar is named after the
servant Hagar of Genesis, whose exile prompts an angel's intercession
with the promise of a great future for her child. (In slave days southern
Negroes referred to themselves as Aunt Hagar's children, presumably
because they, too, were denied status as equals.[5])

III   *"The Class to Which They Had Been Born"*

Mamba's Daughters is the story of the rise of Mamba's daughters
from nothingness on Catfish Row to greatness. It is also the story of
Saint Wentworth's journey to success in a changing society.

Critics were generally right in their displeasure with the second plot
of *Mamba's Daughters:* its weaknesses make for a weaker thematic
statement. Minor scenes in the Negro story, such as Hagar's quiet consolation of the abandoned Rev. Grayson, are more convincing and
moving than the major white scenes: Saint's interview with his
employer, the St. Cecilia Ball with Valerie, his conversation with her
about his painting, and the Wentworths' attendance at the Met. Saint,
like his creator, is full of comment and analyses of the situation that
too often replace action. So, in *Mamba's Daughters*, the external pressures of Heyward's fellow Carolinians wanting a white story from him
and William DeMille anticipating box-office disadvantages in an all-
Negro movie version (when Heyward needed to make from *Mamba*
what money he could) appear to have prevailed where they had not
in *Porgy*.[6] In *Porgy* Heyward had ruthlessly cut out a white Wentworth plot before it began to develop.[7]

Heyward has a problem in aesthetic distance with Saint Wentworth,
the pattern of whose early life largely reflects Heyward's own: family
members, education, dreaminess, interest in ships and Negroes, hard-
ware-store experience, and arrival at maturity in his notice of the
approval of the older people at the St. Cecilia's Ball and appreciation
of his mother's "dauntlessness of spirit" as she had waited patiently for
him to become a real head of the family (136). The narrator is divided,
until the last page, between sentimental attachment to the remnant of
Charleston aristocratic tradition, which includes approval of Saint's
business success story, and criticism of the weakness and sterility, com-
promises and inadequacies, of that world.

In one notable respect Heyward's and Saint's similar paths diverge. Like Heyward, who took up painting as polio therapy, Saint has a strong sense of color, views the dock as a painting, and, though there is no reference to his ever having held a brush, he suddenly tells Valerie that he wants to make a career of painting. But where Heyward abandoned business for writing, partly at his wife's urging, Saint chooses business over penurious art—with an assist from Valerie. On the basis of her father's mistake, she insists that Saint is confusing " 'the love for the thing with the ability to create it' " (162). Her father, she tells him, lacked only " 'the little essential spark' " (162). And, practical little Yankee sweetheart that she is, she traps him into the American success. myth: " 'But don't you see, you can have all that and more when you have succeeded at what you are doing. That's what I want for you, freedom—then beauty' " (163).

Returning home for the St. Cecilia's Ball and finding his clothes laid out for him, Saint appreciates his mother's "determination to hold a place for her children in the class to which they had been born" (122). Saint has found a measure of happiness in books, pictures, geology, art, and his contacts with the Negroes at the phosphate mine, with their "humour, tragedy, and the flattering respect and frank liking they gave him" (122). But now he feels the hand of predestination and, at the ball, experiences "an exhilarating sense of congruity, of measuring up to expectations" (127). Then he meets the enticing Valerie and soon his life is securing things for his mother, Valerie, and their son.

Saint's pursuit of identity and freedom parallels Lissa's. But where his intellectual curiosity, artistic sensibility, and social awareness suggest a capacity for freedom and a fullness of life, Saint succumbs to the pressures of class and meets only the challenge of tradition and a business career. Freedom and fulfillment become for him participation in the rituals of the Charleston aristocracy with the means to do so.

Quickly Saint discovers that business is a "game to be played," rather than a necessary adjunct to social life, as the older aristocracy view it (162). By the Armistice, his fossils, sculpture, and etchings are gone from his office and he is all business: "He was done with abstractions now. He was face to face with something actual, something that yielded results that could be computed upon an adding machine" (204).

And quickly, too, Saint learns that the aristocratic world of Charleston is also changing. Although the Atkinsons "do not exist" for Mrs. Wentworth, Atkinson's three-week campaign to gain an invitation to a St. Cecilia's Ball succeeds (4). Intrigued as Saint is by the world of money, however, the new money is sterile, for, by contrast, there are Hagar's years of savings in which Saint finds "utter beauty" (264).

The difference between the two economic journeys is in the quality of Saint's dream and that of Mamba and her daughters. Beside the magnificent faith of the three women and Lissa's success, Saint can only look enviously at his early efforts with a guitar: "But the past had reached dead hands after him, guiding him imperceptibly this way and that"; by contrast, "Behind Lissa there had been nothing; before her, Mamba's one immovable idea" (265). Mamba and her daughters had transcended economics.

In other forms, the same doubt about the dead hand of tradition as opposed to the quest for freedom occupies Heyward in *Peter Ashley* and *Lost Morning*. Are economic success, social conformity, and being a gentleman compatible with life? Almost desperately, Saint now vows, "Life would still be an adventure" (266).

Saint's relationship to Negroes provides a second measure of his growth and the price he pays for Charleston. "'The right sort of people here do look after their Negroes'" means, for Saint, the modest assistance he gives Mamba, Hagar, Lissa, and Davey (61). But it also means passivity regarding the Negro masses, silent acceptance of the white power structure at the mine, and belief in the general happiness of those who work there, despite the lengths to which the mine owners feel obliged to go to discourage blacks from emigration. Eventually Saint sees the truth about Mamba, Hagar, and Lissa and, in response, "misters" Broaden. But he never challenges the white-supremacy system or appears to recognize that evil and injustice might well be at the heart of the system. When Saint does think to act on principle in opposition to Proc Baggart, prudence not only deters him but appears to argue him out of his position. The one time he does appear to confront the system actively is in his eviction of Bluton, but this is prompted by an angry feeling of uselessness upon receipt of a letter from Valerie.

IV   *The Labyrinth of Race*

Where the two worlds, plots, sets of characters, and their journeys to achievement meet, crucially for each, is in this labyrinth of traditional race relations, social, political, and economic. It is white supremacy that creates Mamba's anxiety for Hagar and Lissa; it is the Negro who will be the measure of Saint's integrity. The meetings end with Lissa's triumph, which reveals both Saint's failure and the numbing truth about Charleston's noblesse oblige: Saint Julian de Chatigny Wentworth and his kind really had little to do with it. Mamba's daughters have done it themselves.

Unlike *Porgy,* in *Mamba's Daughters* both the narrator's and the characters' voices reveal the tension between the black man's increasing claim to dignity and the white man's fear of change. The system's evils are repeatedly exposed, as in Mamba's attitude toward Judge Harkness, which is not one of resignation but bitterness at his righteousness and power: "'Yas, ah seen um once, a-settin' on he bench wid he long black robe on, sendin' nigger tuh jail, like he been Gawd. But don' yuh fergit, onnerneat' dat black wrapper he gots on two-leg pants same like Cook dere'" (19–20). And Mamba clearly begrudges the price she has to pay for the insurance the Atkinsons provide her family. Ironically, it is Atkinson who voices the old rationalization that allows continued oppression of the mass of blacks with a clear conscience:

This negro business; millions and millions of them. Race problem. What to do with the whole mass. You came up to that, and it was there before you like a wall without a gate. One either stood there battering his hands to pieces on it, or he walked away and made it his business to forget. But this old woman, now, and her great ungainly daughter, and that child that they had a way of speaking about with their voices lowered; this was something different. These three were not a race problem. They were individual entities battling with destiny, needing a leg up most terribly. (71–72)

Atkinson will help Mamba's daughters and "leave the race problem to God and the great-grandchildren" (72).

The phosphate mines where Saint runs the store reveal how the masses are treated: " . . . Here in the industrial belt, thronged as it was by the rag-tag and bob-tail of the race, ten, twenty, a hundred of them to a single white, the grip could not be allowed to slacken. White supremacy must remain absolute" (159). The fear that pervades the harsh order here is reflected alike in an ancient crone's fear of being sold into slavery, the company's fear of the alien black clergyman, Grayson, and Hagar's fear of the prying Proc Baggart.

In this racist world mass injustice and suffering are certain to recur, again and again. Curiously, even the narrator turns his back on Saint's humiliating interview with Proc Baggart and saves him from exposure of his embarrassment with a reverie about his irritation at the personal character of southern politics.

The narrator, however, is scrupulously neutral about the phosphate-mine situation, and there is no implication that anyone should be held responsible for its evils. Darwin Turner has observed that Ellen Glasgow avoided admiring the aristocracy.[8] It might be said of Heyward in *Mamba's Daughters* that he determinedly avoids criticizing them.

Yet Charleston nonetheless kicked up a fuss about *Mamba's Daughters:* implicit criticism was enough.[9] The aristocracy emerges pale, dull, and racist.

The chief criticism of the Charleston order of things, however, is its failure to offer hope even to the beneficiaries of white paternalism. One can, like Whaley, be an Uncle Tom, or, like Mamba, abandon her home to pretend to be, for her own purposes, "'an example to the upstart generation of negroes,'" as Mrs. Atkinson puts it (39). One can be the corrupt lackey of the white man, as is Gilly (Prince) Bluton, or a slum landlord, as is Mr. Prescott, with his "faultlessly gloved hands" (219). One can become a sterile parody of the white, as are the pitiful pretenders of the Monday Night Music Club, or an alien among one's own, as is the cerebral Rev. Grayson, who flees to the more rational world of New York City. One can, like Hagar, escape white defeat in death. Or, like Lissa, flee northward to loneliness and struggle there for identity. Mamba, watching the New York steamer move away at the novel's end, symbolizes all. She can die in Catfish Row, but there is no future or it is far away for her daughters. In the changing time, Charleston has become a No-Man's Land for any but the servile Negro. Nor does a mixture of blood help. The mulattoes Bluton, Grayson, Lissa, and North fare no better and, in the long run, worse. And what the Negro clearly cannot expect of the white is a shift in his complacent acceptance of things as they are.

Notably, *Mamba's Daughters* is Heyward's last work treating of the Charleston Negro. It may be that he sensed that he could, honestly, say no more without being dishonest or alienating himself from Charleston. So the next time he confronts the question of race it is miscegenation in a backwoods community. And the next time he writes directly of the Negro he moves to the distant, more primitive, less civilized and far less racist Virgin Islands for a setting.

V   *The Overarching Irony*

What Heyward has to say is said here, in the tension between the races and the balancing of the black and white plots. The Wentworths laugh at Mamba's comic conduct, but Mrs. Wentworth's efforts in Saint's behalf are comparatively weak. Saint achieves economic success among Negro miners, but Hagar's economic success on pitiful white wages makes a great artist. Saint, himself, sees his successful conformity to the aristocratic pattern to be a woefully inferior accomplishment compared with Lissa's. Overcoming racial injustice makes the struggle of Mamba and her daughters heroic while acquiescing in the attitudes of the old order and assuming its economic responsibilities denies heroism to Saint, however sensitive he may be or however much he appreciates Lissa's superiority. Aristocracy leans on racism and decadence results; out of subjugation comes the Negro's strength. Out of the Negro's primitive rhythm comes art; in the white aristocracy the "essential spark" never appears. Apparently, Heyward's last word in *Mamba's Daughters* is this contrapuntal statement, this overarching irony.

As such an ironic statement about Charleston, the novel succeeds. But despite the complex thematic design Heyward gave this book after the hurried *Angel*, he still lacks the craft and intelligence to plumb the depths and complexities of the Negro's search for a place in America and the white man's guilty response. The novel's largely sociological conception does help explain the ultimate failures of the inarticulate Hagar, single-minded Lissa, and Saint, the dreamy compromiser, to be fully realized as characters.

Certain technical flaws are more glaring. The teeth episode, the Whaley-Grayson battle, Whaley's loss of his flask while preaching, and all the World War I references serve some purposes, local color or comedy, perhaps, or weak reinforcement of the thematic forces. But they are not essential. Awkward jumps mar both plots. And the straining for poetic justice in the snobbish Wentworth stream of consciousness monologues at the end is superfluous; if the mode of Lissa's success could be defined otherwise, they would not be missed.

Mamba's Daughters is not, however, the structural disarray some reviewers have implied. Part I focuses on Mamba's emergence from the Row but introduces both plots. After a largely concealed three-year jump, Part II focuses first on Saint's and then on Hagar's exile and years at the mine. Part III is Saint's, as he matures in his experience with

Proc Baggart and at the ball. Part IV, the war years, shifts from Grayson to the war to Lissa's flight. The final part begins with Hagar's flight and death and Lissa's reaction, then jumps seven years to Lissa's debut and ends with Mamba seen back in the Row in her old age. The movement is back and forth, from Mamba to Saint to Hagar to Saint to Hagar and Lissa, then back to Saint in his long interior monologue. Also, at the beginning of Part II, we find Saint lonely, seeking success; balancing it, at the beginning of Part V, Lissa is lonely, seeking success.

The characters and their roles in the action are another matter. Mamba fades to too minor a role after Part I; her response to Hagar's suicide is nowhere noted. Lissa is too little noticed before Part IV, where she becomes and remains central until the end. Saint's story really ends with Part III, so that he is little more than a mere onlooker in IV and a somewhat disillusioned one in V. Hagar is the only character whose role is adequately sustained throughout, from her brief drunken appearance in Part I to Lissa's memorial in Part V. There is, however, some awkwardness in revealing Lissa's response to Hagar's death well before Hagar's last scene. Also, the jumps fragment everyone's story.

Heyward's employment of a sometimes omniscient narrator also presents problems. His shifts in and out of characters' minds are too often arbitrary. The narrator occasionally enters Mamba's or Hagar's consciousness but often looks at the world through Saint's less interesting gaze—except at certain interesting moments. The effect is to emphasize Saint's viewpoint, thus to overemphasize Saint's experience and to come close at times to identifying his viewpoint with the more sophisticated narrator's.

Still, *Mamba's Daughters* is as close as Heyward comes to employing such characteristics of the post-Joyce novel as rapid and complex time changes, shifts in narrative voice, and interior monologue. Another novel published the same year and dealing with several generations of "white folks' niggers" and a shabby aristocratic family, *The Sound and the Fury*, mastered and advanced all of these techniques.

Faulkner is a good touchstone for measuring more pervasive faults in Heyward's novel. After asserting that true regionalists "write of their chosen section as if no other region exists," Donald Davidson's review argues that Heyward does not:

But the voice and tone are not the voice and tone of DuBose Heyward. They are of New York. They echo its fashionable platitudes about the Negro and to some extent play up to its curiosity about Charleston. The book, in brief, though seeming to be an "inside" interpretation, is without the passionate absorption in the subject that we must demand of a regional novelist. It is written as if to order.[10]

Heyward's failures in "passionate absorption," tone, and voice do constitute the novel's chief weaknesses. In *Porgy,* the narrator only glimpses the rich alien world of Catfish Row, but he is intensely interested in it. In *Mamba's Daughters,* the white world is present but never really engaged in the central action of the novel. It *is* a "New York" voice, as Davidson charges, modestly sophisticated, uncommitted, and somewhat patronizing: "One was caught and had sinned; one escaped and was innocent. How marvellously simple. No wonder that even in the noon heat there was song and laughter . . ." (27). The tone here is Atkinson's, the northerner, but the substance is the narrator's. To be less selective, compare the first paragraph of *Sartoris, The Time of Man,* or *The Fathers* with Heyward's opening paragraph:

It was no mere chance that, during the first decade of the new century, brought Mamba out of the darkness of the underworld into the light of the Wentworth's kitchen. Casual as that event seemed, there is good evidence for the belief that it had its origin in some obscure recess of the woman's mind; or in perhaps some deep and but half comprehended instinct that drove her. . . . (3)

Besides the condescension here, by page thirty-six Heyward has given the lie to this interpretation: Mamba is, in reality, hopeful, shrewd, and clever.

Bad writing recurs, as "The rhythm possessed itself of its creators," and overwriting, as in the description of Hagar's grave (13):

All afternoon the September spring tide had been pumping its vast burden of water into the low flat river lands, saturating porous marshes and setting the grass tops awash, piling incalculable tons of brine into salt creeks, brimming secret lagoons. Now the great heart that lay somewhere out beyond the moon turned from systole to diastole and called its tide home. (287)

The movement of the tide serves well, but the confusion of September and spring, the scientific terminology and the weighing of brine are confusing or awkward.

Heyward does not escape the complaint that he offers local color for

its own sake here, and he does lean toward sociologizing. Both, however, enhance the distinctive realism of the novel.

Heyward might be called a memorialist of Low Country society in
this novel, but the implications of the changes in fortune in the course
of the story go beyond the memorialist's fidelity. Again, as were those
elsewhere who turned to the Negro in the 1920s, Heyward is looking
for life. He does not find it in Charleston manners or business success
but among those who are living. And, better than in *Porgy*, he understands what that life is.

VI   *Hagar and Ethel Waters*

Unlike the play *Porgy* and *Porgy and Bess*, which follow the novella
closely, though with significant shifts in thematic emphasis, the 1939
Dorothy and DuBose Heyward dramatization of *Mamba's Daughters*
radically differs from the novel. Major cuts are required. The nonscenic
accounting for years of time could not be staged. The involved plot
had to be simplified, and the number of characters reduced. Thus
Saint's role becomes minor, and the plot focuses on Hagar's sacrifice
rather than more or less equally on Mamba, Hagar, and Lissa.
Mamba's associations with both the Row and the Wentworths are dras-
tically cut, and Lissa's inner conflict disappears along with the whole
Monday Night set, leaving her role the exhibition of moral shame after
being raped. The social order fades into the background; the white
man's injustice is unrecognized or remote, his paternalism generous.
The single real villain is now Gilly Bluton. The slightly self-conscious
sophistication and sometimes dullness of the narrative style are, of
course, gone, too. In its stead, there is drama, song, and the somewhat
slick flashback from the first scene, in which Mamba and assorted
friends listen to Lissa's radio network debut.

Now Hagar is not nearly so inarticulate: Heyward does not preempt
her dramatic scenes for narrative as in the novel. And the chief, the
single effect of the play is her lonely suffering, realized through a dramatically heightened conflict. She becomes, pretty much as Ethel
Waters, for whom the role was written, saw her, "all Negro women
lost and lonely in the white man's antagonistic world."[11] Her loss of
Lissa is more poignant: "I can see um so plain some day. Jus' lak she
was standin' dere five mont' ago. So pretty, so sweet. Didn't 'member
her ma bery well dough, but I don't min' when I can see um. Don't
eber let nobody hurt um, Ma."[12] Heyward adds a poignant scene in

which the sophisticated Lissa brings her friends to meet her ex-convict mother. Hagar's deliberate murder of Gilly is not adequately motivated, but Hagar's words in the final scene are particularly effective on the stage: "Fifteen year ago dat Gilly Bluton daid. Dey say at the hospital five mo' minutes an' he ain't got a chance. Not a Gawd's t'ing between dat yaller nigger an' he Gawd 'cept only me. I gib um back he life. He life belong to me, enty" (177).

The first of Hagar's adversaries in the play is plural: men, not the men like the one who fathered Lissa, but the men who tricked her when she delivered the wash, the judge and prosecutor who failed to appreciate the meaning of five years of separation from her child, the fictional man in "Lonesome Walls," her prison lyric, who promised to come visit every Christmas but did not, and, of course, Gilly, the archetypal male villain, Negro-style, who takes from women what he wants on the assumption that they are for his convenience, without reciprocal love or gratitude. Gilly's blackmail is only another form of rape.

The second adversary is, again, the white race, although the evil of the system is so muted and accepted with resignation as to be barely recognized. Yet, neither when Hagar is given five years for beating the stevedore nor when she is obliged to serve her sentence for coming into town is the punishment just. There is also, as a reflection of race relations, Gilly's special role in the plantation order: " 'He stan's *so* . . .' " (50).

Gilly should not, however, be viewed simply as a white instrument. Mamba and Hagar fear him because "he stan's so" with the police, but the trouble he causes Ned, Hagar, and Lissa is extracurricular. To the blacks he is a "bad nigger," almost Evil personified. To the reader he is a black Simon Legree. The implication is that it is Gilly, the sinner, not so much white society, who is the antagonist.

Here as in the novel the ordinary or honest black man's great hope of freedom remains escape. But Hagar's great counterforce to injustice is not escape. It is her patience, resignation, simple justice, and love, her single-minded pursuit of her end. She also has that virtue Heyward had noticed in *Porgy* in all its forms, the power of song. This power is her undoing when she gets the boat rocking "wid pure song" and loses track of how much she is drinking (37). But it is her consolation when Mamba does not bring Lissa to visit. It expresses her loneliness in prison. It is, she explains to Lissa, half her philosophy of life: "We culled people got one t'ing over de white folks. Dere ain't no trouble so big that we can't sing about um. Bes' t'ing fo' trouble is singin'—an'

workin'. And when yo' work is singin' den yo' is holdin' a charm 'gainst
trouble" (141). Hagar's song is more essential than that in the *Porgy*
play, and more personal. It is not an adjunct to that of the chorus; her
voice, even in chorus, is never swallowed up or absorbed. Song is invariably her best, most personal means of communication, with the sailors,
in disappointment, in her love for Lissa, and in anticipation of death.
It is more than rhythm, however defined. It is a strongly personal and
dramatic expression of loneliness, fear, and love.

While Hagar becomes a tragic figure whose dumb wounds all can
feel, the play falls well short of tragedy. It is more clearly melodrama
than the novel. Fight, trial, exile, razor-slashing, rescue, punishment,
rape, chase, radio triumph, blackmail, murder, and suicide—the play
is all melodrama.

Heyward has plot problems as well. The Prologue, the group gathered at the radio, establishes the situation, but most of the antics of
those present are irrelevant to the action. The shift from "Lonesome
Walls" to the courtroom is confusing as Hagar is not there en route to
jail, nor is it as effective an introduction of Hagar as the meeting with
the sailors. The coincidences regarding Gilly and Prince, who rapes
Lissa, stretch credulity, and a potentially great scene is missed when
Gilly's fate is at stake. Gilly's blackmail is almost as unconvincing as
Saint's response: "We'll have to think hard" (157). And Hagar need not
openly carry the gun into the store; it is too obvious for us to then
believe that only the blind Maum Vina senses what is to come. Hagar's
five years in the penitentiary are also glossed over too quickly.

But the play's inadequacies as literature are secondary to its overall
dramatic effect. As the *New Republic* reviewer wrote:

It makes a play of charm, difference and numerous faults; but the main thing
of the evening is the success of its reality—even through melodrama it retains
that mixture of earnestness, rightness and its own dignity. . . . And that would
be all, excepting some bits of comfortable wisdom from time to time, if it
weren't for the music, the motion, the good ringing speech all through and
the heartening sight of real people. . . . But the show focuses on Ethel Waters.
. . . As Hagar, lusty, tender, bewildered, raging, she has the chance to show
how constant and intelligent that sincere quality in her is. The part makes no
demands of a complex nature but it does demand something of the heroic,
steadfast throughout; the patient incomprehension of the trial scene, the
invective at the meetinghouse, the humbleness here and there and the child's
sweetness over her first "party" at the end—these require not only to be managed by themselves but to be tied together and all sustained.[13]

Hagar's faith is the furthest Heyward progresses from his barren philosophy, "We're here because we're here because we're here." In the more terrestial terms of Heyward's search for life, here, even more than in the Mamba plot of the novel, love is life, love transcending race, rhythm, and community.

The novel version of *Mamba's Daughters* had been a great success, selling 40,157 copies. The play ran 162 performances in the first six months of 1939 before going on tour.[14] It was Heyward's last play. A few weeks after it closed in April 1940, he was dead.

CHAPTER 7

Tragic Mulatto, or The Lemmings:
Brass Ankle

I "Black's Black an' White's White"

TWO of Heyward's three plays, *Porgy* and *Mamba's Daughters*, began as Charleston novels. With his wife's assistance, they were turned into pulsating dramas of simple Negro folk. Appearing a dozen years apart, in 1927 and 1939, they established Heyward's reputation as a dramatist, though both depended more on pathos, melodrama, group scenes, music, and stagecraft than on characters of some complexity in conflict.

Brass Ankle, produced in 1931, is unlike them in dealing not with Charleston blacks but mainly with humorless, puritanical, small-town whites. It is all Heyward's. It is a play from the start, and it is a clear-cut failure. Also, for the first time Heyward takes up the tragic mulatto theme which has, since publication of *The Beautiful Octoroon* in 1855, given rise to dozens of stories, novels, and plays by white and black authors, including Twain, Cable, Howells, and Chesnutt. *Brass Ankle* involves passing and racial intermarriage, although Ruth Leamer is unaware that she is a "brass ankle," of Indian as well as Negro and white origin. The play continues Heyward's concern with the fate of the Negro in a changing society.

The action involves Larry Leamer's discovery of Ruth's race when she bears a dark-skinned son and the effects of that discovery on them, their new son, and their blonde daughter, June. Larry is torn by contending forces greater than any he has ever met—the racism he shares with his neighbors and which makes him hate his son; his fear that his friends will discover the secret of his son's color; his love for his wife, though he now knows her to be mulatto; and his devotion to his until now white daughter. Ruth is obliged to find a way to keep her son and

118

her husband and to protect her daughter from the stigma of identification as a mulatto.

The antagonist, responsible for forcing the matter, is the southern backwoods culture of Rivertown—a remarkably accurate reflection of the darker side of the backwoods South at any time in the previous half-century; barren, ugly, and racist. Incorporation of the town is underway, but the community is probably incapable of any meaningful progress. No thought has ever violated its cliché-ridden serenity. The beauty of the Negro church music has been banished to the outskirts. The Leamers' privacy has yielded to subdivision of their property, and the moon, the pines, and the sounds of nature have given way to the blare of Mrs. Burton's radio next door. As Ruth sees, it appears to be change for its own sake; she worries that they are selling their happiness by the "front foot."[1]

The town's one absolute is race. The play begins with the town fathers plotting the expulsion of the racially mixed Jackson children from what will be the town school. "Gettin' civilized," Larry calls it (14). "Black's black an' white's white," Jake Darcy, the county constable, puts it (43). Larry's resentment of the aristocratic Dr. Wainwright's more subtle view of race relations and his paralysis in addressing his dilemma show him to be handicapped, as is all Rivertown, by an inability to think about race relations or to find in his church genuine moral guidance. Instead, as Rev. Latterby makes clear when Larry would show compassion for the Jacksons, calling on his neighbors to "think of the other fellow sometimes": "This matter has nothing to do with Christianity, Larry" (100). As Ruth has observed, before the discovery: "They take your life and they pull it this way and that. They are so sure they are right" (16).

By contrast, Dr. Wainwright offers Larry the code of his class. He tells Larry how his father's honor forced him to recognize as white the "brass ankle" John Chaldon, once Chaldon had been drafted as a white into the Confederate army. Both Larry and Wainwright realize, however, that the Leamers' situation is not so simple as the secure aristocrat's in the story. Once Larry knows Ruth's race, Wainwright proposes their flight to the city or "deep country" (67). But, in almost the next breath, he shifts to a proposal that they get away "until some disposition can be made of the child" (71).

The situation is hopeless. The town has not yielded on the one-sixteenth-Negro Jackson children. Larry cannot accept his dark son or

bear to have his daughter branded Negro. Nor can Ruth sacrifice her
baby.

The Leamers' difficulty has real dramatic possibilities. Larry's ignorance is, for a racist Carolina town, as terrible and essential as Oedi-
pus's, and Larry's doom is almost as certain once fate strikes. Or else,
for once, a bigoted redneck, alone or with the help of his wife and
Wainwright, will be forced to unravel the race mess to avoid destruction of his world.

But instead of Larry resolving the dilemma, Ruth sacrifices all—for
half of her family. She places Larry's double-barreled shotgun against
the door frame, then repudiates Wainwright's account of her brass-
ankle ancestry by confessing a liaison with the conveniently dead
Davey, thus subjecting herself to what Wainwright has called Larry's
"inherited code of honor" (63–64). Larry swiftly dispatches her with
one barrel and the baby with the other. This leaves Larry above the
law, if chastened, with his racism intact, his lily-white town, and, ironically, his fair and white but actually mulatto daughter, who can, as a
pure white, continue the purity of the master race. Presumably, Ruth
thinks, if she has thought at all, that Larry will be too stupid to discover—or his interest will prevent his discovering—his deceased wife's
family history, so he will not have to recognize what he harbors under
his roof. Of course, his whole interest was in avoiding having to face
just that very knowledge.

If any sense can be made of the denouement, what Heyward seems
to be suggesting, if unwittingly, is that when the truth is publicly
known in Rivertown, Ruth is, alas, expendable, a proper sacrificial victim on the altar of white racial purity. It is no resolution. Larry has
seen his love for Ruth and his daughter to be greater than his racism
or commitment to Rivertown progress, but with Ruth's demise the possibility of Larry's learning anything is foreclosed. And Ruth, who has
appeared sensitive and intelligent and upon whom the burden of
Larry's conversion falls, reasons neither with herself nor Larry. She
thinks of herself and her son as having "changed and started to be
something different" (116). But she never questions what it is. She
never feels that she is a Negro or brass ankle, and she is altogether
incredible in her suicidal sacrifice of her own blood to hatred: "Larry,
we can't let this terrible thing touch June," she tells him, as if June's
whiteness is the highest of all values. Ruth never seems to know who
she is, only what America is and the town is and who she is not. Accept-

ing white superiority, she goes to her death like a lemming, too unresponsive to her fate and too passive to elicit our sympathy.

The situation has great potentialities, and the subject is not too delicate. *Pudd'nhead Wilson* had addressed it; Faulkner does in the early 1930s, and just before *Brass Ankle* appeared on Broadway, a novel on a white–brass-ankle marriage, *Po' Buckra* by Samuel Gaillard Stoney and Gertrude Mathews Shelby, was published. *Po' Buckra* portrays with considerable success the inner conflicts that rage in Barty Grundsen and Judith Beaufain's journey to discovery in the end of her marriage of what is real and worth saving of her aristocratic heritage. Neither is a strong character, but both have inner strength the Leamers lack. Coincidentally, Heyward's friend Stoney intended to use Heyward's title until he learned of the forthcoming play.[2]

The play's inadequacies are clearly evident, beginning with the characters. As Mark Van Doren observes, Larry is too simple a figure for his ruin to be impressive.[3] And while Ruth is sensitive and more aware, neither is she noble. Structurally, the knot of complication Heyward carefully ties in Act I and begins to untie in Act II, Larry and Ruth leave secure in Act III.

Act I suffers seriously because Heyward's chief interest there is employment of irony to prepare for the crisis of discovery of Ruth's mixed blood that ends the act. Yet the irony's effectiveness is lost because neither Larry, Ruth, nor the audience senses the double meaning of almost every word and gesture in Act I. The waste is most conspicuous: The militant Mrs. Burton, who would not socialize with people "we all know's got nigger blood" but does, is also unknowingly prophetic (8): "Husbands are all right in their way, Ruth, but when a woman's hour comes, I say, when her *hour comes*" (10). Larry's inadequacy when Ruth's "hour comes" will, of course, be far more serious than Agnes's cliché mentality can imagine. Larry observes, "I guess we usually get the kind of wives we want, honey. . . ." He goes on to say he always swore he'd "marry a lady," and concludes, "I ain't got no kick comin'" (11). Ruth replies, "I'm neither china nor glass." She is, in fact, an alloy, brass, although as breakable as what she disclaims being. Ruth is antagonistic toward Pink Jones because he had trapped a mother fox, which chewed off its own foot to return to its young; this produces Lee Burton's comment on females: "They positively like to suffer" (35). Larry dismisses the one-sixteenth theory, the practicality of which June's situation demonstrates. Larry makes much of his friends, who are only skin-deep friends—while the Leamers are lily

white. Ruth's uneasiness about her neighbors' righteousness turns to
fatalism when she sees the Jackson world disintegrating, and there is
no suggestion of fear as she approaches her own fate. Burton's sole
claim to dignity is as a bootlegger. He calls Larry, who sugars his mash,
a likely candidate for mayor because he is "progressive," which means
he "thinks like we do" (23). Larry insists, "There's certain bedrock
things we got to start with" (26). Bootlegging is in; integration abed is
out.

But the irony of the situation is revealed only when Larry hears the
mulatto baby's cry and Wainwright reveals what has befallen him.
Until then, the only hint has been the doctor's awkward turn to the
subject of the brass ankles the night Ruth is in labor and his awkward
persistence in finishing the story when Larry urges him to look in on
Ruth. Ironically, the doctor's talk not only fails to prepare Larry for
the news but reaffirms his suspicion and hatred for aristocracy and his
own sense of inferiority.

II   *The Sacrifice of Ruth*

The failings of Act II are of a different sort. The first difficulty is that
the knot Larry Leamer must untie calls for a single choice rather than
an action. Once Larry understands Ruth's refusal to give up her
"throwback" son, he must leave Rivertown with his family or turn
Ruth and her son out. When Ruth follows Dr. Wainwright's advice to
appeal to Larry's emotions by luring him onto the balcony he had
made for her, into the past of other moonrises, into the dark dreams
where "nothing exists" except the distant past, Larry still balks at
accepting his son in his puritanical identification of whiteness and
cleanliness and his inability to imagine Ruth's mother love (78). "I ain't
runnin' no competition with a nigger baby," he emphasizes (84).
Throughout the act, Larry and Ruth only add to one another's misery.
The act does come to a climax at the end in Larry's courageous revelation of the truth because, he explains, he won't let Rivertown "make
a damn fool of Ruth" (108).

In the third act both Larry and Ruth should confront their fate and
the community—and act accordingly. Because neither does—the community is equally passive except for Agnes Burton's gesture of rejection
in sending June home—the act misfires. It is also truncated, less than
half the length of Acts I and II. Nor can the audience be satisfied that
Ruth has no other options. And unless Ruth's suicidal resolution is taken

as despair of life outside the white race, there is no insight or recognition.

Why must Ruth and little Larry be punished? Is Ruth's seeming despair based on her belief that the righteous whites of Rivertown, including Larry, are unable to confront guilt, an inability which forces them to seek scapegoats? Is it enough to leave Larry the illusion of righteousness at such an expense? As tragedy it lacks necessity. What it does offer, until Ruth turns melodramatic, is the real impasse the situation creates for Larry and, in occasional moments, the reality of his agony. But the only dramatic resolution for that agony is truth, awareness, growth, sight, whatever fate demands as the price for the vision.

In *Brass Ankle*, the backwoods scene with its stunted folk provides an excuse for humorless, cliché-ridden speech. The set piece with Latterby about whether Negroes have souls, the race clichés, Wainwright's lectures about brass ankles and Dr. Mendel, Ruth's farewell to June, and Mrs. Burton's calm, apologetic break with Ruth only underscore the general ineptness of the dialogue. Even Ruth's sentiments about their earlier years in Rivertown lack lyrical merit.

Heyward, for once, faces the race theme head on, but he lacks the courage to see it through. He cannot even recognize Ruth's superiority in a white society, so sacrifices her to the appearance of white racial purity.

Also, *Brass Ankle* does not take place in Charleston, where the atmosphere might have pressed in to relieve the play of its unreality. Rivertown is only a few miles away, and Heyward surely knew the Leamers and Burtons, at least secondhand. But he does not know them well. For Rivertown is still the Southern frontier, a foreign world to the Charleston aristocrat, where fears are magnified and produce the harsh controls and fierce bitterness of which Ruth complains. Heyward lacks respect for the Rivertown folk; the town becomes an unambiguous image of all he finds inhuman in the backwoods South and in Progress. Perhaps Charleston manners could have saved the Leamers, for manners are moral forms, and Charleston knew pigmentation to be less than the Absolute, however close it might come. It is to Heyward's credit that he never again wrote of people for whom he had no real sympathy.

Brass Ankle does reveal once more Heyward's interest in social change and, less emphatically, in the rhythms of life. Rivertown is too culturally barren to resist the demands of Progress. Moreover, except for Ruth, the whites are as spiritually barren as Charleston aristocrats. Ruth, different in that her cultural roots are Indian and Negro as well as white, is also different in finding joy and peace in family love and harmony with nature—in trees, birds, moon, and silence. But Progress begins the destruction of Ruth's peace, and Larry's commitment to the progress in reverse of racism completes it. As there is no life for Lissa in Charleston, there is no life for Ruth, the Jacksons, or anyone in Rivertown. This is the play's final disappointment. In *Brass Ankle*, Heyward does not, as in *Porgy* and *Mamba's Daughters*, seriously explore the possibilities of life.

CHAPTER 8

The Choice of Doom: Peter Ashley

I *Sophisticated Perspectives*

A half-dozen years before *Peter Ashley* appeared in 1932, DuBose
Heyward wrote Carolina historian Yates Snowden that doing "the
epic novel" was his "greatest ambition," but while such a novel was
"taking form slowly" in his mind and would deal with "the period just
before, and during the war," he was not yet prepared to start it.[1]

By the time Heyward began working on his "epic novel," sometime
after completing *Mamba's Daughters,* he was much more ready. He
had worked in the longer novel form and had begun to treat of his own
aristocratic white Charleston. With the dramatization of *Porgy* and
travel abroad, he had also seen something of the world beyond the
confluence of the Ashley and Cooper rivers. Some of the world, as
Frank Durham observes, had rubbed off on him.[2]

In *Peter Ashley* Heyward for the first time approaches his material
as a serious craftsman, a seriousness reflected particularly in his careful
concern for narrative voice. One of the first things the reader of *Peter
Ashley* notices is that the pretentious manner of the self-consciously
but modestly condescending and enlightened Charleston aristocrat
whose voice prevails in *Porgy* and *Mamba's Daughters* is missing in
the narration. Once he had decided to be faithful to the contemporary
knowledge and attitudes of Charleston, 1861, there was little place for
the intrusive voice of his earlier Charleston novels.[3] Also, where the
narrator is involved, there is little or no sense of the passage of time
between event and telling. At most there is an April summary of March
events or a character's reflections on his own lifetime or the events of
the recent past. Even more important is the disciplining influence of
the two characters whose points of view Heyward offers. Pierre Chardon, the wise old aristocratic Huguenot ex-soldier, Unionist, and aes-
thete, and his Harvard- and Oxford-educated nephew, Peter Ashley,
are far more intelligent, sensitive, and articulate than any of Hey-

ward's previous characters. As both are keen observers and interpreters
of the proximate as well as the larger scene, there is simply less need
for the narrator's interpretation. For example, Pierre is quite in control
in understanding young Damaris Gordon:

> In another age and setting, Chardon thought, her temperament would
> have made of her a great courtesan. For she could have given more than
> mere physical satisfaction. She could have fostered some great ego, by con-
> tinually presenting its own glorified reflection. But her spirit was as com-
> pletely armored in the Southern gentlewoman tradition of chastity as was her
> body in its stays and hoops. Her expression of fresh and serene innocence, her
> instinctive withdrawal from the obviously and crudely physical, was funda-
> mentally sincere, Chardon concluded.[4]

When this sophisticated narrator's voice does appear, the transition
is smoothly effected, as in the narrator's interpretation of the sweep of
Secession events at the beginning of Chapter 7:

> Always as a prelude to war there comes a time when the rhythm of the life
> of a people changes. A man sensitive to such influences can almost mark the
> hour that saw the passing of the old, the arrival of the new. Before this
> moment isolated events possess the power to disturb the forward measured
> swing of time, but the dominant beat persists. Destiny, while it is not subject
> to the will of the people, is at least influenced by it. Then suddenly the
> rhythm quickens. The human equation disappears. It is the event that deter-
> mines destiny. (102–103)

This passage comes as a prelude to a meditation appropriate to Peter,
though not his, on his hesitation to conform to Secessionist thinking:

> Now for the individual the final moment of decision has arrived. There is
> no turning back. There is no standing still. He must conform or he must be
> destroyed.
> In the face of these simple alternatives, why should he hesitate? He has but
> to march into camp and lay down his arms. He is acclaimed a hero. He at
> once surrenders his will to that of the mass. He has thrown from his shoulders
> the intolerable burden of deciding for himself which act is right, and which
> act wrong. He is of that number which, having delivered themselves over to
> the new, frantic rhythm of life, are possessed by it—are given in this brief
> interval which precedes the crash over the brink, their priceless hour of
> romance, their illusion of great and imperishable splendor.
> And for the nonconformist—what? Only the approval of a small, stubborn,

inner voice that will not be silenced. And for food, the bread of that utter loneliness that is possible only in the press of a crowd. (103)

Wiser than Heyward's earlier narrators, this one also finds the design in the flow of events, a design which explains Peter's mood of the moment but eventually reveals also why Peter does, at last, conform. Moreover, a little wiser than Pierre and Peter, the narrator's perspective adds a patina of gentle but precise irony to the account which indicates that Charleston is, alas, sadly innocent.

Another effect of the superior narration of *Peter Ashley* is that the major characters are almost invariably far better realized than their latter-day counterparts in the skimpy white plot of *Mamba's Daughters.* None of the voices around Saint can be confused with Pierre Chardon's. And Peter's transformation—he is far more involved in the action—is much more fully seen than Saint's.

The success of *Peter Ashley,* then, is a question of thematic development, action, and characterization, not the handling of the narrative or language as with his earlier novels.

II *The Pressure to Conform*

After studying at Oxford, Peter Ashley returns to Charleston with a jaundiced view of slavery and a conviction that Secession will fail. He is just in time to encounter the irrational fervor of the first weeks of separation from the Union. The novel moves through the months before the firing on Sumter to the departure of the Ashley Mounted Rifles two months later.

Peter is the son of a typical Carolina planter, but he has been raised by Pierre Chardon, whose wife and baby had died while Pierre was patriotically engaged in the Mexican War. As independent as his uncle, Peter is still embarrassed by his alienation from the Secession spirit. He works for a newspaper, but only until his reportage of a central Race Week event is emasculated. He falls in love with Damaris and survives a duel with the vulgar Archie Holcombe, another suitor, ostensibly over Peter's doubts about slavery. Recuperating from his wound and rewarded with Damaris's acceptance of his proposal of marriage, Peter feels himself "letting go" (253). As a messenger, he is in the thick of the artillery duel for Sumter. Then he hastens to wed Damaris, puts theory aside, and goes blithely off to war.

The central conflict revolves around Peter's imported perspective on slavery, his determination to go his own way, and the pressure of the aristocratic community upon him to rejoin "his own," whatever folly they may be about in precipitating a war. This pressure develops in two ways. Heyward portrays the aristocratic class with enough sympathy for its ordered and traditional practice of the arts of leisure to make its appeal to Peter formidable, and with enough objectivity for the reader to see its flaws more clearly than Peter can. At the same time, Heyward is revealing, incident by incident, the erosion of Peter's freedom under the pressure upon him to conform.

The formidability of the Charleston aristocracy is sufficiently in evidence: Pierre's reserve and class-consciousness; Judge Mcgra̧th's boutonniere; planters fleeing the fever every May 15; strict observance of good manners at all times; the ritual St. Cecilia's Ball; the proper treatment of slaves. At sixteen, Peter wants nothing to do with a man who is "'not our kind'" (35). Even when Peter forgets Damaris in his excitement following the horse race, the breach of manners is serious: motive is no excuse. Women must be feminine, serene, efficient, stoic, and, Pierre emphasizes, sexual but divine and immaculate.

At its best, this elaborate aristocratic code produces not repressed neurotics but a superior example of the human species: "They were a thoroughbred lot, Peter thought," on meeting other planters' sons at the slave mart (74). Even their weaknesses do not diminish their impressiveness, "massed solidly," awaiting the unscrupulous Magrew:

They looked remarkably alike, bearing as they did the marks of their class. Clean cut, high bred, erect. Movements free, easy, assured. Eyes direct and candid. Not the eyes of analysts, but of a people with an enormous capacity for faith in its accepted beliefs. Faces singularly free from the marks of mental conflict, hale and ruddy from good whiskey, offset by hard riding under a semi-tropical sun. (80)

At the Jockey Club lunch before the races, Peter sees them whole; they are a strongly united, traditional community:

Generation succeeding generation in the same surroundings, facing the same problems, old faces fading away at the hunting club dinners, the race meets, their places filled by young faces varying little from the hereditary mold. Cousins marrying each other with shocking regularity, intensifying neighborhood loyalties, welding the whole into something more than merely a neighborhood, endowing it with a common personality that dominated its individual egos, and that looked upon its own with a certain possessive pride that somehow could not be ignored. This was the thing that he felt most strongly as he stood answering their greetings. This solidarity. (135)

Near the end of the novel, when Peter has succumbed to this spirit of solidarity, the narrator repeats the eighteenth-century Low Country aristocracy's view that no one escapes, that experience only proves, as Uncle Porcher observed in a letter to Peter in England, that nowhere in the world compares to Middle St. John's Parish.

The aristocrats are not, however, altogether unchanging. Damaris introduces a new fashion, the garibaldi blouse. Proctor Gordon is a conscientious objector to dueling. And Chardon sees the universal implications of change in Holcombe's conduct: "'He has taken our virtues and by his excesses has made them vices. He has caricatured us and made us seem ignoble. I always thought him a braggart and a waster, but now he emerges as a revolutionary, and a revolutionary may be an even more vital factor in life than a gentleman'" (34). Later, Chardon notes that his prophecy has come true: "'Everyone's gone wild over him. And why not?—he's a perfect barbarian, and although we may all not realize it, our civilization has ended. This is his world—not ours'" (100). So the images of demure southern womanhood, the code of honor, and manners are all under attack.

Neither are the aristocrats flawless. Their romantic blindness leads to dueling and war. And their minds are closed. No one, least of all William Gilmore Simms, (the major nineteenth-century novelist and militant Secessionist, one of several historical figures Heyward employs peripherally), will attend Peter's reasonable views on Secession at St. Andrew's Hall the night Holcombe provokes the duel. Thomas and Wake Ashley are incapable of introspection or analytical thought. No one will listen to Chardon, Peter, or Petigru. Only Peter appears conscious of any responsibility for precipitating violence: "All about Chardon staid and respectable citizens were behaving as though demented, wringing each other's hands, slapping backs, brandishing canes and hats" (9). This hotheadedness and fanaticism, Robert A. Lively observes, is the fruit of the planter's unchecked pride which produced an "irresponsible indulgence of individualism" oblivious of its effect on society.[5] Twenty years before Lively, Heyward saw it. Yet, his narrator carefully balances this critical view with Chardon's reflection on the sun-drenched troops: "The glory that lay about them was not that of high summer, but the light which slants long-shadowed across an

autumn field" (316). They are going to the harvest; the St. John's way
of life is doomed.

The pattern of Peter's day to day experience also carries him inexorably toward conformity, despite his freedom and good sense and his
continuing problem of conscience. For events allow Peter little exercise
of the freedom his Harvard-Oxford education and Chardon's foster
parentage have given him. Still, as he observes to Chardon, before he
can join in, he says, "'I've got to feel it here inside me'" (62).

Soon enough the reorientation process begins. His experience at the
slave market reminds him that slavery can work humanely. His identification with the Race Week crowd; the feeling of belonging when
Albino wins the third heat; his sense of the neighborhood's "common
personality," its "solidarity," and its "possessive interest" in him at
Wakefield's; and his observation of the "great middle class" singing
"Dixie" at a minstrel show bring him to wonder if we do not all "eventually conform to an unknown and preordained pattern" (136, 165,
171–72). For Peter it is the realization that he is happy only when in
harmony with the crowd.

The turning point comes when he responds as a Charleston gentleman to Holcombe's charge that he is a traitor:

> Behind Holcombe the austere soaring beauty of the great Georgian Hall
> caught at his gaze, pulling it away from the heavy sneering face of his antag-
> onist. It was a part of the incomparable beauty that was in turn a part of him.
> His town, his state. And these men about him, waiting, headstrong, blind
> perhaps, but generous, impulsive, passionate, surrounding him, pressing in
> upon him with the weight of a single unalterable idea. He felt it seize him.
> The rhythm of the crowd pounded in his blood. His moment of clarity passed;
> for a vertiginous second he felt his brain swing. Then he was stepping back-
> ward—a single, quick, watchful step, his body at an aching tension. His right
> hand was tingling—quivers running along the arm to the elbow. His gaze
> was focused on Holcombe's face, gone ashen on one side and scarlet on the
> other where the blow had fallen. (207–208)

Moments before, Peter had realized that it is an "'illusion that slavery
can continue to survive in a civilized democracy'" (206). But blood has
told, and on leaving St. Andrew's Hall old Petigru (modeled on a notable Charleston Unionist whose attitudes were tolerated throughout the
war) calls him a fool for trying to use reason with Simms and the others, then notes that Peter's challenge is another emotional act:

"I'm sorry," Petigru hastened on. "But I wanted to show you that you're not far behind your friends. It comes like that, you see—not through any process of logic, but through instinct, and a capacity for faith. It is like a religious conversion. Some day, like St. Paul, you will see a great light; or even more appropriate to this situation, you will be like Balaam—you will hear an ass speak and you'll believe him. Then your troubles will be over. You can believe miracles, even the one that a Confederacy of Southern States can whip the Union." (214)

Chardon now recognizes that he must give Peter up to a rush to live his life quickly, as Chardon had his before going off to war. The process of Peter's transformation accelerates. He thinks of his responsibility to a "world full of lunatics . . . bent upon self-destruction," then "ceased to care" (245–46). His love for Damaris is all that matters. He senses that his fate is predestined. He accepts the gift of a slave. But Peter is letting go of more than his neutrality or ethical reservation; now he would live for today: "His experience had brought him to a realization of the impermanence of life, the fragility of human happiness, the ridiculous futility of arguing with Destiny. He had Damaris" (253). His "lyric days" at home, recovering, courting Damaris, escaping reality, reflect Peter's abandonment of mind (256).

Ironically, it is in the very hours that Chardon and his company, waiting for news of the bombardment, recognize the grim reality of war that Peter finally hears the ass speak in full voice. Chardon sees the change: "How unaffectedly emotional he had become, how unquestionably he accepted what he was told, how complete had been his escape from the tyranny of reality" (302). Pierre wonders if "the comfort of a present illusion was worth the terror of the ultimate tragic awakening" (303).

By spring, Peter's self-inflicted lobotomy is complete. He had, before, been a prig. "Actual conditions" have "educated him" (308). In the hands of gentlemen, slavery is not so evil. His protests had been wasted: the war and defeat were inevitable. Now he resents "outside interference" in a "life that was completely satisfactory, that had beauty, harmony, dignity, continuity" (310). So Peter becomes a symbol of the last gasp of the old order. He has forgotten the story he had told Damaris of how the sight of a bloody fox had sickened him. Now, his youthful pacifism and rational reservations behind him, he rides off to war, last in the cavalcade of Charlestonians.

Heyward's carefully developed argument for Peter Ashley's conversion, the heart of the novel, is convincing to a point. But Peter's dis-

missals of the evils of slavery and the futility of war are too facile as
are his acceptance of the illusion that their life had been "completely
satisfactory" and his adoption of the argument that they "had always
been their own master" as justifications for war (310). Instead of other
arguments gaining weight, the reader is repeatedly informed that
Peter is now ruled by emotion, fatalism, and hedonism and that he
rejects his earlier views as never having had any merit when the reader
knows that Peter knows better.

In *Absalom, Absalom!*, when Quentin Compson has seen too much
of what has cursed the South, he answers his roommate: " 'I dont hate
it,' Quentin said, quickly, at once, immediately; I dont hate it,' he
said."[6] The continued thought ends the novel. The difference reveals
what is lacking in Peter's "fulfillment." Quentin is left in the tension
of love and hate. Peter is not, because, as John Chamberlain observes,
Heyward seems to be saying, if with some irony, that to live with one's
fellows, one must accept and share society's values, whatever they are,
so that social conformity becomes the ironic hero of the novel, with
power over the heart and will.[7] Head and heart do not meet in Peter
Ashley as they do in Pierre, Petigru, or in his less thinking fellow
Charlestonians. Peter is last seen as a knight riding off to do battle with
yet another dragon—for his lady, having become the first dragon he
had fought.

Heyward's intention is clear, however. He would draw Peter back
into the womb through the ordinary lures of home and the quiet pressures of the clan, however unconvincing, romanticized, sentimentalized, and irrelevant the celebrant is forced to become in the ironic context of the South's suicidal hour.

III   *Chivalric Love, History, and Vocation*

Peter Ashley is another testing and criticism of the Charleston aristocratic code, a chivalric love story, a history of the coming of the Civil
War, and, to a lesser degree, an account of a writer's apprenticeship.
But how completely subordinate are these other levels of the novel,
which have been subsumed into Peter's Progress, and what effect do
they have on the central action?

The courtship of Damaris is a poorly handled romance of clichés,
and it gets very much in the way of the historical crisis at the novel's
center. Damaris is introduced as the dangerous sort who "breaks down
resistance, disarms at a glance, and endows the process of surrender

with a strange sensual delight" (91). Since Peter is conquered in an instant, the only important moments in the courtship are the monologue proposal, Peter's hopeful interpretation afterward, and Damaris's reply following the duel, to which Peter apparently makes no response because he is out of his wits: "'I'll never leave you,' she whispered, 'never. And if you ever go away from me, you'll carry all of me that matters away with you. If it's the war. If you're in torment again, you will know that I am there every single minute. And when you come back, if it isn't until the end of the world, you'll find my empty shell here waiting for you to fill it'" (249). No wonder Damaris seems unbothered by Peter's clichés!

The reader is left in doubt that Damaris becomes a woman and that she, too, is an independent spirit. It is easier to believe that she simply seduces Peter from his high moral plane into the romantic folly of bearing her colors into battle—except for the fact that Peter has been from the beginning determined to be seduced. Heyward repeatedly calls her mysterious and enigmatic, when she is brainless, apparently to explain Peter's fascination. The effect of her presence is to turn the story into stock melodrama.

In the last forty-six pages of *Peter Ashley,* the history of the war's beginning overshadows both Peter's conversion and the love story. Six years after the novel appeared Heyward confesses as much: by linking the war sections of their novels, *Peter Ashley* and *Look Back To Glory,* Heyward and Herbert Ravenel Sass got up *Fort Sumter,* which they advertised as the most detailed account of the two major Sumter actions in the Civil War.[8] These chapters provide a running account of the events of March and early April 1861, the firing on Sumter, the Sumter action, its conclusion, and the surrender byplay. *Fort Sumter*—Heyward's part—omits only the possibly spurious account of confusion regarding the surrender, a paragraph of Pinckney's sermon, and passages involving Heyward's characters. The Sumter engagement occasions Peter's final conversion, but Heyward makes little effort to absorb the battle into the story. Consequently, the effect is to dissipate further the modest tension of the earlier struggle between Peter's mind and class attachment.

Peter's pursuit of his vocation as a writer is so truncated that it serves mainly as another reflection of the romantic sickness of Carolina society: there is no audience for detached reporting so that Peter must join in the prostitution of ideas and words or give up writing, as important as it is to him:

He had known so many moments when, with body weary and brain lax from the exhaustion of thinking, he had stepped suddenly across the threshold into a new dimension, and for a brief moment had touched the universal. The things that he had written then throbbed with life. (224)

Certain weaknesses in *Peter Ashley* are by now evident. The courtship and history both overburden the main action. Several characters, especially Damaris, lack development, and Peter is unconscious when the most important phase of his conversion occurs.

IV   *The Epic Novel and "The Little Cavalcade"*

As for Heyward's "epic novel," neither Peter Ashley's character nor his deeds suggest an epic hero. Some examination of the demands of the epic genre, however, can serve to focus more clearly the broader implications of the novel as well as the failings of its hero as a hero.

The moment before the Civil War begins is a potentially epic hour, like the periods of historic change Scott and Tolstoy examine. Chardon and Peter are aware of a rising middle class that is intruding upon the sacred environs of the Charleston aristocracy. Old, somnolent Charleston has lost a sense of time, lives outside of time in a cycle of exactly recurrent rituals such as Race Week, and flares at any serious challenge to that static order from within or without. Heyward does not give his Charleston a full historical context but the threats of northern industrialism and the abolition of slavery are sufficient to indicate the impending doom of its secure world.

In *Peter Ashley*, however, the issue is joined not in a civil war of epic proportions as in Scott's novels, where, as Georg Lukács observes, two social forces clash in the popular march of progress or in a national struggle that essentially reveals and begins to purge the evils in the social structure as in the Russia of *War and Peace*.[9] Union is not such a progressive cause nor, for most of those involved in the novel, is slavery a grave social evil. The slaves do not rise nor do yeoman emerge as the undeniable force of the people. Rather, the battle is joined, as Charlestonians see it, simply because the Union threatens their timeless world of agriculture, custom, and status. Or, as Chardon sees it, because such a threat triggers irrational passions.

Consequently, Heyward's hour of secession in Charleston focuses on an aging society choosing suicide over awakening. The epic antagonist, the Unionist hegemony that will come with defeat, is not represented

in the struggle. The historical action in Charleston at the outset of the
Civil War is too much a single class's reaction to its fancied antagonists
to represent the disintegration of a social order and so qualify as an
epic struggle on the grand scale. The progressive features of the age
are not to be found in such a closed aristocratic society, nor are they in
Peter Ashley. Even those who oppose slavery and secession hardly represent the forces of change, with the partial exception of Peter Ashley
upon his return.

Heyward's narrator does not pretend that the novel treats such an
epic struggle; still, he is ambivalent about the situation: "It is at this
moment that the civilization which has grown slowly through centuries
of patient cultivation pours its life into a last incomparable flowering.
For those who have tended it, and watched it spread and bud, it is all
too often the moment of delirium that precedes the oblivion of death"
(103). "Two centuries had gone into the making of the little cavalcade," the narrator observes (316). In the adjective we see that Charleston's finest hour is also its most pathetic. The narrator sees in full, Peter
in part, Charleston's choice of death. Anti-intellectualism, pride, hot-
headed irrationality, moral compromise, lack of wise leadership,
hedonism, and insulation from the outside world doom the aristocracy.
Peter Ashley celebrates the sunset of any heroic claim Charleston has.
Still, present, too, is the capacity for sacrifice, the loyalty, the inner
strength that makes for the tragic struggle to come. This is particularly
evident in the clans sending their men off to war.

As an epic struggle, *Peter Ashley* does not fit the mold of the modern
epic novel. It is, of course, doubtful that Heyward understood the epic
form as anything more than giving the historical moment authenticity
and life through characters and portrayal of events. By his definition,
he met considerable success. And *Peter Ashley* fits Lukács's description
of the classic historical novel's action as built upon "a broad delineation
of the manners and circumstances attendant upon events."[10] Heyward
touches all the bases, and the color and texture of Charleston life in the
novel credit his knowledge and love of the old city.

Notably, three of the best, most carefully realized episodes are those
recognized to be the most historically significant of the period. The
novel begins with the disappointed Chardon, on the occasion of the
signing of the Ordinance of Secession, mingling with the crowds he
generally avoided while reflecting on the disruption of the Union he
loved and had served. In contrast to the frenzied crowd, bent on self-
destruction, a wiser, nostalgic Chardon watches Judge Magrath, bou-

tonniere in lapel, close the federal court building upon abandoning his
office and thinks of how, thereafter, the blooming of the French rose
will remind him of that act. And he wonders "why, as we grow old,
the things that we love most are one by one poisoned for us by new
and painful associations" (5). It is a fine perspective.

The second historic event, the firing on *The Star of the West*, occurs
as, aboard the brig *Kiawah*, the sensitive young scholar peers through
the mist in "a faint lemon-colored sunlight" for signs of Charleston
harbor (37). The fog clears:

It was so incomparably lovely—so exactly as he remembered it all. Off the
starboard bow lay Long Island crowned by its palmetto forests, and dead
ahead Sullivan's Island with the bulk of Fort Moultrie an ominous note at its
center. To port lay Morris Island, and beyond, Fort Sumter, with the town on
the horizon behind it, showing in faint gleams of light, where the sun caught
the spires. It was all a part of him, as he was flesh of its flesh. God! It was
good to be coming home! And then he was struck by something odd. The
landscape lay fixed—static. The harbor was without movement. The few
boats that could be seen in the distance of the inner harbor lay at anchor.
Over the broad flat country and the still bay the sky arched vacant and enormous. All life seemed gathered up in the steamer that preceded them into
the waiting silence. In search of some explanation, Peter's gaze turned toward
the fortification on the point of Morris Island. In that moment he saw a flash
of orange light at the muzzle of one of the cannon. A fountain of spray broke
the blue of the water before the bows of the advancing steamer, then a second
splash, and third, as the ricocheting projectile lost velocity. Across the water
came a rumbling detonation. (42–43)

Heyward captures here the very unreality of the experience that poses
the conflict Peter Ashley must face.

The battle for Fort Sumter is more the historian's remote narration.
An almost staccato beat of short sentences summarizes and interprets—
like a process—the chronology of events, hesitating only for such odd-
ities as Rev. Pinckney's sermon:

March fourth. General Beauregard arrives at Charleston and assumes command of the military forces. On the fifth, he appears publicly with Governor
Pickens and his aides at a performance at the Charleston Theater. Little
Misses Fanny and Julia dance and sing. A competent cast performs *The Lady
of Lyons*. But the sensation of the evening is the glittering presence in the
proscenium box, and Charleston, remembering Jacques Toutant-Beauregard
and François Marie Chevalier de Reggio, feels safe in taking the general

unreservedly to its heart. Overnight he becomes the fashion. Ladies denude their gardens and convert headquarters at Institute Hall into a bower. Lads who have patiently cultivated fierce and warlike beards trim them down without a quiver to the Beauregard mustache and goatee. Huguenots with one accord forget that the general is a Catholic, and remember only that he is French. (262)

In each instance, a sensitive observer, Pierre or Peter, records the event, the mood of the hour, and something of his own feeling. The same care goes into the fictional scene in St. Andrew's Hall with Simms and Petigru that leads to the duel.

The advantages in the choice of Pierre Chardon and Peter Ashley as the major character-voices have already been seen, but those in the choice of the wry all-knowing ageless eighteenth-century man of reason for narrator are equally fortunate. For example, the Rev. Pinckney's sermon account:

The rector is known as a man of independent thought. He says what he pleases; and that, within limits, is right and proper, for is he not a man of God and a Pinckney? But with the announcement of the text, the congregation begins to have misgivings. Protected by his cloth, and by that monopoly of vocal expression which the Church bestows upon its priests, the speaker at once likens the South to Nebuchadnezzar whom, because of his pride and vainglory, God had reduced to the level of a beast of the field. He points to the fate of the Chaldean Monarchy, the Roman Empire, the Greek Republic, and, because they had been slave-holding civilizations, likens them to the Confederacy, and predicts a similar disintegration; and lastly, under the intoxication of his own oratory, he utters the ultimate blasphemy: He says that cotton cannot be depended upon to force the world to kneel and pay tribute to the South.

The congregation leaves in silence. The affair is neither infuriating nor amusing, but actually distressing. It is remembered that brilliant mentalities sometimes go like that. But after all, it is a matter to be handled by the family. The Pinckney connection is large and well-to-do, and what steps should be taken as to the care of their unfortunate member is a matter for them and not the community. Decidedly the proper attitude is that of tactfully ignoring the fact that a sermon had been preached at Grace Church on the morning of March twenty-ninth. (263–64)

The voice here is neither Pierre's nor Peter's but that of an omniscient narrator, rational, detached, and with a slightly amused and fatalistic tolerance of man's repetitious follies, a voice useful in giving fictive life to such broadly social and political scenes.

Heyward also shows an appreciation for many of the conventions of the classical historical novel of the death of a civilization. He does not involve us in too wide or large a stage: here is one "battle" in one place, a single representative action that focuses the historic issue, and the concrete action of the novel rises from it and the surrounding tension. And actual historical figures are kept in minor roles.

Still, two of the most important characteristics of the historical novel as its most successful creators achieve it are missing. Social class interaction, save that between Holcombe and the true-blue but weary aristocracy, is lacking, and when we look closely, Sumter is too preliminary, its significance too unclear, to be the representative large-scale conflict. Second, because Peter's progress, while leading to defense of the homeland, is essentially toward irrational compromise, there is no real epic hero. And instead of a view after the explosion of the Civil War to complete the epic action, we have only a view of Peter after his conversion to conformity.

Peter does promise the genuinely heroic in the duel episode. Name, reputation, vocation, happiness, and life, as well as the aristocratic order Holcombe threatens, are at stake. The event is placed in an heroic context. Holcombe takes on monstrous dimensions when Peter has a vision in the moments of exhaustion near the end of his night of pistol practice. Having arrived from England in a winter mist, Peter experiences a "quickening to the rhythm of spring" moments before the duel: the seasons conspire with him (235). His victory counters the helplessness and impotence of Chardon's view, saves Charleston from its immediate foe, wins Peter the hand of its favored daughter, and gives him new strength as, back at Wakefield's, he "feels resurgent life" (250). Here Peter fulfills the basic requirements of the romantic hero—love, adventure, and combat—at least minimally. And there is a kind of epic necessity about Peter's involvement in both the duel and the war: he is not responsible for either but when it is necessary that he do his thing, he does it.[11]

Yet Peter is invariably more observer or passive participant than romantic hero. He observes the firing on *The Star of the West*, is drawn into purchasing the slave Washington and pushed into buying the old free woman, reports on the horse races, listens to the middle-class singing of "Dixie," and listens to the St. Andrew's Hall discussion until dragged in. After the duel, he is altogether passive until he energetically witnesses the Sumter engagement. Consequently, the hero's scenes lack the dramatic emphasis they should have.

Still, while Peter is not the average self-sacrificing type from which epic heroes develop, he does concentrate, upon his return, what is otherwise dispersed in the national character. He encompasses tradition but also reason and a social sense. And so, for a time, anyway, he remains free. But he comes by this concentration in an unrepresentative way, through his atypical uncle's intellectual legacy and his travels. Moreover, that freedom does not lead to greatness because by yielding to those he represents he fragments himself and ceases to be free. If he can enter both sides—North and South, the schools of passion and reason, old and new, upper and middle classes, it is not as Ivanhoe and Rob Roy can. For he can enter only one at a time. Lukács would explain his failure as bourgeois in several respects: he is a class representative, a man of ideas and feelings rather than action, and interesting in large part for his personal psychological struggle, which is quite private: his courtship and writing. Fragmented and bourgeois, he fails in the historical role in which he should concentrate the passions of the people of his time. And because he turns off his intellect, he cannot do what the epic hero must do for his people: save them.

The failure to join convincingly matters of consequence and Peter's romance within a character capable of development is a major weakness of a novel that proposes to be more than the ordinary historical novel. This fault, however, remains subordinate to that of the ending, where the courtship and marriage have become part of the antiheroic conversion. There is here no tragic recognition and no narrator's gentle irony in viewing the gallant little cavalcade. Peter rides off to war all too eagerly. It is Heyward himself who sits the prancing Starling, waving farewell to the Charleston he has written three novels about, a place befitting the great lover of the city if not the author of an "epic novel."

It is, however, only at the end that the narrator's double perspective—ironic and understanding—breaks down. Peter is heroic in ably and successfully defending the Charleston code, winning the king's daughter, and succeeding to the kingdom. The only trouble is that he wins the wrong battle; the reality of the epic moment is in the public, political crisis that reaches a climax with the firing on Sumter. This is neatly illustrated by the narrator's observation that at the moment of civilization's "last incomparable flowering," a choice must be made: "He must conform or he must be destroyed" (103). Conform to what? Heyward says to the "will of the mass." But Peter knows that slavery is evil and that a gentleman's "good form" will not pass for a clear

conscience, and he knows the war to be suicidal madness. Northrop
Frye says that in the romantic myth the "reader's values are bound up
with the hero's."[12] They are not bound up with Peter in his acquiescence to the claims of local mores. Instead, the reader chafes at Heyward's awkwardness in rendering the psychological process of conversion and remembers the narrator's wry voice and Peter's own
statements which attest to the folly of secession. The reader simply cannot share the narrator's second view, that the call of the clan is, finally,
compelling and may be answered unashamed.

While Peter's course does not adequately serve the purposes of the
epic and merits so long a consideration of its inadequacies as epic only
because it provides an interesting demonstration of the several
demands of a genre beyond Heyward's understanding, it does serve
the purpose of the memorialist of an aristocratic society. The tracing
of Peter Ashley's increasingly uncritical rediscovery of "his own" shows
the reader in some detail what St. John's was, what it was not, and
what it was in danger of becoming. And Heyward skillfully employs
local color, the concentrated narrative thrust of events in a little place
that came to have such wide and tragic repercussions, and the sense of
pathos beneath the narrator's irony and cool wisdom to this end. Moreover, the conflict that pits Peter Ashley and Pierre Chardon against
that which threatens aristocratic values and customs is well realized,
and it accounts for half of the book. Consequently, in its concern with
values and the social order, *Peter Ashley* transcends the superficial
quaintness of many local color stories and historical novels. Again,
Heyward is very much concerned with the participants' experience of
a moment of social change. Peter Ashley fails as an epic hero because
he is *only* a more sensitive and temporarily detached member of a
doomed, irrational world. Like Saint Wentworth, he displays independence of mind and moral responsibility, but hardly enough. He would
pursue the arts. He would follow reason and serve the cause of culture.
But the Charleston aristocracy squelches him as it does Saint; like
Saint's, his pursuit of life ends in a zombie role. But the cause of it all,
the reality and the tragedy of antebellum Charleston, is all there.

In one sense, though, Heyward wrought better than he knew. As a
prospective writer compromised by the closing of the southern mind
in the contradiction between slavery and Christian values, Peter serves
as a fictional reflection of the historical development Lewis P. Simpson
has seen as compromising the southern mind for a century—until the
Southern Renascence set about recovering memory and history, from

which the southern mind had committed apostasy before the Civil War, in order to see the South in historical classical-Christian terms.[13] Heyward's appreciation of the Negro's humanity, the sterility of the Charleston aristocracy, the evils of racism, and now the compromise of Peter Ashley's mind, all signify his participation in the emergence of the southern mind from bondage.

CHAPTER 9

A *"Sahara of the Bozart"*: Lost Morning

I   *The Exeter Etcher*

IN *Lost Morning*, which appeared in 1936, the setting is not Charleston but the Piedmont, where a major social change has already occurred and the forces of the new order are indisputably in command. What *Lost Morning* has in common with Heyward's Charleston fiction is that its hero is a frustrated artist, in conflict as are the would-be artists of *Mamba's Daughters* and *Peter Ashley* with the Establishment, here the vulgar, nouveau-riche emergent South.

For three-quarters of its length, *Lost Morning* focuses on one character and his struggle through one season to free himself and his art from the modern business environment of Exeter which has all but destroyed his artistic integrity. For once, Heyward is more interested in telling his story, developing the characters essential to that story, and realizing a single, well-focused theme, the artist's struggle for integrity in an alien society, than he is in memorializing the past, celebrating the virtues of a people, or making broad arguments about racial progress or the folly of secession from the Union. Even the slips near the end are more problems in the handling of point of view than uncertainty of purpose. The story holds together remarkably well, and once the reader is caught up in Felix Hollister's critical conflict, Heyward sustains that interest.

The action of *Lost Morning* is concentrated in a single season. Hollister's wife and business manager, Miriam, has been in Europe with their two nearly grown children, Aubrey and Felicia. One August evening, his studio assistant, Leslie Morgan, candidly criticizes Felix for his compromise of his talent by etching for money rather than pursuing his early inclinations to paint or sculpt. This conversation and subsequent chores Felix does for Leslie and her convalescent mother at the Hollister camp upset his old equilibrium. By Miriam's September return, he has become restless and is finding in Leslie's sympathy and friendship a goad to break out of his chains.

The course of Hollister's revolt is swift and eventful. For a time he is engaged in a nostalgic, sentimental quest for the lost youth he sacrificed for a family and economic security. But in Leslie's faith in his ability, then her love and willingness to leave Exeter with him, he finds real hope that he can make a fresh start. The increasingly distasteful commercial schemes Miriam cooks up, the phony snob values, and the sacrifice of human responses to money, power, or social status on the part of Miriam and her country club friends hurry him to a decision. He goes, even after Leslie's apparent suicide, and he stays gone.

The situation is deliberately established—the potential scandal of his visits to Leslie's apartment; the fact of Miriam's drive, singleness of purpose, and acquisitive impulse; and the necessary past: Felix's choice of her managerial, decision-making talents and return home to Exeter over the "worship of beauty" and the "heart beat" in the lump of clay.[1] Felix is a citizen of Exeter and the South before he is an artist, and his antagonist is home.

Later, Felix rationalizes about his abandonment of his dedication to sculpture in Paris. In the tide of life, you "mastered the rhythm" or, "if you had been born out of your generation maybe," you were lucky if "you had someone who could get you through" (87). But he had begun to "master the rhythm"—of his art, anyway, so that his ready sacrifice of his art for Miriam's figure is hardly, in the context of the novel, simply being "born out of your generation maybe." Giving up the struggle and returning home is not what the generation of Hemingway and Fitzgerald did. So what Hollister is suggesting is that the difference between himself and the other lucky students of Matisse and between himself and Hemingway and Faulkner is that being born in Exeter is being born out of the generation that could escape the ties of the old home town's dead clichés. The country club "aristocracy" of Exeter is just what the expatriate writers were fleeing.

So Felix had gone home. He had apparently never questioned Miriam's decision that he should be the Exeter etcher or the decision to abandon a chance to work under Matisse. Now they would travel from town to town, Miriam would pick his subjects, and "Hollister then would be put furiously to work" (34). Apparently, Hollister only briefly questioned his wife's separate bedroom after Felicia's birth and became content to draw a "vicarious and sensuous satisfaction" from hearing other men lust after Miriam's near voluptuousness (35).

This account is the least satisfactory thing in the novel, for the reader must believe that a talented young artist could thoughtlessly abandon his idealism for security, give up his wife's bed, live in a stupor for twenty years, and then, the moment his blood is sufficiently warmed by Leslie's femininity and humanity, come out fighting.

The following chapter occasions Hollister's first comparisons of Leslie's genuine humor with the "counterfeit coin" of Miriam's carefully rehearsed jokes, which serves as a preparation for his greater displeasure at her proposal that they recoup the losses from his unproductive summer by having his prints executed in New York, a challenge to Hollister's artistic integrity he cannot ignore.

In each of the following scenes the pattern established here is repeated. Exeter and its money values, the tension between Miriam's force and Felix's pain, an actual attack on what self-respect he has left, and Leslie. In this instance, Felicia's repetition of Leslie's criticism both heightens and extends his misery and completes the assault on his self-respect begun by Miriam.

Felix tries to put the blame on his family by arguing that their support and sacrifice would be necessary for him to break new ground. But the voices of Exeter respectability do not impress Felicia; she is determined to be free herself.

In this scene, Miriam would compromise his craft, but it isn't nearly as serious a compromise as the one she next proposes; the difference shows how rapidly the stakes are rising in the game Felix must play to Miriam's tune.

Double-edged as the last difference, it develops out of the tableau of the six former Exeter High schoolmates, Felix, Miriam, Jarvis and Mame Maxton, Dr. Pendleton, and Jerry Enfield, partying at the country club. Maxton is a ruthless, hated banker whose victims pay "long and painfully" for crossing him (66): "Early in his career he had realized that a man could best attain stature by devouring his fellows, and this he had done, systematically and with relish." Pendleton has also spent his life desiring Miriam, resenting Felix, gossiping, and condescending to poorer patients. Enfield is a selfish and eternally adolescent former football star, boxing champion, war hero, and air racer now engaged in auto racing. Miriam, apart from managing Felix's affairs with a "shrewd calculating smile," throws her weight around in politics, and the local Episcopal church is her "personal possession" (154, 92). As Felix sees the church, God is "a tenant whose occupancy was strictly contingent upon good behavior" (92). In Exeter, the affluence and power of the group spells success: " 'We have an aristocratic tradition here,' " Miriam remarks, characterized, she admits, by " 'social snobbery' " (87).

The one of the group at all like himself, Felix finds, is Enfield. Sitting quietly on the veranda, Enfield alludes to his loss of nerve the year before, then enviously admires Hollister's security. Felix "flinched visibly under the word" and lashes out bitterly at the sacrifice he has made for it (70). Enfield reveals his own life to be a vacuum of protracted adolescence, spent in pursuit of speed.

The second attack comes when, en route home, Miriam explains how she would capitalize on the South's sense of tradition by turning Hollister's etchings and the "publicity value" of his name into cigarette advertising for Maxton's products. While she talks, Felix recalls the "intoxicating elation" in his early work and the peaceful dignity of a more rural Exeter and its simple folk in his boyhood (84). In contrast, they pass through the "incandescent hideousness of Main Street," a wasteland of robotlike people drifting in a phony world (85). By a neat coincidence, they also pass Leslie's, and Felix feels some envy and resentment of her top-floor escape from Exeter. For the first time, Felix identifies Miriam and himself with the alien town—in the ugliest image of all Heyward's work, sensing that the change in Exeter parallels that in himself.

In the "Sunday" chapters that follow, another pattern, one of self-assertion and freedom, overlays this one.

The Sunday after the advertisement proposal, Felix's memories of walking with Leslie that summer, her "young confident body leaning outward against the weight of the wind" like the Winged Victory of Samothrace, suddenly lifts him from a sense of defeat, and he sets about painting recklessly. When Miriam, the minister, and his wife enter, before them are the "exaggerated breasts and long white limbs of a woman," over whom is hanging "a form, obese, lewd," a form of "lust incarnate, unleashed and gloating over its prey" (109). Miriam is ashamed and makes excuses. For a moment, Hollister has given his imagination free rein, and when the rector's poetess sister-in-law, a "follower of beauty," reveals herself to be a "profane egotist" by rhyming his favorite psalm, Felix flees in open rebellion (114, 115).

Instinctively, he arrives at Leslie's, pursued, he tells her, by a posse and bloodhounds. Exeter, Miriam's dominance, Leslie: the assault is less strong this time, but a major change is occurring in Felix. Now he is taking the initiative. In return, Leslie begins to reveal her feelings and Felix discovers that her formality stems from concern for the necessary proprieties in Exeter, violation of which would cost her job. The scene ends with a reassertion of Exeter's influence. As Felix leaves, across the hall, door open, sits a family listening to a radio church service; what Felix notices is a pair of "narrow close-set eyes that glinted spitefully . . ." (125). He flees.

The final two "Sunday" chapters, occasioned by the death of Leslie's mother that same evening, drive Felix into still more open and righteous revolt. The ugliness of Miriam's response to the death, in her fear of scandal, shows Felix quite clearly that in Exeter social appearances are more important than human decency. Almost frightened, Felix realizes, too, that Leslie's support of his resistance to Miriam is all that stands between him and defeat in the advertising scheme at the hands of Miriam, Maxton, and Exeter.

II   *"The Outcast's Kiss Upon the Hand of Sweet, Naked Truth"*

At the midpoint of the novel, Felix has withstood an ultimatum. But though he still sees his relationship with Leslie as innocent in Chapter 13, his relationships with Miriam, Exeter, and his artistic compromise are radically changed.

In Maxton's sterile office of phony antique plushness the next afternoon, Felix has a glimpse of why Exeter in all of its vulgarity has conquered him rather than he it. Thinking of Leslie's resignation and her explanation that Miriam's conduct at the funeral was designed to force her to go, he notices the view of Exeter in the late afternoon light:

Beyond the window which framed Miriam's silhouette the light was changing. A moment ago the bright square had showed a foreground of treetops, with here and there a gable or a spire, the whole dominated, almost crushed, by a vast blue hemisphere of sky. Now the values had shifted. The late sun, already below the range of distant hills, had plunged the foreground into shadow and was drenching the upper air with yellow light. From a fold in the rolling country where the factories lay, a dark smudge commenced to take form, drawing itself out in a thin line of deep violet, then flowing downward to mingle with the shadows, and blurring the horizon until sky and earth seemed to melt into each other.

Moved irresistibly by the sudden and unexpected revelation of beauty, Hollister rose and walked to the window, and stood there with his back to the others, his head bowed, and his hands in his pockets, looking out into the gathering twilight. Now seen from his lofty perch, the sky had become a vast hollow sphere with night rising like a slow tide to fill it. And he saw Exeter far below him, looking small and lonely, flinging out her first lights against the encroaching darkness.

An emotion somber yet exquisite invaded him, a sort of nostalgia for a home that might have been his yet which somehow he had missed. Exeter, even this strident new Exeter, was beautiful, and he had never guessed it. But it should be painted like this, lying subdued and quiescent beneath an immeasurable sky. (156–57)

The image of Miriam is superimposed upon the town, which, in turn, is disappearing into darkness and industrial smoke. Its beauty, Felix realizes, he has failed to see, trapped within its harsh nearness. He needs perspective. The scene prefigures his situation and foreshadows his flight. The bargainers, however, see only something to be exploited—for cheap, commercial ends. He is, he feels, trapped, possessed; that other Exeter appears beyond his reach.

Felix slips away from Miriam's birthday party to hear Leslie challenge him to come out of hiding. Hearing Pendleton's voice the next morning, Felix comes downstairs prepared to vanquish Miriam and the doctor, only to learn that someone—it was Enfield—had run down Leslie the night before. Pendleton and Miriam have already established an alibi for Felix, manipulating the law, witnesses, and the mass media. Despite his shock, Felix sees that they are an irresponsible, materialistic, cowardly, vicious, destructive pack, prepared to abuse their power in any way to protect their respectability. In these same hours, Felix moves from his dependence on Leslie and, again, momentarily, on Miriam to a newfound strength to go it alone, a legacy of his evening with Leslie.

Enfield has killed Leslie in confusing her with a vision of his first love: another refusal to grow up. Discovering Leslie's letter in his car—evidence that her death was not suicide as Felix has been told, he decides not to incriminate himself as he drives into the chill autumn night. His one difference from his old classmates is that he has a bad conscience.

Exeter's essential immorality is exposed in the cover-up, but it is more pervasive than one hit-run accident, as Miriam's education of Pendleton about her marriage reveals:

"What you call living together as man and wife hasn't much to do with it. At any rate not after the first twenty years. It's learning to pull together. It's an all-round partnership, children, the home, business. You don't junk a corpo-

ration just because there is a breakdown in one department—do you? No, of
course you don't. You patch it up and you keep on doing business. Well, if a
woman's wise, she does the same thing with her marriage. . . . Felix has a
certain gift—so have I. We supplement each other. We're a going concern
with a future." (232–33)

Ironically, this speech on the coldness and calculation that are her substitutes for love prefaces Felix's decision to leave.

In contrast, before hearing the news of Leslie's death, Felix has
waked to a new world, alive to the autumn's colors, sounds, and odors,
thinking of his work, Leslie, becoming himself. With the news, he feels
frozen, so insensitive his cigarette burns his palm. But he has learned
his lesson and fights back the despair that thought of Leslie's suicide
prompts.

Fittingly, the cigarette advertising vulgarization of his art becomes
a double victory, first for Miriam whose triumph provokes his
imagination:

And from them [the presses] in an irresistible gush, signed Hollisters, pouring
wave after wave across the continent. Pulps and slicks stacked on street cor-
ners. A bulbous girl in a bathing suit—a Hollister, a smut weekly—a Hollister, a pink screamer—a Hollister—He saw them caught up from the stands,
as though by a great wind, and sent whirling away to settle upon the face of
the land. . . . He saw the submissive public, fed on him, gorged on him, sick-
ening on him unto death, yet having him pumped into it until one year, two
years, from now, nauseated beyond endurance, it would rise and vomit him
forth into oblivion. (248–49)

Second, the vulgar deal is, for Felix a means to escape. It will provide
him an annuity that will make him independent.

But there is yet one major hurdle—his old inability to stand alone.
On the title page of the novel Heyward has quoted a passage from
Sidney Lanier's *Poem Outlines:*

A man does not reach any stature of manhood until like Moses he kills an
Egyptian (i.e. murders some oppresive prejudice of the all-crushing Tyrant
Society or Custom or Orthodoxy) and flies into the desert of his own soul
. . . and begins to look with his own eyes, and first knows unspeakable joy of
the outcast's kiss upon the hand of sweet, naked Truth.

The Egyptian that Hollister has had to slay is Exeter's oppressive hold
on him.

In New York City, Felix realizes what art requires: "If you could stand alone, fight through and win, you were free" (259). Good work, he sees now, is done by "'a man who has given himself to life and let it eat him. A man who has explored the exquisite and illimitable resources of pain, and who has known joy . . . as a sudden release from despair, when the thing that he has striven for breaks into life under his hands—'" (268–69). Now, he says, "'I have to take sorrow, and despair, and loneliness'" (269).

Once the reader gets past Felix's initial compromise and the first stages of his renewal, the developing tension between one creative citizen and the sterile society to which he is wedded moves relentlessly to the break with Exeter and Felix's recognition of his lonely role. Thus, as a single action, *Lost Morning* succeeds where *Peter Ashley* fails. And with a protagonist who is increasingly conscious that the changed Exeter is his major antagonist, it stands as Heyward's major assault upon the new southern plutocracy as well as his most concentrated treatment of the conflict between the individual seeking life and his society.

Felix's mistake may seem to be his marriage to Miriam in the first place. But in the end she is only a representative of all that is puritanical, materialistic, false, corrupt, and dead about Exeter—Miriam, Pendleton, Maxton, Enfield, and the bourgeois Felix himself. He realizes that men cannot live by bread—or lies—alone; certainly the artist cannot. He needs heart, and the sculpture of Maternity and the lustful Sunday oil are not merely a celibate's erotic expressions. They speak of life and love, of inner experience. But there is no love in Miriam or in Exeter; there is no appreciation of art because there is no inner life. Exeter is, at best, a society of manners, but not the "good form" of *Peter Ashley*. They are the appearances by which the power structure guards against criticism while pretending to embody the highest values.

When Enfield leaves Exeter, he looks back: "There, over a fold in the hills, a smoke pall hung suspended, marking the metropolis of Exeter" (214–15). Felix is not there to see it; he has to discover it himself, alone: that all of Exeter is under the pall—and that the artist needs light, pure light. Felix cannot make a crutch of Exeter or hide in its smoke, nor can he make a crutch of Leslie or Felicia. His first promising work was done alone, and he must again work out of himself, even if he has lost his morning.

III   *Developing Craft*

Generally, the two stock conflicts—the love triangle and the artist at odds with society—are woven together effectively here, and the result is an interesting story. The thematic conflict is realized, and Heyward is also more effective than before in both the handling of action and the development of character. The novel develops scenically, and what is said and thought and done, in Hollister's studio or with Enfield on the highway, shows Heyward's characters changing as they act and react. The narrative is minute, approaching drama or becoming drama. For once, Heyward's characters talk. And even minor figures such as the obnoxious Pendleton and the pathetic coroner are etched clearly through their brief but close scrutiny. Listen to the coroner on the absence of a suicide note: "'Bodies can make a lot of truth,' he concluded sadly, 'by not exercisin' a little forethought'" (230). Certainly, the narrator is more self-effacing than in any of Heyward's previous novels.

In his three Charleston novels, the names of a number of characters echo those of old Charleston families—Archdale, Ashley, Pinckney, Petigru, and Pringle. A few in every story are chosen for their suggestiveness: Crown, Gabriel, Hagar. But the names in *Lost Morning* are all richly, elaborately suggestive of the characters' roles and personalities, so that Heyward virtually outlines the story in the names. The Exeter (exit-or) etcher, Felix Hollister—Holly to his wife—is hollow, having sacrificed his imagination in order to etch his way to felix-ity or prosperity (*felix* also means happy). His wife, Miriam (= Mary = marry), whom he sees as his need at the dawn of his career, was formerly an Aubery (*aube* = dawn). Her family's prosperity had dawned with the first Piedmont Aubery. Among other associations, Leslie Morgan offers Felix a less-protected new life (less lee) or morning (the German *Morgen*). Jerry Enfield, a former broken-field runner, comes to the end of his adolescence when he loses his nerve. The "lost morning" is certainly the lost dawn of Hollister's life and art, but it also suggests the lost love (morning is later than dawn). Ironically, his second morning is indebted to the profits from the lost morning.

One weakness of the novel has already been noted, the dubious motivation for Hollister's sudden need for Miriam's security and for his twenty years of endurance and then sudden bristling at every vulgarism. Blair Rouse complains that the reader is not shown the wearing process of time.[2] But it is Hollister's staying power that we need to understand. He has instantly identified Leslie as a model for the

Winged Victory and a reincarnation of the "Young Diana" who modeled for him in Paris (178). And what of Leslie's love for a weak, self-pitying if somewhat talented man older than her mother? The sexual relationships are all unconvincing.

Also, contrivances and coincidences are too many and too obvious. Leslie's mother is virtually a stage prop. And Leslie's note landing in Enfield's car when she is hit overstrains credulity. Nor is such extraneous matter as the beauty of Leslie's mother and the weather reports functional. Heyward also does not escape here the old complaint of overwriting, as in Leslie's trite paean to the mailbox: "Into it had gone the dreams, ambitions, pitiful frustrations, of so many lives—and from it, like pebbles thrown into still water . . ." (184).

These failings are not of equal seriousness. Perhaps chief of them is that Hollister has inured himself to being the Exeter etcher for too long to go to pieces in self-pity or to rediscover the thirst for the grail quite so suddenly.

The most notable artistic flaw in *Lost Morning*, though, is the departure from Felix as center of consciousness in Chapters 19, 20, and 21. Except for a brief view of Felix through Leslie's eyes in the beginning of Chapter 1 and again at the outset of the seduction scene, the point of view has been consistently limited to a narrator who knows no more than Felix thinks, sees, remembers, or surmises. Now Heyward gives us Leslie's sentiments after Felix leaves at the end of Chapter 18; the narrator takes the disastrous spin with Enfield in the disproportionately long next chapter; then he eavesdrops on Miriam and Pendleton the following morning. The Enfield chapter is a good episode and the coroner scene adds an important dimension to the ugly display of Establishment power in the novel. But none of these scenes is completely assimilated because it is too late in the novel for a series of prolonged shifts in narrative voice that could all have been avoided.

IV   *A Credo for the Artist*

One of the many possible prototypes for Felix Hollister must be Heyward himself. This may explain his compassion and respect for Felix, who, after all, is really pretty much a self-pitying bore. Heyward, too, found himself selling the same goods over and over, even, as Felix, in more popular forms. And just as Hollister must escape Exeter and Miriam, so did Heyward need to escape the stultifying influence of Charleston society, an escape he never made. And so did

Alfred Hutty and other Charleston artists need to escape the economic bonds that diverted their talent from original expression to the repetition of quaint old scenes that would sell.

Hollister realizes finally, with Lanier, that art is born only out of the lonely suffering and pain of trying to give form to one's poetic intuitions. It is a significant credo for a southern artist at the beginning of the Southern Renascence. Too many southern writers between Lanier and Heyward, in Charleston as often as anywhere in Dixie, persisted in the view that art was an avocation or, as those under John Bennett's influence in Charleston, busied themselves capturing a popular audience. Unfortunately, for Hollister and Heyward, the discovery comes late, after a lost morning. Ironically, *Lost Morning* is perhaps more finished than any of Heyward's novels. Still, it is a mild and unoriginal statement.

Like Felix Hollister, after *Lost Morning* Heyward set sail in a new direction, to the Virgin Islands, scene of *Star Spangled Virgin*, his last novel. Like Felix's new start, it is a return to his first love, the primitive Negro world.

CHAPTER 10

The Universal Rhythm:
Star Spangled Virgin

I *St. Croix and Noodeal*

IN *Lost Morning* Heyward returns to a theme that appears variously in each of his first three longer works of fiction: those who remain in harmony with the rhythms of nature in the corrupted atmosphere of civilization and progress are purer, wiser, and happier—and to be envied. In *Star Spangled Virgin*, published in 1939, this theme receives one of its strongest, yet least obtrusive, expressions.

When Heyward discovered the natives of St. Croix in the Virgin Islands on a yachting voyage with Huntington Hartford for the National Geographic Society, which resulted in a survey of the three larger islands in the September 1940 issue of *National Geographic*, he found a ready-made story of a more general black victory over the evils accompanying white change. For the best in the strongly traditional Crucians had survived Prohibition, the Depression, and "Noodeal."

Fittingly, *Star Spangled Virgin* is an idyll, a comic conquest of time, fate, human weakness, and the remote but benevolent god of social welfare, Noodeal, which is personified and identified with President Roosevelt. But for its historical origins, the story would border on fantasy. The ultimate victory may belong to progress, but for the moment Rhoda and the St. Croix natives have asserted their identity, have been reunited with the land, and Noodeal has faded into the background.

The story is simple and, like *Porgy* and *Angel*, hardly novel-length, consisting of no more than 44,000 words. Adam Work suddenly returns with his son to St. Croix after living on Tortola for five years with a church-wed wife, Victoria, who bore him Ramsey MacDonald and two daughters. He has some difficulty regaining the favor of his earthy former common-law wife, Rhoda Berg, who is mother of his two nearly

153

grown daughters, Crystal and Treasure, and now of two sons who are
not his, Hoover and Patrick. The period of his effort to recapture
Rhoda parallels and is interwoven with the period of Prohibition,
which means in the Virgins no rum production, extreme depression,
and various American relief efforts.

Adam succeeds only after Rhoda has successfully challenged the
new-fangled insistence that couples living together marry. Such a shift
would have endangered the traditional matriarchy that had only
shortly before been reinforced by U.S. Navy–government insistence
upon paternal child-support, whoever be the incumbent man of the
house. Almost simultaneous with this victory, the generosity of Noodeal, the dole, ends with repeal of Prohibition. Their older daughter
lost to the States and its exported corruption, the younger marrying a
solid homesteader and faced with the challenge of self-support, Rhoda
finally accepts Adam again, and they become homesteaders, too, opti-
mistic about a future in harmony with the past and secure on their
own land.

What Heyward is doing in *Star Spangled Virgin* is quite clear. The
call of Rhoda "with the tang of earth and hard labor upon her" and
the call of the soil of St. Croix finally lure Adam home.[1] He senses it in
the face of nature:

Far overhead the roofless tower framed a circle of stars—nearer and
warmer, Adam thought, than those he had watched on Tortola while Victoria
had identified them conscientiously in her Guide to Astronomy. Through the
wide empty windows a breeze—soft, earthy, and singularly lulling—came
and went rhythmically, as though the island were breathing in its sleep. (20)

But Adam Work, the natural man destined to sweat for his bread—
but who complains of never sweating on Tortola—quickly learns that
he can't go home again. Poor rainfall, a hurricane, the Depression, and
the dire effect of Prohibition on the sugar-cane market have changed
everything, destroying the orderly natural cycle of life:

"Dat was a good life we had," he said simply.
She answered, looking out to sea, and with a great hunger in her voice, "In
dem days dere was always something it was time to do; time to break land,
time to set new canes, time to cut de full crop, to tie de canes, to hoist de
bundle to yo' head an' feel de good weight press down on you till yo' feet
bog in de wet places." She raised her head and her voice took on color. "Den
you use to step out proud an' handsome 'cause you know what you's totin' is

a man's load an' dere's money in it for you an yo' young." She paused, and when she spoke again the longing in her voice had given place to bitterness. "But now dere ain't nuthin' but time, and nuthin' to do with it. De ole folks sits down in it an' rots, an' de young ones uses it to get into trouble." (51–52)

So what appears to be the story of Adam's return to Eden becomes a chronicle of St. Croix's unhappy experiences with the white man's art, institutions, and dole. The narrator withdraws, in this large middle, from Rhoda and Adam to a third-person external view. Only in the last three pages of the novel does the focus again become Adam's view. Between, history becomes plot, and because that history, a little rearranged for Heyward's purposes, provides a neatly developing conflict between native Crucian life and the threat to that life of change, history rather than Adam's pursuit of Rhoda's favor carries the action forward toward the happy end.

The second section focuses on the fumbling arrival of government bureaucracy and the relief it brings. Adam earns five dollars by miraculously changing five bulls into five saddle horses and avoiding yards of red tape. The agent who comes to register Adam, Rhoda, and the children for the dole is thoroughly confused by the matriarchal arrangement of Rhoda's household. The last mango gone, the visit of the white-clad Noodeal, presumably Roosevelt himself, prompts Adam and any other reticent natives to accept the new Eden.

The full significance of these changes and the characters' roles is not clear, even in Part III, where the natives respond slowly to the basic demands of citizenry, Oliver begins his marriage campaign, Crystal is attracted to the local opera production, and Rhoda notices the uneasiness of those living in the clean, new, concrete block cottages.

But in Part IV the shape of the new order and its effects are finally seen, first in the *H.M.S. Pinafore* production:

The full moon cleared Mount Welcome.
A royal palm caught it, cut a black stencil into its heart, then released it to ride magnificently up the eastern heavens. Its light flooded down and stippled the bay with cold white fire, patterned the square in sharp whites and blacks, and streamed across the deck of H.M.S. *Pinafore,* making it suddenly incongruous and false, its glaring incandescence cheap and tawdry. (131)

Adam and Rhoda had been proud of Crystal's half-cultivated, half-dialect song and half-disciplined, half-African movements on the stage, but her departure for New York with Sullivan a week later reveals how vulnerable the country-bred Crystal is to the lures of the new ways.

By Part V the corruption is advanced. Supplication Day, formerly dedicated to prayer for safety in the hurricane season, is scoffed at by young street dancers who place their faith in Noodeal. Oliver now introduces the discomfort of alien social and moral class distinctions with his plans for a parade of the married elect. The full negative effects of Noodeal are not seen, however, until after Rhoda has scored a major victory for tradition by turning Oliver's parade back with such ridicule that he flees the island. Peace reestablished, first Adam and then Rhoda slips into the drunken stupor of the coconut wine. While bureaucratic and somewhat misguided relief efforts have fed the former cane workers, they have at the same time threatened Crucian institutions and corrupted the Crucians.

In no instances is it the direct pressure of the white bureaucracy to change Crucian life that is really at fault, however, inept though some of the Americanizing efforts are. But the indirect pressures, beginning with Prohibition itself, do serious damage. The dole inevitably leads to idleness. And the presence of white customs prompts imitation. The Americans have no design to create a native middle class or a native social register, but it begins to happen.

The history plot even provides Heyward with a neat polemical resolution for this dilemma. With the end of Prohibition comes the end of the dole and a new approach which is one part wise government assistance—the homestead program directed by Tom Lyndall, the rest an engagement of the native virtues of industry and love of the land. The Crucians' old way of life is now changed only in that they will own their own land and have the use of tractors. The welfare state is bad; freedom through private ownership of one's livelihood on the land is good. Clearly, the center of the novel is an encounter between the Crucians and the new American influence.

Curiously, race relations are not an important factor in the encounter, although the old relationships were distinctly paternal so that at the end Rhoda fears that Mr. Lyndall will embrace her when she asks if she can sleep that night on her own land:

She hoped he wouldn't, because she knew he would be sorry afterward, and God knew she wouldn't know what to say or do: but he didn't do anything. He just sat and looked at her for a long time with a little water in his eyes. Then she felt it slackening off; and presently he said in a voice that shook a little, "Sure, you can spend the night here if you want to. It's going to be clear." (225)

There is no apparent racial injustice; what is notable is the seeming unconsciousness of race on the part of almost everyone, perhaps because the white population then was only about 6 percent and a fourth of the population was of mixed ancestry. Six years before Heyward's novel appeared, Claude McKay's *Banana Bottom* suggested that the cultures do clash in the Indies. But the absence of racial tension here is a great convenience to Heyward's comic approach to the situation. For once he had escaped that nemesis: the suffering and inequality for which the white man was responsible.

II   *The Rhythms of Nature*

The countervailing forces throughout *Star Spangled Virgin* are the earth and the rhythm of its people. Living on Tortola, Adam had become a sailor. But St. Croix, the most arable of the Virgins, lures him back. The sun that "hung poised for its dive into the Atlantic" tells Adam to be patient (96). The birdlike girl who conveniently appears to satisfy his lust is first noticed because she sings "an old St. Croix song that went far back into his memory" (99).

Adam and Rhoda experience life in terms of nature, and Rhoda has faith in the ways of nature: " 'You can't hold runnin' water back with yo' naked hand. You got to let it keep on runnin' till it finds a place to settle, then it will rest still' " (116).

Nature again plays a role in Rhoda's campaign to mobilize the island's unmarried mothers. Oliver would capitalize on the white custom of marriage between parents to establish a snob class, and Rhoda is determined to thwart and humble him. But the trade winds have failed to bring their usual coolness, which proves a particular challenge to Rhoda:

In the thickets and cane fields a lush whispering gave place to an intermittent metallic rustling. Frogs were silent, and cicadas drilled monotonously through the heat. Travel on the paved highways was not bad, but on the side roads the dust was appalling, and it took a stout heart to negotiate them afoot during the torrid hours of midday. (148–49)

But the night before the showdown with Oliver, when Rhoda has done her work well despite the dust, a thunder squall "swept the island with a rush of cold, revivifying cleanness" (154). The morning brings the light mood her plot requires. And then, at its critical moment, when Rhoda's boisterous forces have driven Oliver into full retreat from the bandshell to the banquet hall, Rhoda uses nature again, distracting the guard, Adolphus, by rubbing her breasts against him until she can unlatch the hall door.

Nature can also play a villainous role, as it does in providing the cheap coconut wine that fills the leisure hours while the dole is in effect. Nature smiles on him who works in harmony with her to foster life; it frowns on those who step outside the work-harvest rhythm.

Heyward is also quite attentive to the rhythmic harmony of the Crucians with nature and their past. Adam "in action became instantly a harmonious whole, at one with the sea or the land" (18). The "syncopated rhythm of African speech" and Crystal's "untamed grace" show through in the opera (122, 124). Rhoda notices the natural rhythms of the women along the road, carrying the heavy loads on their heads. The cacophony of color of Rhoda's following, wearing their traditional dress, harmonizes with the scarlet flamboyant tree, yellow jasmine, and crimson poinsettias of the landscape. The close proximity of the two references suggests that the "raucous rhythm" of the scratchy band is but an amplification of the shrilling cicadas.

But in *Star Spangled Virgin* Heyward is not, as narrator, so self-conscious about the black man's special rhythm. It is an integral part of a set of defining cultural characteristics—the work relationship to the land, harmony with nature, the familial order. It is one part of the black St. Croix life-style.

Notably, it is from the land and its tradition that the leader of the resistance to alien change comes. The savior is Rhoda Berg, the cane-worker mother, a rose of the earth, a mountain of strength, who insists upon all relationships growing organically out of an inner harmony. Her parade places an emphasis upon nature and tradition, scorning the artificial and alien.

The final victory for Adam and Rhoda does not come until all is ripe for it. Adam has earned Rhoda's forgiveness for his flight to Tortola. Rhoda has secured her equality. Now both are humbled by the drugging wine. She sees her need for him; he recognizes the futility of his idleness, and both see clearly again their relationship in the family. Homesteading at Adventure is the panacea that gives them a future.

(In his *National Geographic* article, Heyward notes the poetry of the names of St. Croix estates: "All-for-the-Better, Contentment, Wheel of Fortune, Catherine's Rest, Work and Rest, Betsy's Jewel, Lower Love, Upper Love, Jealousy, Prosperity Garden."[2]) Conveniently, young Woolsey's appearance as Treasure's lover and his news of a new order consistent with Crucian tradition—marriage and homesteading—serve to dispel Rhoda's fears.

The final scene brings to a culmination all of the conflicts and motifs of the novel. The Crucians' economic dilemma is resolved in a dignified way. And, clearly in charge, Rhoda prepares for a ritual of reunion with Adam and the land—white dress, headkerchief, quilt, package of food. Rhoda and Adam, man and earth mother, come together under the open sky, their rhythm joining that of the land. She sighs in happiness. "'It's time for you an' me to rest still,'" she says (230):

> He felt the old irresistible pull and sweep of her in the dark beside him. It communicated itself to the earth upon which he lay, and set it rocking. It poured into his body, and for a moment he choked with the beat of it in his throat. Then the separate elements yielded themselves to the march of a universal rhythm, and he could not have said which was the woman, which the man, and which the earth that bore their weight upon its sustaining hand. (230)

It is a simple melodramatic scene but an effective dream-fulfillment—for Adam, Rhoda, and DuBose Heyward.

III   *Memorializing the Old and Young*

Unfortunately, the historical chronicle overwhelms the story of Rhoda and Adam's reunion—until the last few pages. Adam is caught in the web of the economic forces which he finds on return to St. Croix. He needs to be more an agent than a bystander as the movement of these forces is seen, and yet his role is inevitably a passive one. Still, had Heyward known the Crucians more intimately, he might at least have seen the changes through Adam and Rhoda's consciousness a greater part of the time.

An explanation for Adam's abandonment of Rhoda for Tortola is never given. Since Victoria is clearly a symbol of late nineteenth-century white English culture, why should Adam have chosen her and her staid ways? All we have is Adam's vow to Ramsey that he is through

with women: "'We is goin' to live we own life, free an' natchell
...'" (8). He notices the tibet trees or "Women's Tongues" that have
taken over the ruin and are, like women, never quiet. Yet, in the next
breath he is carefully rationalizing his guilt so he can justify Rhoda's
accepting him again. He more or less forcibly takes the birdlike girl,
and then he waits long for Rhoda's favor, which comes on her terms.
But the feminist-freedom theme is not fully developed, as is the free-
dom-in-work argument that prevails in the end.

Heyward encounters something of a problem in handling Rhoda,
too. In the early pages, she is a simple mother of a mixed brood, stubbornly resisting her errant lover. Suddenly she blooms into a Joan of
Arc, shrewd and full of wiles. But the earth mother's matriarchal pre-
rogatives had not been challenged until Oliver plans his parade; when
they are, she must pick up the gauntlet one of her "ex-husbands" has
laid down.

Heyward's foreword confesses the difficulty he had with the Crucian
dialect, which emerges as "Standard Southern Negro," by pointing out
that he could not transcribe the "sophisticated tonal quality, the syncopated rhythms, the fantastically misplaced accents" which constitute
the Crucian speech.

But the central critical question about the novel remains Heyward's
divided intention. For again he has sacrificed his characters and their
story to memorialize a time and place. The page given to the legend
that as a boy Alexander Hamilton once managed Adventure, quite
irrelevant to anything in the novel, is a glaring if not representative
example of how this local color, travelogue intention possesses Heyward, at whatever cost to his narrative structure. It is as if in culling
the *National Geographic* article notes for details of Crucian life that
would be useful to the novel—the "obeah" conjure, Martinique headkerchief, scratchy band, gait of women with skirts tucked high—he
inadvertently clipped the Hamilton passage and did not consider that
he might omit it. For what he includes in *Star Spangled Virgin* of the
magazine account of St. Croix is largely the local color, seldom the
historical.

But the explanation for Heyward's divided intention is not that simple. Despite its economic and social focus, Heyward's narrative moves
forward with notable succinctness. While Adam and Rhoda are subordinate to the social movement, that movement is seen largely in

terms of their involvement in it, and several scenes are well realized. Yet only Rhoda's march is an integral part of the history plot.

The effectiveness of the march scene, with its concentration of detail and local color, is a unique achievement in the novel. Rhoda's group, as she observes, "'ain't goin' to be nothin' today but St. Croix'" (156). "'Us ain't married and we is proud of it,'" the sign of Rhoda's forces reads (161). Oliver's concession speech is from the deck of a departing boat: "Noodeal had need of his services in a broader field" (178).

The feminist is in clear command during Rhoda's campaign. But afterwards, victorious over a new marriage order that would rob the mother of her power to guarantee child support, now Rhoda "was a woman of her word" (177). That word is, in effect, to sacrifice her power, to be taken. So, ironically, her word takes her to the dull-eyed, weak-mouthed male, Adolphus. The next day, he "trod the earth like a god," and, returning home, slapped his wife's false teeth out and kicked them under the bed (177). So much for the feminist victory.

Too many other scenes, however, are dramatically weak or hardly dramatic at all.

Generally the style of the novel is no radical departure from the somewhat heavy-handed narrator's command of the situation found in most of Heyward's novels. But the narrator's voice is less noticeable in the handling of the history plot and less obtrusive throughout than in most of his fiction. Heyward's cosmic pretensions seem to have disappeared, or they become functional, as the night Rhoda joins Adam in a coconut-wine sleep and Treasure slips out of the cabin to become a woman, another generation in the cycle of life:

Overhead the constellations wheeled in slow procession, pulling at length over the eastern hills the half-empty shell of the last full moon. Down at Rhoda's cabin the door opened cautiously and Treasure came out under the night sky. She was wearing a white nightgown. . . . (188)

The almost but not quite successfully ironic overwriting is still in evidence, as in the coming of Noodeal:

Now the western sun striking athwart the minute suspended particles converted the public highway into a veritable Glory Road, and down the dazzling perspective, like Elijah in his chariot of fire, came an incandescent presence surrounded by a shining white company. (74)

The narrator's attitude does occasion one question about Heyward's intentions, the narrator being the vehicle for a good-humored but nonetheless condescending attitude toward the primitive natural order of things on St. Croix: they are children, if wise and enviable.

IV   *Another Gershwin Opera*

From the outset Heyward probably saw *Star Spangled Virgin* as material for a second Heyward-Gershwin opera. A month before Heyward's 1937 trip to the Virgin Islands, Gershwin's letter proposing a serious musical came.[3] According to Frank Durham, they also discussed the West Indies as a setting.[4] Mrs. Heyward explained that after considering that the work should go the novel, play, opera route, they soon agreed to proceed with an opera.[5] Gershwin's death ended this plan. Heyward then considered doing the musical with Arthur Schwartz, casting Ethel Waters as Rhoda and building the musical around the character of Rhoda as he had the *Mamba's Daughters* play around Hagar.[6] The musical possibilities are present in the novel, particularly in the music, color, and motion of the clash between Oliver's and Rhoda's forces, the H.M.S. *Pinafore* and Supplication Day scenes, and the domestic scenes at Rhoda's, where the guitar and song are common sounds.

But it would be misleading to find fictional inadequacy in *Star Spangled Virgin*'s operatic potentialities. The novel's faults are not here but in that intention which places something else above what Henry James calls "felt life." Still, the lightness of the novel makes it appealing, and Rhoda and Adam do achieve a primitive resolution of Heyward's favorite themes. For once progress is subverted to human purposes. So in the end there is life on the land, in the present and future, for a Negro couple capable of aspiring to and gaining the past.

CHAPTER 11

The Vision and the Achievement

I A Transitional Figure of Importance

WHEN DuBose Heyward began to write in earnest, at the end of the First World War, the recognized contemporary Southern writers were long-lived nineteenth-century figures, Mark Twain, George Washington Cable, and Joel Chandler Harris, and two of these were émigrés to the North. By 1925, all of these, as well as Thomas Nelson Page, Mary Noailles Murfree, and James Lane Allen, had gone to the grave. Glasgow and the more recently published James Branch Cabell appeared almost as sports in Mr. Mencken's Sahara; he could account for them in his notorious article only by ignoring them. No middle class had developed in the hard times of Reconstruction to produce writers, and the southern mind still labored under its fealty to ideas irreconcilable with its classical-Christian heritage.[1]

Yet, a dozen years after the Great War, the Southern Renaissance was in full progress; Heyward had been off only a moment ahead of the pack. Since much of the Fugitives' best work, *The Time of Man*, and *Soldier's Pay* were published within a year of *Porgy*'s appearance, Heyward had certainly exercised no appreciable influence as a writer on this burst of new creative energy in the South. Rather, because he was a decade or more older than all in that group except Miss Roberts and because, unlike them, he was little aware, if aware at all, of new currents in thought and technique, Heyward should be viewed as a transitional figure between the propaganda and Old South myth-making of Page and the renascence that appeared in the late 1920s. To appreciate his place in that transition is largely to define his achievement as a writer.

Heyward's place and his achievement are modest, first because he was not the serious writer such contemporaries in the 1920s as Glasgow, Cabell, Ransom, Tate, Faulkner, and Roberts were. He was poorly educated. Unlike the midwesterners who gravitated to Chicago as journalists at the turn of the century or who, after World War I, went abroad and enlarged their experience, he remained largely unaffected by what lay beyond Broad Street until well after he became an established writer. Hervey Allen found that limiting, indeed: "Nobody outside the plank road gives a damn about what is thought in that strange little antipodes which thinks deity has congealed in it."[2]

Heyward wrote as if modern literature did not exist. We see no influence of the major figures whose work was appearing at about the time Heyward reached maturity. He probably read the more popular G. P. R. James, Walter Scott, Bulwer-Lytton, and Kipling. Timrod's mark on his poetry is evident, and the Harlem stage at least indirectly influenced the Heywards' plays and the libretto for *Porgy and Bess*. But Heyward seems to have had little interest in contemporary literature; Louis Rubin finds this true of the Charleston group in general.[3]

Certainly, as a fiction writer, he would not have understood what was meant by the claim of the modern novelist to discover the intellectual and moral implications of the subject through technique. Only the ironic fatalism in the narrative voice of *Peter Ashley*, so close to that of Pierre Chardon, suggests that Heyward could employ point of view as a technique to reveal the truth more fully. Rather, writing in the nineteenth-century tradition, with the omniscient narrator often front and center, too often ostentatiously, he came much closer to the decadent but popular fiction style of Joseph Hergesheimer, with its weak shifts in point of view, pretentious and decorative language, narrow and imprecise vocabulary, a high proportion of abstract and formal words, frequent adjective and adverb qualifiers, careless sentence structures, too condensed action, disconnected structure, and a tone out of character, literary, or condescending.[4] Add plot contrivances, sententious philosophy, irrelevancies, diffusion of focus, and a weakness for melodrama, and one has a fair catalog of the weaknesses of Heyward's fiction style.

As a dramatist, Heyward relies heavily on melodrama and local color, particularly crowd effects and music. Action is not sustained, nor does it lead to awareness. His poetry is too often fragmentary, ordinary, and sometimes unclear. His drama and fiction characters are often inadequately developed. And while he learns from his experience and mistakes, as evidenced by the handling of point of view in *Peter Ashley*, the developed conflict of *Lost Morning*, and the focusing of the *Mamba's Daughters* play on Hagar, these works are flawed, too.

Yet, Heyward connot be dismissed. In his fiction he was capable of honest observation and was saved by it. In historical perspective, he successfully carried local color farther in poetry than anyone else in his time, without succumbing to quaintness or mere folklore. The Negro folk life, song, and crowd scenes of the Heywards' two plays assisted in opening the American stage to black music, new materials, and greater realism. *Porgy and Bess* is the first great American folk opera. Moreover, Heyward's realistic and sympathetic handling of the Negro, particularly the Negro community, and his Charleston aristocrat's sober and realistic view of the changing southern scene in fiction provide important new perspectives in the Negro Renaissance of the 1920s and the Southern Renascence that followed.

II *Memorialist, Stoic, Realist—and Mencken Iconoclast*

Heyward's role in the Southern Renascence is a minor but special one. Ellen Glasgow argued that the South's greatest needs were "blood and irony," the one "because Southern culture had strained too far from its roots in the earth," the other because she thought irony "the safest antidote to sentimental decay."[5] Faulkner's Negroes, yeoman farmers, and tragic vision provided the blood, and Glasgow's ironic vision, as Hugh Holman observes, "lay bare the inner nature of the social order" of the South which was the subject of her novels of manners.[6] A Charlestonian, Heyward could not share the mythical vision of Faulkner's South; he belonged to that city's eighteenth-century conservative tradition to which the Civil War was not the Apocalypse; Charleston, after all, was "the city that care forgot." Heyward could see the evils of crass commercialism and feel some of Mencken's barbs hit home, but he did not, as Allen Tate, see the South as a peculiar battleground of Western values and the modern spirit. He could not distance himself enough from Charleston's decadent aristocracy to offer the ironic criticism of his world that Glasgow could of hers.

The voice frequently heard in *Peter Ashley* suggests that Heyward might have been an ironist. But there is as much sentimentality as irony in Heyward, and he is more often and better defined as a memorialist and as often as a realist.

Like Faulkner, Heyward sees from without and feels from within, but the ambiguous response in Heyward lacks the creative conflict; Heyward's perspective remains more discrete.[7] His feelings have more to do with manners than moral passion.

Heyward's role, then, is transitional, memorializing and criticizing, telling the truth—not all of it but enough to be called courageous for his time. He is less the Glasgow ironist, Faulkner moralist, or Stribling satirist than the mannered Charleston stoic who is largely resigned to the imperfections of the world in his gratitude for its blessings or to the hopelessness of affecting the future—but not quite always resigned. Heyward's special brew was a combination of this inborn aristocratic conservatism; the local colorist's nostalgia for the traditional, particularly the primitive qualities of the Negro; that eighteenth-century southern stoicism that hesitates to judge or strongly criticize; an honest recognition of the practical evils that follow from the doctrine of white supremacy; and a recognition of the change that was upon the region, whether it wanted such change or not, and of the inability of the aristocracy to meet such change effectively. It might be called social realism.

Central in Heyward's contribution to the Southern Renascence is his truth-telling, in the first years after it had become possible to "tell the actual truth about any phase of life in the South."[8] Latter-day readers will find Heyward's truth selective and pallid, and his style and point of view are sometimes a challenge to that truth. But "Gamesters All," *Porgy*, *Angel*, and *Mamba's Daughters* are not lacking in a certain investment of courage. At least enough of Catfish Row, the elemental mountaineers' struggle, and the phosphate mines is there to guess the whole truth. Then, in *Peter Ashley*, he dares tell the less than heroic truth about how some—at least one—of the gallant heroes of the Confederate army came to be there in the first place: against his better judgment. And in *Lost Morning* there is no mistaking the vulgar nouveau-riche decadence that has engulfed whole communities and the frustration of the artist caught in it. Still, by viewing the reality of Negro urban life in *Porgy* largely apart from the moral issues involved in white exploitation and social irresponsibility—and apart from the historical context of black experience, Heyward has his truth . . . without alienating a Southern audience. The same strategy carries over into *Mamba's Daughters* where Saint's class, ineffectual conventional Christianity, and a stoic acceptance of the status quo obscure the burning social questions raised by the difficulties Mamba and her daughters face. It is truth within limits: the reader does not encounter anywhere an adequate image of that oppressive and brutal conformity experienced throughout the South in the early twentieth century. *Brass Ankle* is the nearest approximation.

Yet, Heyward's work reflects the truth of his childhood experience of poverty, of his clerkship in a hardware store, of his waterfront observation, of his summers in the mountains, of the firsthand accounts he heard of what the Sumter prelude was really like, and of the new aristocracy he as surely met in the 1930s as a defeated Felix Hollister met it in Exeter.

Assessment of Heyward's criticism of his world—and appreciation of the origin of that criticism—is assisted by returning to Donald Davidson's question about why Heyward's studies of Negro life are "so palpably tinged with latter-day abolitionism." Davidson's concern was what he saw, in certain southern works, Heyward's included, to be "a dissociation of the artist from his environment, resulting in a literature of mingled protest and escape."[9] Davidson answers his own question about Heyward extremely well: "The Southern tradition in which these writers would share has been discredited and made artistically inaccessible; and the ideas, modes, attitudes that discredited it, largely not southern, have been current and could be used."[10]

And whose ideas discredited it? Ironically, where the Nashville academics could discount H. L. Mencken as a "vulgar rhetorician," DuBose Heyward, as this study has shown, repeatedly adopts a perspective consistent with Mencken's iconoclastic stance and his campaign to "free" the Southern mind.[11] *Angel* is a good example. Heyward sees little of value in the backwoods life of Thunder Cove; in ridiculing Thornley's revival as an emotional orgy, he fails to acknowledge anything genuine in Fundamentalist Protestantism; he scorns the mechanical and uniformly tawdry lives of the mill folk. And, like Mencken, he has nothing to put in place of what he scorns, save the indomitable spirits of Buck and Angel. Again, in *Mamba's Daughters*, Heyward sees the inadequacies of the life Charleston's whites inherit but offers only a healthy mercantile career as an inferior alternative— and escape for blacks. Nor are the religious values of Mamba and Hagar duly credited as motives until the play version. *Peter Ashley* probes the closed Southern mind—sympathetically but without mercy. Southern provincialism in Rivertown has no redeeming features, and in Exeter the modern secular world is fully realized and dominant; Hollister at his best is part of it, too, if hostile to the commercialism. As Davidson observes, Heyward's treatment of the South—the Negro, race relations, Puritanism, or whatever—serves to confirm Mencken's narrow view of the South as reflecting "bigotry, ignorance, hatred, superstition, every sort of blackness" as opposed to "sense."[12] Heyward appears to need Mencken to begin to see meanings in what he so well observes.

Whatever prompts Heyward's insight, when he is finished, the illusion of the white aristocracy's superiority is dispelled. But Heyward also goes beyond Mencken's concerns to recognize certain primitive Negro strengths and qualities, particularly rhythm, community spirit, and a *joie de vivre*, as well as such sad realities of black life as Hagar's pathetic self-hatred and the self-deprecation of Row inhabitants who see themselves as "just niggers." Also, the relentless inroads of modern industrialism and progress are reflected in the changing economics of the aristocracy, the aspirations of the urban Negroes, the invasion of the mountains, the incorporation of Rivertown, the modernization of the city ("Chant for an Old Town"), and the bourgeois respectability that rules Exeter. The truth of Heyward's vision is primarily social, for the struggles of his characters are chiefly with society or representatives of it.

III   *The Search for Life*

But the social reality is not all that Heyward sees. His main characters all seek identity, self-realization, and fulfillment, and their experiences—in large part painful encounters with the social reality of Heyward's changing South—both define the requisites for human life and reveal the narrow possibilities of its realization here.

Black, crippled, and alone, Porgy finds life in Catfish Row, and his mysterious sense of expectation finds fulfillment in his love for Bess. But that personal happiness is contingent upon reconciling the primitive and the rubrics of white society, and when that reconciliation fails, Porgy is left alone with his awareness that the juices of life no longer flow for him.

Angel must meet the challenges of her father's religious fanaticism and the mountains' harshness by escaping the one, surviving the other, and facing the challenge of the future in town with Buck.

In *Mamba's Daughters*, Lissa discovers herself only when she fully appreciates the sacrifices that have brought her to New York and reconciles her racial spirit and her art. Hagar, particularly in the play, finds self-realization in total sacrifice—first of her daughter and then of her life. Saint discovers in Lissa's success that his fate, the achievement of creature comforts within the Charleston aristocratic mold, is to have missed the more genuine fulfillment.

Ruth Leamer looks for life in the sounds of nature and her family, Larry in the doubtful progress of moonshine profits, segregation, and incorporation. For both race becomes the destructive absolute.

In *Peter Ashley*, Peter's youthful dreams give way to the realization that he would sacrifice anything for his past, his place, and his people—to his participation in the southern mind of his time.

In *Lost Morning*, Felix Hollister learns that business and art, compromise and integrity, are incompatible, that he must honor his experience of life in sculpture and that this experience of life is necessarily a lonely one.

In *Star Spangled Virgin*, Rhoda and Adam Work find bliss only when they are in harmony with the land.

Southern society and social institutions invariably fail Heyward's characters: noblesse oblige and the white man's law in *Porgy*, religion and married respectability in *Angel*, the unbridgeable gulf between the races and the bondage of the aristocracy's code in *Mamba's Daughters*, the racist religion of Rivertown, the magnetic power of placeways in *Peter Ashley*, and the cultural decadence of the new moneyed aristocracy of the South in *Lost Morning*. The homestead in *Star Spangled Virgin* may appear to be a Noodeal reality, but it follows the failure of Noodeal and comes via the grace of the Nineteenth Amendment, which permits a reunion with the past. It is, in truth, a wish that answers Heyward's yearning for a traditional life of primitive rhythm, sex, and harmony with the earth.

Southern society and white social institutions are the major enemies of life, chiefly in that they command conformity. The Charleston past, which is for Heyward an inescapable part of the present, more often than not is a dead hand that kills whatever it touches and denies the possibility of life. For Peter Ashley and Saint Wentworth—but also for Felix Hollister, Angel Thornley, and the Leamers—the demand for conformity frustrates the harmony with nature, community, love, spirit of sacrifice, and dedication Heyward's blacks know as life. Those few whites who refuse to conform—Buck, Angel, and Hollister—must abandon the past and their own people, which foreshadows a poorer success for them. Ruth Leamer contemplates flight, as do Hagar and the play Porgy. Lissa does flee, and Saint and Peter should.

Catfish Row, on the other hand, has made the necessary accommodations to the urban white world. And with common values and faith that weather death and defeat, it lives—uninhibited, a real community. Only here is there the freedom to pursue and realize a meaningful personal life. Perhaps Heyward's first poem, "Gambler's All," should be read in this context: the black gambler seeks freedom at any cost; the policeman who shoots him is actually enslaved by his racist role. The Ediwander blacks brook no interference with the harmony of their lives.

Unlike the major figures of the Southern Renascence who seek to recover the classical-Christian values of history, Heyward finds the meaning of life empirically, in observing the contemporary black community where man's tie to nature has not been broken, where dead social codes do not frustrate freedom, and where rhythm and religion, courage and community, give meaning to the struggle for survival and dignity in the white man's world.

The vision of life that emerges from the several searches of Heyward's characters lacks full definition. His whites are too passive about their fates, too easily compromised, or, in the Leamers' case, too uncomplicated and unintelligent for the struggle to be fully engaged. While his black characters have a sense of direction and values, in the pursuit of which they achieve identity and freedom, they are simple, elemental folk in pursuit of simple objectives—a woman, a career, a place on the land. Hagar's inner pain is seen, but she remains Heyward's simplest character.

This lack of moral engagement shows the limitations of Heyward's work more than anything else. But what we see of the pursuit of life in his work at least sketches a vision. Like Faulkner, he sees the paralyzing influence of a closed society and rigid caste system upon his characters. But his interest in his black characters is less in the conflict between the white social code and the individual, less in moral conflict, than in the individual's capacity to find life despite white supremacy and Noodeal. Life is found in harmony with the earth, in the bond of community suffering, in joy and its expression in song and dance which constitutes rhythm, and in integrity and love. All are achievable apart from white society. Heyward's whites seek life and expression in art, but they lack the depth of feeling, the rhythm, and, save Felix Hollister, Porgy's and Hagar's integrity of purpose.

All of Heyward's whites share a deep alienation from their world. Heyward's vision of life may be defined by envy both of the black rhythm of Charleston and, the crowning irony of his Charleston aristocrat's vision, of the black man's relative insularity from white society. The rhythms of Charleston are not only different; they are, Heyward sees, essentially antithetical.

In *A Certain Measure*, Ellen Glasgow observes that she was, in her "humble place and way, beginning a solitary revolt against the formal, the false, the affected, the sentimental, and the pretentious, in Southern writing," solitary because she "had no guide."[13] Heyward could have used her for a guide—or Balzac and Flaubert, who did guide her. John Bennett had other ideas, so Glasgow does not save Heyward from the occasionally affected and pretentious in style. But when Miss Glasgow goes on to say that her revolt came because "life had broken through these elegiac tones," she is striking the note of Heyward's fiction as well.[14] He, too, could recount what life had shown him. And certainly his fiction and plays facilitate the serious criticism of the South and modern man that was to follow in the Southern Renascence.

IV *"A Member of Harlem's Intellectual Colony"*

Heyward's contributions to the image of the black man in the Harlem Renaissance may be more precisely defined.

As Negro writers have been saying for years—and more recently, white scholars, too—the historical image of the Negro in American literature is largely one of distortion.[15] The Harlem Renaissance occurs against a background of demeaning stereotypes and exaggerated primitivism that deny the black man's dignity. These distortions and others—fancied primitivism, exoticism, and indulgence in varying forms—continue through the 1930s. But in the early 1920s southerners Heyward, T. S. Stribling, and Julia Peterkin, as well as Jean Toomer and others, begin to see the human qualities of the black man with a truth that changes that image significantly. Heyward's special place in this group is his portrayal of southern Negroes who are relatively contemporary, urban, involved in the white man's world—the Negroes white men encounter or expect to encounter, neither historically remote as Stribling's nor geographically remote as Peterkin's rural folk, seen through the double perspective of a paternalistic white Southern aristocrat and an honest observer who satisfies even Negro critics in his fidelity to the truth of what he observes. If Heyward's paternalism is sometimes condescending, so is it sympathetic and understanding. The reader does not escape with his complacency.

Moreover, in his close observation and awareness of the complexity of what he sees within the Negro community, Heyward corrects a host of stereotypes and rescues Negro primitive qualities from the distortions of the work of his contemporaries to reveal the elements that make the Negro more responsive to life and nature than his mannered white Charleston neighbors. Specifically, the rhythm Heyward sees is neither primitive exuberance, the echo of atavistic drums, nor both but the essential element in the cultural expression of a folk close to the earth and their God and joined in suffering and misery, joy and hope. Nathan Huggins tells us that in the Harlem Renaissance, "The Negro was in the process of telling himself and the world that he was worthy, had a rich culture, and could make contributions of value."[16] Heyward was showing the Negro—and the world.

Most important of all, he shows us Porgy and Hagar performing in the intimacy of a black world, an opportunity seldom given Faulkner's Negroes. Thus Heyward won an audience for fiction that treated the Negro seriously and sympathetically as a human being that no American writer since Twain and Joel Chandler Harris had reached.

One need not argue with Ralph Ellison's contention that the Negro playwrights and musical-comedy writers of the 1920s came closer to reality than *Porgy and Bess* or *Emperor Jones*.[17] One could even accept Ellison's view that *Porgy and Bess* is pretty much a "a negative contribution except as a vehicle for excellent singers and actors."[18] But such a judgment about *Porgy*, the novel, and *Mamba's Daughters* would be an unfortunate confusion of Heyward's fiction with the simplified opera story. Certainly Heyward's observation of the Negro is not flawless, but if it is seriously flawed he has fooled a lot of people who should know better. Shortly after the publication of *A Different Drummer*, I heard William Melvin Kelley, upon mention of *Porgy*, quote much of the concluding passage of the novel. Witness one university lecture program statement: "We have great pleasure in presenting this evening Mr. DuBose Heyward, who is not only a member of Harlem's intellectual colony, but who is also a Southern Negro of the old tradition."[19]

In the 1960s and after, a new surge of Negro primitivism as part of a new assertion of racial identity and aspiration occurred. Unfortunately, the same phony primitivism and claim of atavistic ties with the jungle gained ascendancy again, once more Vachel Lindsay's drums were heard, and the American Negro was seen searching for himself in African art, a tradition from which he has been separated for 300 years. Heyward served as an important moderating influence in response to the excesses of primitivism in the 1920s. Placed in an appropriate or "native" habitat in *Porgy* rather than the artificial night world of Harlem, primitivism was something more modest, subtle, and genuine than the white writers visiting Harlem fancied. By the time Heyward had defined it as "rhythm," it was something more positive and admirable.

Likewise, the strength, the determination, the faith that the nation recognized in the civil rights movement in the South in the 1960s Heyward had recognized in the Catfish Row community scenes and in the imposing wills of Mamba and Hagar and Lissa forty years before.

Heyward may have had nothing to say to the civil rights militants of the 1960s, but this somewhat stuffy southern gentleman of the old school could serve to call blacks to a recognition of what is genuinely positive, superior, and real in their American past. For the worn phrase of condescension, "They sho' got rhythm," takes on a different meaning in *Porgy*, "Half Pint Flask," and *Mamba's Daughters*. It serves as a criticism of the creeping paralysis afflicting white Charleston and as the crucial, primary term of praise for the Low Country Negroes.

Heyward's work may be, as Hervey Allen says of Heyward's most loved characters in his poem "DuBose Heyward of Charleston," written on the occasion of Heyward's death, "of simple lives whose mouths were dumb."[20] But Heyward appreciated, as James McBride Dabbs has, so eloquently, since, that there is human value in these dumb ones that should not be lost.[21] As an ardent Low Country memorialist, the loss of that primitive "rhythm" of life was surely his greatest fear.

V   *A Gentleman—But Not Hopelessly*

For DuBose Heyward, whom Emily Clark called "hopelessly a gentleman," respect for the manners and rituals of his society, for the beauty and charm of his locale, and for what was genuine and living in its people was certainly an essential part of the definition of a gentleman—at least of the voice heard in Heyward's poems and stories.[22]

While exploring the Charleston of Heyward's poetry, fiction, and plays, one could not help but notice that the current events of half a century later provide a curious commentary on that now dimming time and place Heyward knew and of which he wrote and on the tension he saw between the dying aristocracy and those struggling to live as they were affected by time and circumstance. One South Carolina U.S. Senator's public complaint of starvation and dire poverty in the Low Country clearly echoes our Charleston gentleman's noblesse oblige as a response to the callous Rivertown spew of the up-country Strom Thurmond. But Senator Hollings was, in those days, an excep-

tion. The racist mouthings of Thurmond shifted hardly a decibel when
state troopers massacred black students at Orangeburg. Almost daily,
the late U.S. Representative Mendel Rivers of Charleston was proving
himself a true heir of Secession Day and, by implication, his constitu-
ents showed themselves to be the most bellicose in the land. Again,
there were echoes of Heyward's phosphate mine in a television report
on worms in Beaufort Country Negro children, which gave a leading
county doctor occasion to call another doctor, who had not learned to
serve blacks discretely, "a liar" who was "trying to be a martyr."[23]
Meanwhile, a Charleston social lion became a lioness and announced
her engagement to her servant, a local Negro, "the first young man I'd
never been afraid of."[24]

Our Charleston gentleman Mr. Heyward would have difficulty with
the stupidity, stridency, vulgarity, inhumanity, and injustice evident in
several of these events and would have understood the last. As an honest observer of his world, which included the often dubious changes
taking place in all areas of southern life, he would not really be surprised. His memorialist stance looks as much to the future as to the
past. It is his anxiety about the future as well as the present, his painful
awareness of the difficulty of finding life in the modern South as he
saw it, that quickens his observations—and makes him more than a
local colorist.

Notes and References

Preface

1. "The Horrible South," *Virginia Quarterly Review* 11(April 1935): 209.
2. "A History of the Charleston Movement," in Marjorie Peale, M.A. thesis, Duke, 1941, Appendix B. p. 205.
3. *Three Modes of Modern Southern Fiction* (Athens: University of Georgia Press, 1966).
4. "The Regional Motive," Seminar: Southern American Literature, Modern Language Association, Denver, December 9, 1969.
5. "A Mirror for Artists," in Twelve Southerners, *I'll Take My Stand* (1930; rpt. New York: Harper, 1962), p. 59. And John Crowe Ransom, "Modern with the Southern Accent," *Virginia Quarterly Review* 2(April 1935): 186.
6. "The Novel in the South," *Harper's*, December 1928, p. 99.
7. Floyd C. Watkins, *The Death of Art: Black and White in the Recent Southern Novel* (Athens: University of Georgia Press, 1970).
8. Herschel Brickell, "Creator and Catfish Row," *New York Herald Tribune Books*, March 10, 1929.
9. Donald Davidson, "Critic's Almanac," *Nashville Tennessean*, February 3, 1929; Cullen, "Book Shelf," *Opportunity* 3(1935): 379.
10. "Writers: Black and White," in *The American Writer and His Roots*, ed. John O. Killens (New York: American Society of African Culture, 1960), p. 43.

Chapter One

1. Heyward's life has received extensive attention in Frank Durham's "DuBose Heyward: Southerner as Literary Artist," Diss., Columbia, 1953; *DuBose Heyward: The Man Who Wrote Porgy* (Columbia, S.C., 1954); and "The Rise of DuBose Heyward and the Rise and Fall of the Poetry Society of South Carolina," *Mississippi Quarterly* 19(1966): 66–78. Other biographical sources for the Chronology and this chapter include Headley Morris Cox, Jr., "The Charleston Poetic Renascence, 1920–1930," Diss., Pennsylvania, 1958; Marjorie Elizabeth Peale, "Charleston as a Literary Center, 1920–1933," M.A. thesis, Duke, 1941; Emily Clark, "DuBose Heyward," *Virginia Quarterly Review* 6(1930): 546–56; Eleanor P. Hart, "Weighing Her Merits," *Preservation Progress* 10(January 1965): 1–6, and "Lo! His Name Led All the Rest," *Preservation Progress* X(March 1965): 8–11; Josephine Pinckney, "DuBose Heyward (1885–1940)," in *Dictionary of American Biography* XXII, Supplement Two, ed. Robert Livingston Schuyler (New York: Scribner,

1958), pp. 302–303; DuBose Heyward Papers, John Bennett Papers, Yates Snowden Papers, Janie Screven Heyward Scrapbook; clipping files of the South Caroliniana Library of the University of South Carolina, South Carolina Historical Society, Charleston Library Society, and *Charleston News and Courier*; and interviews with Charles Mathew, Jeannie Heyward Haskell, Frank Durham, Laura Bragg, Kathleen Drayton Mayrant Simons, and Jenifer Heyward.

2. Interviews with Charles Mathew, Hendersonville, S.C., August 26, 1966, and Mrs. W. E. (Jeannie Heyward) Haskell, Charleston, September 1, 1966. Izard is an old Charleston name, as is the saying.

3. "The Sahara of the Bozart," in *A Mencken Chrestomathy* (New York: Knopf, 1929), pp. 184–85. In shorter form, the essay appeared in the *New York Evening Mail*, November 13, 1917; it was the longer version published in 1920 in *Prejudices: Second Series* that was noticed in the South.

4. "Editor's Note," *Poetry* 40 (May 1932): 92.

5. "Is There a Southern Renaissance?" *Virginia Quarterly Review* 6 (April 1930): 196–97.

6. *A Certain Measure* (New York: Harcourt, 1943), p. 8.

7. "Southern View-Point," *North American Review* 244 (Winter 1937–38): 390; also: *A Certain Measure* pp. 135–37.

8. "The New Provincialism," *On the Limits of Poetry: Selected Essays: 1928–1948* (New York: Swallow, 1948), p. 292.

9. Letter to Mrs. John (Susan Smythe) Bennett, April 4, 1921. Bennett Papers, South Carolina Historical Society, Charleston.

10. Clark, p. 556.

11. Letter to Nannie Creighton, September 9, 1931. Yates Snowden Papers, South Caroliniana Library, Columbia, S.C.

12. DuBose Heyward and Hervey Allen, *Carolina Chansons: Legends of the Low Country* (New York: Macmillan, 1922), from "Two Pages from the Book of the Sea Islands," p. 67.

13. Jessie B. Rittenhouse, *My House of Life: An Autobiography* (Boston and New York: Houghton Mifflin, 1934), pp. 241–42.

14. John Bennett to DuBose Heyward, August 19, 1923. Bennett Papers.

15. In *The Carolina Low-Country*, ed. Augustine T. Smythe et al. (New York: Macmillan, 1932), p. 184.

16. Herbert Marshall McLuhan, "The Southern Quality," in *A Southern Vanguard*, ed. Allen Tate (New York: Prentice-Hall, 1947), pp. 100–21; Donald Davidson, *Still Rebels, Still Yankees and Other Essays* (Baton Rouge: Louisiana State University Press, 1957); Allen Tate, "A Southern Mode of the Imagination," in *Studies in American Culture*, ed. Joseph A. Kwiat and Mary C. Turpie (Minneapolis: University of Minnesota Press, 1960), pp. 96–108; Robert Heilman, "The Southern Temper," in *South: Modern Southern Literature in Its Cultural Setting*, ed. Louis D. Rubin, Jr., and Robert D. Jacobs (Garden City, N.Y.: Doubleday, 1960), pp. 48–59; Cleanth Brooks, *A*

Shaping Joy (New York: Harcourt, 1971); Louis Rubin, Jr., *A Faraway Country* (Seattle: University of Washington Press, 1963); C. Hugh Holman, *Three Modes of Modern Southern Fiction.*

17. John Bennett to DuBose Heyward, November 10, 1918, and February 9, 1934. Bennett Papers.

18. DuBose Heyward to John Bennett, July 30, 1920. Bennett Papers. Also Durham, "DuBose Heyward: Southerner as Literary Artist," p. 113, and *DuBose Heyward*, p. 22; Cox, p. 16.

19. John Bennett to DuBose Heyward, August 22, 1921, and DuBose Heyward to John Bennett, November 28, 1924. Bennett Papers.

20. DuBose Heyward to Hervey Allen, Juyl [*sic*] 15, [1924], and [no date]. DuBose Heyward Papers, South Carolina Historical Society, Charleston.

21. Letter to John Bennett, August 7, 1920. Bennett Papers.

22. Letter to DuBose Heyward, August 23, 1920. Bennett Papers.

23. John Bennett, "Rotten Books and Rotten Plays," *Charleston News and Courier*, February 3, 1925.

24. Letter to Hervey Allen, Thursday [Summer], 1923. Heyward Papers. Heyward admired and championed Allen's verse.

25. Cox, p. 103.

26. Heyward, Allen, and Bennett, "Foreword," *Year Book of the Poetry Society of South Carolina for 1921* (Charleston, 1921), p. 5.

27. "Foreword," *Year Book of the Poetry Society of South Carolina for 1924* (Charleston, 1924), pp. 9–12. How clear the way was is illustrated by a later foreword, which still rejected William Carlos Williams and Gertrude Stein outright. See Josephine Pinckney et al., eds., *Year Book of the Poetry Society of South Carolina for 1927* (Charleston, 1927), pp. 6–7.

28. J. Bryan III, "Hervey Allen—A Copious Fellow," *New York Herald Tribune*, Books, January 26, 1933.

29. William Gilmore Simms, *Simms' Magazine*, May 11, 1945, cited from Jay Hubbell, *The South in American Literature, 1607–1900* (Durham, N.C.: Duke University Press, 1954), p. 578.

30. Durham, "DuBose Heyward: Southerner as Literary Artist," pp. 170–71, based upon an interview with Dorothy Heyward, and Chard Powers Smith, *Where the Light Falls: A Portrait of Edwin Arlington Robinson* (New York: Macmillan, 1965), p. 23.

31. DuBose Heyward, "The MacDowell Colony," *Southwest Review* 9 (January 1926): 165.

32. Conversation between Bennett and Frank Durham, cited in Frank Durham, "DuBose Heyward's 'Lost' Short Stories," *Short Fiction Studies* 2 (Winter 1965): 157.

33. DuBose Heyward, "The Brute," *Pagan* 3 (November 1918): 19–26. This quotation is cited in Durham, *DuBose Heyward*, p. 19.

34. "Beatrice Ravenel," in *Library of Southern Literature*, Supplement I,

ed. Edward Anderson Alderman and Charles Alphonso Smith (Atlanta: Martin and Hoyt Company, 1923), p. 474.

35. Frances Newman, "On the State of Literature in the Late Confederacy," *New York Herald Tribune*, Books, August 16, 1925.

36. "And Once Again—the Negro," *Reviewer* 4 (October 1923): cited from Clark, p. 551.

37. "Introduction," in Dorothy Heyward and DuBose Heyward, *Porgy: A Play in Four Acts*, Theatre Guild Acting Version (Garden City, N.Y.: Doubleday, 1927), pp. ix–xxi.

38. *Bookman* 61 (April 1925): 153.

39. *Woman's Home Companion* 55 (June 1928): clipping without title or pagination in Yates Snowden Papers. These committees were concerned with race tensions, lynching, and legal and welfare services. See also *Crisis* 31 (March 1926): 220.

40. Letter dated December 21, 1931.

41. Clark, p. 556.

42. Interview with Katharine Drayton Mayrant Simons, September 1, 1966.

43. Interview with Frank Durham, August 29, 1966.

44. Alfred Kreymbourg, *Our Singing Strength* (New York: Coward-McCann, 1929), p. 560.

45. [John Bennett et al., eds.?], *The Year Book of the Poetry Society of South Carolina for 1925* (Charleston, 1925), p. 9. Quoted from the *New York Evening World*.

46. Letter to Hervey Allen, n.d. Heyward Papers.

47. H. L. Mencken, "The South Astir," *Virginia Quarterly Review* 11 (January 1935): 58–59.

Chapter Two

1. *Poetry* 20 (April 1922): 47–48.

2. Laura Bragg's private library, Charleston, S.C.

3. Heyward, Allen, and Bennett, "Foreword," *Year Book of the Poetry Society of South Carolina for 1921*, p. 5. Concerning authorship, see Heyward letter to Bennett, May 14, 1921. Bennett Papers.

4. "Contemporary Southern Poetry: I/The Audience," *Bookman* 62 (January 1926): 563.

5. Durham, "DuBose Heyward: Southerner as Literary Artist," p. 57.

6. *Carolina Chansons*, p. 9.

7. Cox, p. 90.

8. Heyward and Allen, "Preface," *Carolina Chansons*, p. 10.

9. Stanhope Sams, *Columbia* [S.C.] *State*, January 29, 1925.

10. DuBose Heyward and Hervey Allen, "Poetry South," *Poetry* 20 (April 1922): 35.

11. Ibid., p. 36.
12. Ibid.
13. Ibid., p. 37.
14. Ibid.
15. Ibid., p. 46.
16. Ibid., p. 43.
17. Hervey Allen to Thomas R. Waring, June 13, 1923, and John Bennett to DuBose Heyward, June 13–14, 1923. Bennett Papers.
18. Durham, "DuBose Heyward: Southerner as Literary Artist," p. 88.
19. "This Southern Number," *Poetry* 20 (April 1922): 31–34.
20. *Fugitive* 2 (June-July 1923): 66. Later, Davidson hedges on this attack on Miss Monroe's "local color program," noting that the chauvinism of the western South presented dangers the "picturesque charm of the Charleston Low Country" did not. See "The Southern Poet and His Tradition," *Poetry* 40 (May 1932): 94–95.
21. *Fugitive* 2 (August-September 1923): 99.
22. "Certain Fallacies in Modern Poetry," *Fugitive* 3 (n.d.): 67.
23. "The Artist as Southerner," *Saturday Review of Literature* 2 (May 15, 1926): 782.
24. In discussing *Carolina Chansons* Edd Winfield Parks echoes Davidson: "What few men seemed to realize was that local color when employed with discretion made an excellent background to give added reality, but a thin and quick-fading foreground." "Introduction," *Southern Poets*, ed. Edd Winfield Parks (New York: American Book Company, 1936), p. lxxviii.
25. "The Southern Poet and His Tradition," p. 99.
26. Ibid.
27. *Virginia Quarterly Review* 2 (April 1935): 186.
28. Ibid., p. 188.
29. Ibid., p. 186.
30. "A Note on Three Southern Poets," *Poetry* 2 (May 1932): 108.
31. *The Spyglass: Views and Reviews, 1924–1930*, ed. John Tyree Fain (Nashville: Vanderbilt University Press, 1963), p. 31. The review, "An Author Divided Against Himself," was originally published in the *Nashville Tennessean*, February 3, 1929.
32. *Nashville Tennessean*, April 20, 1924.
33. Ibid.
34. *Virginia Quarterly Review* 2 (April 1935): 306.
35. Ibid., p. 308.
36. Ibid., pp. 309–12.
37. Ibid., p. 309.
38. Ibid., p. 310.
39. Ibid., p. 316.
40. Ibid., p. 317.
41. Ibid., p. 318. Brooks's criticism of Davidson's poetry may help explain

why Davidson was hardest on the Charlestonians: they are superficial because
they lack his mystique—exclusion at the other extreme.

42. Ibid.

43. *Southern Writers in the Modern World* (Athens: University of Georgia Press, 1958), p. 17.

44. Louis D. Rubin, Jr., "The Southern Muse," in *The Curious Death of
the Novel* (Baton Rouge: Louisiana State University Press, 1967), p. 215.
Originally in *American Quarterly* 13 (1961): 365–75.

45. Donald Davidson, "Two Ways of Poetry," *Fugitive* 4 (September
1925): 95. E. E. Cummings's *XLI Poems* is also considered.

46. Rubin, "The Southern Muse," p. 219.

47. Davidson, *Southern Writers in the Modern World*, pp. 11–13.

48. Cox, pp. 75–76.

49. Thomas Daniel Young, Floyd A. Watkins, and Richard Croom Beatty,
eds., *The Literature of the South*, rev. ed. (Glenview, Ill.: Scott Foresman,
1968).

50. *Columbia* [S.C.] *State*, December 17, 1921.

51. DuBose Heyward, *Skylines and Horizons* (New York: Macmillan,
1924).

52. Robert Frost to DuBose Heyward, January 22, 1921. Heyward Papers.

53. Durham criticizes the lapses into poetic diction. See "DuBose Heyward: Southerner as Literary Artist," p. 138.

54. Review of *Skylines and Horizons*, *Nashville Tennessean*, April 20,
1924.

55. "The Southern Muse," p. 215.

56. Stanley Rinehart to DuBose Heyward, August 3, 1931. Heyward
Papers.

57. "Jasbo Brown," *American Mercury* 6 (September 1925): 7–9; Audrey
Wood to DuBose Heyward, May 5, 1938, May 12, 1938, and March 22, 1939,
Heyward Papers; for *Porgy and Bess*, see Chapter 3, note 52.

58. Durham complains of the treatment of Jasbo being more forced than
that of South Carolina coastal blacks in Heyward's work. "DuBose Heyward:
Southerner as Literary Artist," pp. 151–52.

59. Parks, "Introduction," *Southern Poets*, p. cxxiii.

Chapter Three

1. "The Perennial Rooster," *Virginia Quarterly Review* 2 (January
1926): 153, 155.

2. "Orchestrated," *New York Herald Tribune Books*, October 18, 1925.

3. "The Reputed Demises of Uncle Tom: on the Treatment of the Negro
in Fiction by White Southern Authors in the 1920's," *Southern Literary
Journal* 2 (Spring 1970): 40–45.

4. DuBose Heyward, *Porgy* (New York, 1925), p. 148. Subsequent citations are for this edition.

5. Interview with Jeannie Heyward Haskell, September 1, 1966. Durham quotes the clipping from the *Charleston News and Courier,* without a date, in *DuBose Heyward,* p. 47.

6. "Introduction," *Porgy: A Play in Four Acts,* p. ix.

7. *Charleston News and Courier,* March 11, 1951; July 16, 1959; and November 3, 1961.

8. "Introduction on the American Negro in Art," p. xii. Hervey Allen has recounted his long discussions with Heyward "as the story grew": "It seemed to occur to him in a series of scenes, and we did talk about how to string them together." Edward Weeks, ed., *Great Short Novels* (New York: Literary Guild of America, 1941), p. 562.

9. Heyward, *Porgy* Manuscript, Charleston Library Society.

10. "A Major Musical," *New Republic* 128 (April 6, 1953): 31.

11. Alain Locke, "The Negro in American Literature," *New World Writing* 1 (April 1952): 28. See also Charles Glicksberg, "The Negro Cult of the Primitive," *Antioch Review* 4 (March 1944): 49.

12. *Nigger Heaven* (New York: Knopf, 1926), p. 165.

13. *Home To Harlem* (New York: Harper, 1928), p. 118.

14. Ibid., p. 68.

15. *The Novels of the Harlem Renaissance* (University Park: Pennsylvania State University Press, 1976), pp. 18–22.

16. Telephone interview with Ralph Ellison, October 22, 1967.

17. *Creating the Modern American Novel* (London: Williams and Norgate, Ltd., 1936), p. 145.

18. Alain Locke, "The Legacy of the Ancestral Arts," in *The New Negro,* ed. Locke (New York: Albert and Charles Boni, 1925), p. 153.

19. "A Major Musical," p. 31.

20. *DuBose Heyward,* p. 70.

21. Letter to Horace E. Scudder, March 18, 1899, cited in George Brown Tindall, *The Emergence of the New South: 1913–1945* (Baton Rouge: Louisiana State University Press, 1967), p. 303.

22. "Negritude and Its Relevance to the American Negro Writer," in *The American Negro Writer and His Roots,* p. 15.

23. "Back-Country Novels," *Virginia Quarterly Review* 8 (July 1932): 467.

24. DuBose Heyward to Kathryn Bourne, December 21, 1931. Cited from Frank Durham, "DuBose Heyward's Use of Folklore in His Negro Fiction," *The Citadel: Monograph Series, No. 2* (Charleston: The Citadel, 1961), pp. 18–19.

25. *The Art of Southern Fiction* (Carbondale and Edwardsville: Southern Illinois University Press, 1967), p. 24.

26. Conversation with Leo Rockas, October 28, 1968.

27. "Modern with the Southern Accent," p. 187.

28. "Poetry of the South," in *Anthology of Magazine Verse for 1926*, ed. W. S. B. Braithwaite (Boston: B. J. Brumner and Company, 1926), p. 64.

29. *The Art of Southern Fiction*, p. 24.

30. Conversation between Dorothy Heyward and Frank Durham, cited in "DuBose Heyward: Southerner as Literary Artist," pp. 170–71.

31. John Bennett to DuBose Heyward, November 5, 1924. Bennett Papers.

32. *DuBose Heyward, A Critical and Biographical Sketch, Including Contemporary Estimates of His Work* (New York: George H. Doran Company, n.d. [1926]), p. 13.

33. "Writers: White and Black," in *The American Negro Writer and His Roots*, p. 43.

34. "The Dilemma of the Negro Author," *American Mercury* 15 (December 1928): 478.

35. "Introduction," *Three Negro Classics*, ed. Franklin (New York: Avon, 1965), p. viii.

36. "It Seems To Me," *New York World*, October 14, 1925.

37. "Introduction on the American Negro in the Arts," p. x.

38. "Back-Country Novels," p. 469.

39. Cited in Allen, *DuBose Heyward, a Critical and Biographical Sketch*, p. 17.

40. Program for "An Artistic Triumph," Janie Screven Heyward Scrapbook, and Durham, *DuBose Heyward*, p. 107.

41. Dorothy Heyward, *Love in a Cupboard* (New York: Samuel French, Inc., 1926).

42. Henry Sember, "With 'Porgy' as Their Precedent," *New York Herald-Tribune*, January 1, 1939.

43. "Introduction," Dorothy Heyward and DuBose Heyward, *Porgy: A Play in Four Acts*, Theatre Guild Acting Version (Garden City, N.Y., 1928). Subsequent citations of the Introduction or play in this chapter are indicated in the text and refer to the same edition.

44. "Races," *New Republic* 52 (October 26, 1927): 261.

45. "DuBose Heyward: Southerner as Literary Artist," p. 342.

46. "The Play of the Week," *Saturday Review of Literature* 4 (October 29, 1927): 251.

47. "Lights Down," *Outlook* 147 (November 30, 1927): 402–403.

48. *Porgy* opened October 10, 1927, at the Guild Theatre with a cast of unknown or little-known performers: Frank Wilson as Porgy, Evelyn Ellis as Bess, Percy Verwayne as Sportin' Life, Jack Carter as Crown, and Georgette Harvey as Maria. In 1928, Jack Carter was replaced as Crown by Paul Robeson.

49. *Charleston News and Courier*, November 14, 1952.

50. For the genesis of *Porgy and Bess*, see Durham's longer studies; Edward Jablonski and Lawrence D. Stewart, *The Gershwin Years*, Introduc-

tion by Carl Van Vechten (Garden City, N.Y., 1958); Robert Payne, *Gershwin* (London: Robert Hale, Ltd., 1962); and David Ewen, *A Journey to Greatness* (New York: Holt, 1965).

51. For discussions of the origins of the songs, see Durham, "DuBose Heyward: Southerner as Literary Artist," pp. 373–75, which cites his conversation with Dorothy Heyward and a letter from Ira Gershwin dated June 18, 1951; DuBose Heyward, "Porgy and Bess Return on Wings of Song," *Stage* 13 (October 1935): 27; and, particularly for changes from the spirituals used in the play, John Webb Cooper, "A Comparative Study of *Porgy*, the Novel, *Porgy*, the Play, and *Porgy and Bess*, the Opera," M.A. thesis, Columbia, 1950, pp. 80–82. "A Woman Is a Sometime Thing" echoes a poem, "Venner's Sayings," by Julia Peterkin, which includes the lines, "A man is a some-time thing" and "E sad; e ain' glad." See *Poetry* 23 (November 1923): 63.

52. Theatre Guild, *Porgy and Bess*, music by George Gershwin, libretto by DuBose Heyward, lyrics by DuBose Heyward and Ira Gershwin, settings by Sergei Soudelkine, orchestra conducted by Alexander Smallens, directed by Rouben Mamoulian (New York, n.d. [1935]), pp. 555–59. Subsequent citations are to this publication of the libretto.

53. "Opera Blues," *New Republic* 84 (October 30, 1935): 338.

54. *Charleston News and Courier*, January 19, 1958.

55. "Opera Blues," p. 338.

56. "Gershwin, Part IV," *New Republic* 176 (May 14, 1977): 25.

57. Ibid., p. 24.

58. "Drama," *Nation* 141 (October 30, 1935): 519.

59. "A Major Musical," p. 31.

60. Howard Taubman, "The Faithful Maestro," *New York Times*, April 26, 1953; Ewen, p. 282; John Rosenfield, "A New 'Porgy' in Dallas," *Saturday Review of Literature* 35 (June 28, 1952): 44. Calloway claims Gershwin originally asked him to play Sportin' Life, a figure he saw to be modeled on his performances at the Cotton Club, which Gershwin frequented. See Cab Calloway and Bryant Rollins, *Of Minnie the Moocher & Me* (New York: Crowell, 1976), p. 185.

61. Interview with Frank Durham, August 29, 1966, and Mrs. Jeannie Heyward Haskell, September 1, 1966.

62. Interview with Frank Durham, August 29, 1966.

Chapter Four

1. *Angel* (New York, 1926), p. 9. Subsequent citations are for this edition.

2. "From a Dry Spring," *New York Herald-Tribune Books*, October 31, 1926.

3. Cited in Durham, *DuBose Heyward*, pp. 78–79.

4. *Kenyon Review* 30 (Issue 2, 1968): 169–264.

5. Ibid., p. 170.

6. Letter to John Bennett, December 8, [1926]. Bennett Papers. The letter is dated 1925; the novel was published in August 1926.

7. "From a Dry Spring."

Chapter Five

1. A radio adaptation was presented annually between 1935 and 1937. Douglas Coulter, *Columbia Workshop Plays: Fourteen Radio Dramas* (New York: Whittlesey House, 1939), p. 323.

2. *The Half Pint Flask* (New York, 1929), p. 7. Subsequent page references are to this edition.

3. The other movie script was Irving Thalberg's *The Good Earth*. But since twenty other writers followed Heyward, exactly what is Heyward's about the film is unclear. He said that the final scenario was his—and Pearl Buck's, as he had closely followed the book—almost to the last detail. *Charleston News and Courier*, October 30, 1938, and March 5, 1939.

4. Eugene O'Neill, *The Emperor Jones, With a Study Guide for the Screen Version of the Play* by William Lewin and Max J. Herzberg (New York, 1949), p. 60. No source is given.

5. DuBose Heyward, Movie Scenario of *The Emperor Jones*. Lincoln Center, New York, N.Y. In ditto form, the scenario is eighty-one typed pages; the first sixty-nine constitute Heyward's addition.

6. Lewin and Hersberg in O'Neill, *The Emperor Jones*, p. 61.

7. Interview with Laura Bragg, September 1, 1966.

8. *New Theatre*, July 1935, cited from Peter Noble, *The Negro in Film* (1948; rpt. New York: Arno Press, 1970), p. 57. Gershwin had wanted Robeson to play Crown in *Porgy and Bess* after seeing him as Jones in Amsterdam in 1934. See letter to DuBose Heyward, March 8, 1934. Heyward Papers.

9. "Dramatic Team That Put 'Porgy' and 'Mamba' on Broadway Writes an Original Play Now," *Charleston News and Courier*, March 5, 1939.

10. *Charleston News and Courier*, September 29, 1948.

11. Interview with Herbert Aptheker, March 28, 1968. Both actors consulted Aptheker about accepting a role in the play.

12. "Drama," *Nation* 167 (November 20, 1948): 586.

13. Dorothy Heyward, "Set My People Free," Lincoln Center, New York, N.Y. This is apparently a working script.

Chapter Six

1. DuBose Heyward, *Mamba's Daughters: A Novel of Charleston* (New York, 1929), p. 36. Subsequent page references are to this edition.

2. Frances Lamont Robbins, "Grand Melodrama," *Outlook and Independent* 151 (February 6, 1929): 228.

3. *Reviewer*, 4 (October 1923), cited from Clark, p. 551.

4. "The Negro in the Low Country," pp. 186–87.

5. Carl Van Vechten, "The Black Blues: Negro Songs of Disappointment in Love—Their Pathos Hardened with Laughter," in *Cavalcade of the 1920s and 1930s*, ed. Cleveland Amory and Frederick Bradlee (London: The Bodley Head, 1960), p. 96.

6. John Bennett to DuBose Heyward, October 26, 1925. Bennett Papers. Mrs. Heyward discussed DeMille's proposals with Frank Durham; see "DuBose Heyward: Southerner as Literary Artist," pp. 267–68.

7. Durham, "DuBose Heyward: Southerner as Literary Artist," pp. 188–92, 194.

8. "The Forgotten Decade of Southern Literature: 1900–1910," Conference on Southern Literature, Modern Language Association Meeting, Chicago, Ill., December 27, 1967.

9. In a letter to Hervey Allen from Dawn Hill, August 9, 1929, Heyward writes: "Mamba's Daughters continues to sell, and to kick up much turmoil among my folks in and about S.C. But I rather expected the latter." Heyward Papers.

10. *The Spyglass*, pp. 31–32.

11. Ethel Waters with Charles Samuels, *His Eye Is on the Sparrow* (Garden City, N.Y.: Doubleday, 1951), p. 239.

12. Dorothy and DuBose Heyward, *Mamba's Daughters: A Play* (New York, 1939), p. 24. Subsequent page references are to this edition.

13. Otis Ferguson, "Daughters and Others," *New Republic* 97 (January 18, 1939): 315.

14. Durham, "DuBose Heyward: Southerner as Literary Artist," p. 282, and *DuBose Heyward*, p. 134.

Chapter Seven

1. DuBose Heyward, *Brass Ankle* (New York, 1931), p. 15. Subsequent page references are to this edition.

2. Robert M. Wallace to the author, February 23, 1968, and August 26, 1968. His source is his father, D. D. Wallace, a South Carolina historian who knew Stoney.

3. "The Color Line," *Nation* 132 (May 13, 1931): 538.

Chapter Eight

1. Letter dated November 2, [n.d.]. Snowden Papers.

2. Interview with Frank Durham, August 29, 1966.

3. DuBose Heyward, "A New Theory of Historical Fiction," *Publishers Weekly* 122 (August 13, 1932): 511–12.

4. DuBose Heyward, *Peter Ashley* (New Yok, 1932), p. 92. Subsequent page references are to this edition.

5. *Fiction Fights the Civil War* (Chapel Hill: University of North Carolina Press, 1957), p. 126.

6. William Faulkner, *Absalom, Absalom!* (1936; rpt. New York: Random House, 1951), p. 378.

7. "DuBose Heyward's Civil War Novel," *New York Times Book Review*, October 23, 1936.

8. *Fort Sumter* (New York, 1938).

9. *The Historical Novel*, trans. Hannah and Stanley Mitchell (London: Merlin Press, 1962), p. 36 and passim.

10. Ibid., p. 31.

11. Paul Goodman, "Epical Actions," reprinted from *The Structure of Literature* (Chicago: University of Chicago Press, 1954) in *Perspectives on Epic*, ed. Frederick H. Candelaria and William C. Strange (Boston: Allyn and Bacon, 1965), pp. 122, 125.

12. *Anatomy of Criticism* (Princeton, N.J.: Princeton University Press, 1957), pp. 186–87.

13. Lewis P. Simpson, *The Dispossessed Garden: Pastoral and History in Southern Literature* (Athens: University of Georgia Press, 1975), passim, but notably pp. 34–64, 69, 75–76.

Chapter Nine

1. DuBose Heyward, *Lost Morning* (New York, 1936), p. 12. Subsequent references are to this edition.

2. "Time and Place in Southern Fiction," in *Southern Renascence*, pp. 130–31.

Chapter Ten

1. DuBose Heyward, *Star Spangled Virgin* (New York, 1939), p. 11. Subsequent references are to this edition.

2. With Daisy Reck, "The American Virgins," *National Geographic* 78 (September 1940): 305.

3. Letter to DuBose Heyward, January 26, 1937. Heyward Papers.

4. "The Opera That Didn't Get to the Metropolitan," *South Atlantic Quarterly* 53 (October 1954): 505.

5. Frank Durham, "DuBose Heyward: The Southerner as Literary Artist," p. 401. Mrs. Heyward is Durham's source.

6. DuBose Heyward to Audrey Wood, February 9, 1940, and DuBose Heyward to Ethel Waters, November 8, 1940. Heyward Papers.

Chapter Eleven

1. Newman, "On the State of Literature in the Late Confederacy."
2. Letter to John Bennett, May 19, 1925. Bennett Papers.
3. "The Southern Muse," p. 216.
4. See Ronald E. Martin, *The Fiction of Joseph Hergesheimer* (Philadelphia: University of Pennsylvania Press, 1965), pp. 164, 196, 230–242, 267.
5. *A Certain Measure*, p. 28.
6. *Three Modes of Modern Southern Fiction*, p. 19.
7. See Frank Durham, "The Southern Literary Tradition: Shadow or Substance," *South Atlantic Quarterly* 67 (Summer 1968): 467.
8. Julia Peterkin, "Southern View-Point," p. 392.
9. Donald Davidson, "The Artist as Southerner," *Saturday Review of Literature* 2 (May 15, 1926): 782.
10. "A Mirror for Artists," pp. 58–59.
11. Davidson, *Southern Writers in the Modern World*, p. 30; Fred C. Hobson, *Serpent in Eden: H. L. Mencken and the South* (Chapel Hill: University of North Carolina Press, 1973), pp. 109, 148–52.
12. The characterization of Mencken's view is his, not Davidson's. See "Aftermath," *Baltimore Evening Sun*, September 14, 1925, cited in Hobson, p. 151.
13. *A Certain Measure*, p. 8.
14. Ibid.
15. See Seymour L. Gross, "Stereotype to Archetype: The Negro in American Literary Criticism"; Theodore L. Gross, "The Negro in the Literature of the Reconstruction"; and Leslie A. Fiedler, "The Blackness of Darkness: The Negro in the Development of Anerican Gothic," in *Images of the Negro in American Literature*, ed. Seymour L. Gross and John Edward Hardy (Chicago: University of Chicago Press, 1966).
16. Nathan Irvin Huggins, *Harlem Renaissance* (New York: Oxford, 1971), p. 59.
17. Telephone interview, October 22, 1967.
18. Ibid.
19. Brickell, "Creator and Catfish Row."
20. "For DuBose Heyward of Charleston," *Saturday Review of Literature* 22 (June 29, 1940): 8.
21. *Who Speaks for the South?* (New York: Funk and Wagnalls, 1964), passim. This study is also invaluable in providing a perspective on white stoicism in the South.
22. Clark, p. 556.
23. Columbia Broadcasting Company television newscast, December 23, 1968.
24. *Milwaukee Journal*, November 21, 1968.

Selected Bibliography

PRIMARY SOURCES

1. Books

Carolina Chansons: Legends of the Low Country (with Hervey Allen). New
York: Macmillan Company, 1922.
Skylines and Horizons. New York: Macmillan Company, 1924.
Porgy. New York: George H. Doran Company, 1925.
Angel. New York: George H. Doran Company, 1926.
Porgy: A Play in Four Acts (with Dorothy Heyward). With an Introduction
on the American Negro in Art. Theatre Guild Acting Version. New York:
Doubleday, Page & Company, 1928.
Mamba's Daughters: A Novel of Charleston. New York: Doubleday, Doran,
and Company, 1929.
The Half Pint Flask. New York: Farrar & Rinehart, Inc., 1929.
Jasbo Brown and Selected Poems. New York: Farrar & Rinehart, Inc., 1931.
Brass Ankle. New York: Farrar & Rinehart, Inc., 1931.
Peter Ashley. New York: Farrar & Rinehart, Inc., 1932.
Porgy and Bess (music by George Gershwin, libretto by DuBose Heyward,
lyrics by DuBose Heyward and Ira Gershwin, settings by Sergei Sou-
delkine, orchestra conducted by Alexander Smallens, directed by
Rouben Mamoulian). Theatre Guild Presentation. New York: Gershwin
Publishing Corporation, n.d. [1935]. Also Limited Edition. New York:
Random House, Inc., 1935.
Lost Morning. New York: Farrar & Rinehart, Inc., 1936.
Fort Sumter (with Herbert Ravenel Sass). New York: Farrar & Rinehart, Inc.,
1938.
Star Spangled Virgin. New York: Farrar & Rinehart, Inc., 1939.
Mamba's Daughters: A Play (with Dorothy Heyward). New York: Farrar
& Rinehart, Inc., 1939.
The Country Bunny and the Little Gold Shoes, as told to Jenifer. Boston and
New York: Houghton, Mifflin Company, 1939.

2. Editing

The Carolina Low-Country, ed. Augustine T. Smythe, Ravenel Sass, Alfred
    Huger, Beatrice Ravenel, Thomas Waring, Archibald Rutledge, Jose-
    phine Pinckney, Caroline Pinckney Rutledge, DuBose Heyward, Kath-
    erine C. Hutson, Robert W. Gordon. New York: Macmillan Company,
    1932. Includes an essay by Heyward, "The Negro in the Low-Country,"
    pp. 171–87.
Year Book of the Poetry Society of South Carolina for 1921 (with Hervey
    Allen and John Bennett). Charleston, S.C., 1921. Includes Foreword by
    the editors, pp. 5–7.
Year Book of the Poetry Society of South Carolina for 1922 (with Hervey
    Allen and John Bennett). Charleston, S.C., 1922.
Year Book of the Poetry Society of South Carolina for 1923. Charleston,
    S.C., 1923. Includes Foreword by Heyward, pp. 9–13.
Year Book of the Poetry Society of South Carolina for 1924. Charleston,
    S.C., 1924. Includes Foreword by Heyward, pp. 9–12.

3. Articles

"Poetry South" (with Hervey Allen), *Poetry* 20 (April 1922): 35–48.
"And Once Again—the Negro," *Reviewer* 4 (October 1923): 39–42.
"Beatrice Ravenel," in *Library of Southern Literature*, Supplement No. 1,
    ed. Edwin Anderson Alderman and Charles Alphonso Smith. Atlanta:
    Martin and Hoyt Company, 1923, pp. 473–75.
"The New Note in Southern Literature," *Bookman* 61 (April 1925): 153–56.
"The MacDowell Colony," *Southwest Review* 11 (January 1926): 162–68.
"Contemporary Southern Poetry," *Bookman* 62 (January 1926): 561–64; 63
    (March 1926): 273–312.
Review of Beatrice Ravenel, *Arrow of Lightning*, *Charleston News and
    Courier*, December 12, 1926.
"Foreword," Samuel Gaillard Stoney and Gertrude Mathews Shelby, *Black
    Genesis: A Chronicle*. New York: Macmillan Company, 1930.
"A New Theory of Historical Fiction," *Publishers Weekly* 122 (August 13,
    1932): 511.
"Porgy and Bess Return on Wings of Song," *Stage* 13 (October 1935): 25–28.
"Dock Street Theatre," *Magazine of Art* 31 (January 1938): 10–15.
"Charleston: Where Mellow Past and Present Meet," *National Geographic*
    75 (March 1939): 273–312.
"The American Virgins" (with Daisy Reck), *National Geographic* 78 (Sep-
    tember 1940): 273–308.

SECONDARY SOURCES

The most complete list of Heyward and related studies and book reviews is in my "DuBose Heyward: The Rhythms of Charleston." The following list includes only those scholarly studies—books, dissertations, and articles—particularly concerned with Heyward's work, as well as two discussions of use of the Gullah dialect in literature.

ALLEN, HERVEY. *DuBose Heyward, a Critical and Biographical Sketch, Including Contemporary Estimates of His Work.* New York: George H. Doran Company, n.d. [1926]. A pamphlet.

BENNETT, JOHN. "A Negro Patois," *South Atlantic Quarterly* 7 (October 1908): 332–47; 8 (June 1909): 39–52.

BROOKS, CLEANTH, JR. "The Modern Southern Poet and Tradition," *Virginia Quarterly Review* 2 (April 1935): 305–20.

CLARK, EMILY. "DuBose Heyward," *Virginia Quarterly Review* 6 (October 1930): 546–56. Reprinted in *Innocents Abroad.* New York: A. A. Knopf, Inc., 1931.

COOPER, JOHN WEBB. "A Comparative Study of *Porgy*, the Novel, *Porgy*, the Play, and *Porgy and Bess*, the Opera." Unpublished master's thesis. English Department, Columbia University, 1950.

COX, HEADLEY MORRIS, JR. "The Charleston Poetic Renascence, 1920–1930." Unpublished doctoral dissertation. English Department, University of Pennsylvania, 1958.

CREIGHTON, NANNIE ELIZABETH. "DuBose Heyward and His Contribution to Literature." Unpublished master's thesis. English Department, University of South Carolina, 1933.

DAVIDSON, DONALD. "The Other Half of Verse," *Fugitive* 2 (August-September 1923): 99. Initiates the Nashville criticism of local color poetry.

———. *Southern Writers in the Modern World.* Athens: University of Georgia Press, 1958.

———. *The Spyglass: Views and Reviews, 1924–1930*, ed. John Tyree Fain. Nashville: Vanderbilt University Press, 1963.

DURHAM, FRANK. "DuBose Heyward: Southerner as Literary Artist." Unpublished doctoral dissertation. English Department, Columbia University, 1953.

———. *DuBose Heyward: The Man Who Wrote Porgy.* Columbia: University of South Carolina Press, 1954. New edition with 1965 Preface. Port Washington, N.Y.: Kennikat Press, 1965. An informal version of his dissertation, the most useful biographical source.

———. "DuBose Heyward's 'Lost' Stories," *Short Fiction Studies* 2 (Winter 1965): 157–63. Reviews Heyward's apprentice work.

———. *DuBose Heyward's Use of Folklore in His Negro Fiction.* The Citadel Monograph Series, No. 2. Charleston, S.C.: The Citadel, 1961. A pamphlet: one treatment of Heyward's use of the Gullah dialect.

———. "English-French Huguenot," *Huguenot Society of South Carolina Transactions*, No. 58. Charleston, S.C., 1953, pp. 5–12.

———. "The Opera That Didn't Get to the Metropolitan," *South Atlantic Quarterly* 53 (October 1954): 497–507.

———. "The Reputed Demises of Uncle Tom: On the Treatment of the Negro in Fiction by White Authors in the 1920's," *Southern Literary Journal* 2 (Spring 1970): 26–50.

———. "The Rise of DuBose Heyward and the Rise and Fall of the Poetry Society of South Carolina," *Mississippi Quarterly* 19 (Spring 1966): 66–78.

———. "South Carolina Poetry Society," *South Atlantic Quarterly* 52 (1953): 277–85.

HARRIGAN, ANTHONY. "DuBose Heyward: Memorialist and Realist," *Georgia Review* 5 (Fall 1951): 335–44.

HEYWARD, DOROTHY. "'Porgy's' Native Tongue: A Dissertation on Gullah, the Negro Language of the Play," *New York Times*, December 4, 1927.

JABLONSKI, EDWARD, and STEWART, LAWRENCE D. *The Gershwin Years.* Introduction by Carl Van Vechten. Garden City, N.Y.: Doubleday & Company, Inc., 1958.

MACFIE, ANNE ELIZABETH. "The Representation of Aristocracy in the Novels of DuBose Heyward." Unpublished master's thesis. English Department, University of North Carolina, 1958.

O'NEILL, EUGENE. *The Emperor Jones.* With a Study Guide for the Screen Version of the Play by William Lewin and Max J. Herzberg. Student Edition. New York: Appleton-Century-Crofts, Inc., 1949.

PEALE, MARJORIE ELIZABETH. "Charleston as a Literary Center, 1920–1933." Unpublished master's thesis. English Department, Duke University, 1941.

PINCKNEY, JOSEPHINE. "Charleston's Poetry Society," *Sewanee Review* 38 (January 1930): 50–56.

RANSOM, JOHN CROWE. "Modern with the Southern Accent," *Virginia Quarterly Review* 11 (April 1935): 184–200.

RUBIN, LOUIS D., JR. "The Southern Muse: Two Poetry Societies," *American Quarterly* 13 (1961): 365–75. Reprinted in *The Curious Death of the Novel: Essays in American Literature.* Baton Rouge: Louisiana State University Press, 1967.

SLAVICK, WILLIAM H. "DuBose Heyward's Names," in *Love & Wrestling, Butch & O.K.* South Central Names Association Publication No. 3. Commerce, Texas: 1974, pp. 119–24.

———. "DuBose Heyward: The Rhythms of Charleston." Unpublished doctoral dissertation. English Department, University of Notre Dame, 1971. A critical study of Heyward's work.

————. "Going to School to DuBose Heyward," *Studies in the Literary Imagination* 7 (Fall 1974): 105–29. Focuses on the treatment of Negro characters in *Porgy* and *Mamba's Daughters*.

THOMSON, KEITH, and DURHAM, FRANK. "The Impact of *Porgy and Bess* in New Zealand," *Mississippi Quarterly* 20 (Fall 1967): 207–16.

WARREN, ROBERT PENN. "A Note on Three Southern Poets," *Poetry* 40 (May 1932): 103–13.

WILLIAMS, GEORGE. "Peregrinations of a Goat Cart," *Sandlapper* 6 (October 1973): 41–49.

YOUNGREN, WILLIAM. "Gershwin, Part IV," *New Republic* 176 (May 14, 1977): 23–27.

Index

Negro spirituals, 31. *See also* Heyward,
  DuBose
New Deal, 153, 156, 161, 169–70
Newman, Frances, 20, 30, 57, 90–91

O'Connor, Flannery, 29
O. Henry, 26, 29
O'Neill, Eugene, 12, 67, 96

Page, Thomas Nelson, 163
Page, Walter Hines, 70
Parks, Edd Winfield, 43
Peale, Marjorie Elizabeth, 26
Percy, William Alexander, 34
Peterkin, Julia, 20–21, 31, 38, 67, 171,
  183
Petigru, James, 129–32
Pinckney, Josephine, 26–27, 42
Po' Buckra (Stoney and Shelby), 121
Poe, Edgar Allan, 35, 43, 48, 93
Poem Outlines (Lanier), 148
Poetry Society of South Carolina, 9, 20,
  23, 26–28, 34–36, 42–43, 52, 56. *See
  also* Heyward, DuBose
Poitier, Sidney, 82, 84
Price, Leontyne, 83
primitivism, 66–68, 171–72. *See also*
  Heyward, DuBose
Prohibition, 153–54, 156
Pudd'nhead Wilson, 121
Puritanism, 67

race relations, 23. *See also* Heyward,
  DuBose
racial stereotypes, 75, 171. *See also*
  Heyward, DuBose
Ransom, John Crowe, 31, 37, 39–40, 42–
  43, 52–53, 56, 73, 163
Ravenel, Beatrice, 26, 30, 38, 42, 48, 74
Reese, Lizette, 34
Reviewer, The, 30
Rice, Cale Young, 34
Rivers, Rep. Mendel, 174
Roberts, Elizabeth Madox, 34, 91, 113,
  163
Robeson, Paul, 67, 97
Robinson, Edgar Arlington, 20, 28, 36–
  37, 52
Rockas, Leo, 73

Roosevelt, Franklin D., 153
Rourke, Constance, 20, 28, 74
Rouse, Blair, 150
Rubin, Louis D., Jr., 27–28, 42, 52, 164
Ryan, Fr. Abraham, 34

"Sahara of the Bozarts, The," 19–20,
  163, 176
Sandburg, Carl, 23, 39, 41
Sartoris, 113
Sass, Herbert Ravenel, 133
Sayler, Oliver M., 80
Schwartz, Arthur, 162
Scopes trial, 43
Scott, Lester, 83
Scott, Walter, 134, 164
Secession, 22, 126, 129, 135, 142
sentimentality, 39, 41. *See also*
  Heyward, DuBose
"Set My People Free" (Dorothy
  Heyward), 97–98
Shelby, Gertrude Mathews, 121
Simms, William Gilmore, 28, 129–30,
  137
Simons, Katherine Drayton Mayrant, 26,
  32
Simpson, Lewis P. 140–41, 163
Singh, Anrit, 67
Smalls, Samuel, 60–61, 102, 109
Smith, Chard Powers, 28
Snowden, Yates, 125
Society for the Preservation of Spirituals,
  28
Sound and the Fury, The, 112
Southern poetry, 34
Southern Poets (Parks), 43
Southern religion, 21
Southern renascence, 24, 35, 38, 140,
  152, 163, 165–171. *See also* Heyward,
  DuBose
Stallings, Lawrence, 31
Stand in the Mountains, A (Peter
  Taylor), 91
Stebbins, Robert, 97
Stein, Gertrude, 67
stoicism, 23
Stoney, Samuel Gaillard, 121
Stribling, T. S., 38, 166, 171
Stuart, Jesse, 38, 40